REMARKABLE SERVICE

Remarkable Service

SECOND EDITION

The Culinary Institute of America

WILEY

JOHN WILEY & SONS, INC.

THE CULINARY INSTITUTE OF AMERICA

President: Dr. Tim Ryan
Vice President, Dean of Culinary Education: Mark Erickson
Director of Publishing: Nathalie Fischer
Associate Dean of Restaurant Education and Operations: Jennifer Purcell
Lead Writers: Ezra Eichelberger, John Fischer
Reviewers: Douglas Miller, Kenneth Carlson
Photographers: Keith Ferris, Ben Fink
Editorial Project Manager: Mary Donovan
Editor: Ann Martin Rolke

Published by John Wiley & Sons, Inc., Hoboken, New Jersey
Published simultaneously in Canada

LIBRARY OF CONGRESS CATALOGING-IN-PUBLICATION DATA:

Remarkable service / The Culinary Institute of America. — 2nd ed.
    p. cm.
Includes bibliographical references and index.
ISBN 978-0-470-19740-0 (pbk.)
1. Food service management. I. Culinary Institute of America.
TX911.3.M27R453 2009
647.95068—dc22
                          2009000399

Printed in the United States of America
10 9 8 7 6 5 4 3 2 1

WE DEDICATE THIS BOOK to the students and graduates who have learned the meaning of remarkable service. By applying its principles on a daily basis, they endow our chosen career with the unmistakable hallmarks of a true profession.

Guest Check

31	5		37317	Pat

2	Sal	① BC ③ side oy y
1	Terr	4
1	Crab	5
1	Soup dj.	2
1	Rav	4
1	Ling	2
1	Sole	①
1	Ck	③
1	Chop m.w.	4
2	Stk	5 m 2 mR

Contents

Foreword

REMARKABLE SERVICE IS A SIMPLE CONCEPT, one that can be achieved with no more dramatic cost than that of a welcoming smile, knowledge of the menu, and the willingness to pay attention to your guests for the entire time that they are in your dining room.

This book, with its grounding in nine basic principles of service, demonstrates the underpinnings of a style of professional service that can only enhance the entire industry, both in terms of the respect with which it is held and the revenues it can generate for dedicated professionals. It behooves every member of the restaurant's staff to try to make the customer's experience as rewarding as possible so that the customer comes back again and again as a source of ongoing revenue, as opposed to working against you as a source of bad word-of-mouth. In the front lines, of course, is the professional server.

Knowledge of your responsibilities and a sense of what is important are prerequisites for professionalism. Good service is friendly and courteous, knowledgeable, efficient, timely, consistent, informative, and trustworthy. Remarkable service is that which has the goal of delighting the guest by exceeding those expectations.

This book is designed to be a reference work on all aspects of front-of-the-house service, from setting up an appropriate reservations system to equipment identification. Even the most veteran server, faced with a new situation, can use this book as a source for solutions.

In this book we describe the attributes of remarkable service and the standards that such service must meet or exceed. Like principles, attributes can be difficult to define. Everyone knows courteous service when experiencing it, but how to set guidelines for courtesy? Not all aspects of great service are based on abstract concepts. There are right and wrong ways of doing things. No matter what the setting, from the most informal to the height of fine dining, there are dos and don'ts. These rules and their rationales are clearly explained.

It is vital to realize the importance of your job and to take pride in it. If you are a true professional, then you know what you must do to provide remarkable service. You must learn as much as you can about your profession, your dining room, and your colleagues in the kitchen. You'll feel good about yourself, the restaurant, and your guests. You will know that you are doing the right thing.

The goal of this book is to turn every comment into a compliment. The delivery of remarkable service is the only way to ensure a steady stream of positive remarks. "remarkable service" refers to a system that not only is worthy of praise but also is above and beyond expected levels. Remarkable service engenders the word-of-mouth promotion that no amount of money can buy.

1

The Principles of Remarkable Service

AT ITS BEST, WHEN EVERYTHING comes together, working in a restaurant's dining room feels like you're giving the best dinner party ever. Trained cooks and a great chef send out delicious food; beautiful surroundings and the right music coax guests into an expansive mood; a professional, highly trained staff brings the guests whatever they need, ideally before they even know they need it. In the dining room we have the opportunity to bring complete strangers into our warm, welcoming space and make them feel like they are a part of our family, so that they will want to return over and over again.

We are in the hospitality business. And making hospitality a business involves identifying what takes service from acceptable to remarkable and then reliably performing those actions whenever necessary.

This book addresses both practical service skills (sometimes referred to as "hard skills"), such as setting the table, serving food, and presenting the check, as well as the less tangible hospitality skills ("soft skills"). Keep in mind that less tangible does not mean "less important." In fact, attention to the intangibles is exactly what separates remarkable service from ordinary service.

What Does the Word *Hospitality* Mean to a Professional Server?

IN ORDER TO SUCCEED in the service industry, you need to first understand the concept of hospitality.

HOSPITALITY (hospi'tæliti). [a. OF. hospitalité (12–13th c. in Hatz-Darm.), ad. L. hospitalitas, f. hospitalis (see HOSPITAL a.).] 1. a. The act or practice of being hospitable; the reception and entertainment of guests, visitors, or strangers, with liberality and goodwill. (Oxford English Dictionary)

It is not easy to arrive at a succinct definition of what *hospitality* means for the professional server. You can study and master the smallest details of fine table service, but hospitality extends beyond such professional skills. Hospitality in the restaurant can be expressed in a number of ways, such as making eye contact with the guest; anticipating a guest's need based upon body language or facial expression; adapting easily and unobtrusively to the needs of the guest; and similar actions aimed at creating a relaxing, positive experience. (These skills are often referred to as the "innate skills" that servers should already possess.) Hospitality implies constant concern for the welfare and enjoyment of the guest. To convince the guest that you are really concerned for their happiness, every action you perform needs to come across as genuine. You can say all of the right words, but if you don't convey a certain warmth, your guest will feel the lack of sincerity.

What Does the Word *Service* Mean to a Professional Server?

THE QUALITY OF SERVICE plays a very large part in determining the long-term survival of a restaurant and its market share of the available business.

The most common sense of the word *service* refers to the manner of presenting a meal to the guest. There are other meanings of the term service when it is used by a professional server. Traditionally, a service was the group of dishes composing a given part of a meal, such as a tea service. Service can also signify the utensils necessary to serve a particular part of a meal. Service in this sense would encompass the whole ensemble of objects used at the table: linens, plates, glasses, silver, and hollowware. Guests will often use the term service to refer to the timeliness in which the food was served, as in "Wasn't that amazingly quick service?"

Specific actions on the server's part can lead to desired feelings and emotions on the guest's part. These actions can be singled out, defined, described, and put into simple, trainable terms—for example, anticipating the pace of a meal and bringing successive courses at just the right time; avoiding bare-handed contact with plates or glass rims; suggesting menu items that will complement dishes already ordered; and presenting the check at the appropriate moment when the meal is done. The skills needed to deliver remarkable service, which includes all aspects of restaurant service, from greeting to order taking, service to check presentation, as well as reservations and special challenges in the dining room, are described throughout this book.

Combining Hospitality and Service Skills for Remarkable Service

THE NINE PRINCIPLES OF REMARKABLE SERVICE

Remarkable Service Is Courteous, Friendly, and Welcoming

Remarkable Service Instills Trust

Remarkable Service Comes from Knowledgeable Servers

Remarkable Service Depends on Effective Communication

Remarkable Service Is Performed Efficiently

Remarkable Service Is Well-Timed

Remarkable Service Is Flexible

Remarkable Service Is Consistent

Remarkable Service Exceeds Expectations

Hospitality has to do with attitudes and behaviors, which can be expressed through actions; in other words, through service. When you combine hospitality skills with service skills, you are delivering remarkable service.

A high level of caring for the comfort of guests—remarkable service, in other words—is the distinctive attribute of the best dining establishments. Providing service is at the heart of all businesses, from auto repair shops to hairdressers to restaurants. The more personal the service, the more the guest or client will feel comfortable and confident that they are being treated with respect and care.

Hospitality and service may seem, at first glance, to represent very different kinds of activities. Hospitality depends on feelings and impressions, while the essence of service resides in actions. Service is being able to carry four dinner plates without spilling the sauce, or opening a bottle of Champagne without spewing foam onto the floor. While the service tasks themselves do not involve emotion, they can evoke positive feelings in guests when they are carried out in a professional manner. We have identified nine basic principles of remarkable service that are the foundation of the lessons throughout this book. Since the principles represent various aspects of caring and share the common objective of making the guest feel comfortable, it should not come as a surprise when two or more of the principles overlap. Nor should it come as a surprise that remarkable service draws upon both the hospitality and service skills in the professional server's tool kit.

REMARKABLE SERVICE IS COURTEOUS, FRIENDLY, AND WELCOMING

"You only have one chance to make a first impression." This is the rallying cry for every quality-oriented service business. In the food-service business, guests make decisions within their first minute of contact with the restaurant. Thus, a good server never forgets this oft-quoted but still essential maxim. When guests are met by friendly, welcoming hosts, they are assured that they can relax and enjoy their meal.

Good servers are attentive to the guests' needs, not only with the dishes served, but also with the dining environment. Most guests do not come to a restaurant to chat with the service staff. Reading the table (discussed in chapter 6) can tell the server which guests want to talk and ask questions about the restaurant and which prefer to be left alone. Regular customers may develop a more informal relationship with the staff—and will perhaps think of the restaurant as their second dining room. Courteous servers are attentive, but not intrusive with these guests.

One cannot appreciate a meal in a hostile environment. Proper manners smooth uncertain social interactions, subconsciously informing people that they have nothing to fear. Courteous behavior tells the guests that they are in a caring, comforting environment. The server's fine manners signal a sincere concern for the guests' happiness.

When the meal is over, a thank-you for the guests—as well as a thoughtful farewell—is essential.

REMARKABLE SERVICE INSTILLS TRUST

A state of trust must be maintained between the server and the guest. The guest needs to know that menu items are described accurately and that health and sanitary codes are being obeyed. As an illustration, when guests order decaffeinated coffee, they have only the server's word that they are, in fact, getting decaffeinated coffee. If a guest notices that the coffee machine has only two carafes and both of them have brown handles (which indicate regular coffee—while orange or green are often used for decaffeinated coffee), doubts arise that can affect the trust in the relationship with the server throughout the rest of their meal.

When a restaurant (the space, equipment, furnishings, and staff) presents a clean and neat appearance, it comforts guests by banishing their worries about the sanitary conditions in the part of the restaurant they can't see: the kitchen. A single grease stain on the carpet, a crumb on a chair, or a spot on the wall can adversely affect the way guests feel about the meal they are about to enjoy.

Just as the guest must have trust in the server, the server must have trust in the guest. The server needs to believe that the guests will be reasonable—that they won't make impossible demands, nor reject food or wine capriciously, nor "stiff the waiter" and leave without paying for the meal.

Dealing with guests in a straightforward and honest manner puts them at ease. When they are relaxed, they are happy. When they are happy, they order more freely—and they tip more generously. Trust enhances the dining experience.

REMARKABLE SERVICE COMES FROM KNOWLEDGEABLE SERVERS

Servers who are knowledgeable about the menu (i.e., the ingredients, preparation, and portion size of menu items; the wine list) assure the guests that they will be able to get the information they need in order to make informed decisions about their meal. Guests cannot order dishes they don't know exist. Servers make the guest feel

What Makes It Extra-Virgin?

This is an example of the kind of question that a server should be prepared for. Although a witty waiter may have several clever retorts for this question, a professional server has the correct answer:

Olives are pressed much like grapes. The best olive oil is extra-virgin olive oil, then the next grade is virgin olive oil. Cold-pressed oil from the first pressing of the olive (if under 1 percent acid) is considered extra-virgin olive oil. If the oil from the first pressing contains from 1 to 3.3 percent acid, it is labeled "virgin olive oil." The subsequent pressings of the same olives produce "pure olive oil." Usually a good year for grapes is not as good for olives and vice versa.

"We were halfway through our main course and my wineglass was empty, though everyone else had plenty. I didn't want to order another bottle of wine. The waiter came to me and told me about a wine they had by the glass that was just perfect with my steak."

comfortable by becoming trusted guides through what might otherwise be unknown territory for the guest. Guests often need information about menu items or, more generally, about upcoming events at the restaurant, transportation and other services, and points of interest in the vicinity. When servers share their knowledge with the guests, it assures them that they won't miss something special.

A remarkable server not only needs to know about the menu items, but also has to understand what the guests are really asking. For example, if the guests ask the server what is in the spinach and goat cheese quiche, and the server replies, "spinach and goat cheese," this is technically accurate, but it is far from being hospitable, and certainly doesn't make the customer feel appreciated enough to spend their money. What the customer wants to know is: "What else is in the quiche? Does it contain onions? Is the goat cheese local? " They want to know something more than what is written on the menu.

REMARKABLE SERVICE DEPENDS ON EFFECTIVE COMMUNICATION

It is not enough to be well informed; good servers must be able to communicate effectively with guests as well as with the rest of the restaurant staff. Jargon that eliminates confusion in the kitchen has the opposite effect when spoken to guests and should be avoided. The art of communication consists of transmitting just the right amount of information exactly when it is needed.

Remarkable servers recognize what guests need to know, and provide it in an unobtrusive manner. Rather than an ostentatious "showing off" of knowledge, it is the quiet, confident, sensitive, sincere, and tactful delivery of facts that best serves the guests. Neither more nor less is required, or desired.

While some guests respond well to humor, some prefer more formality. Remarkable servers adapt their communication styles to the situation and the guests to whom they are speaking. The type of establishment very often determines the form and style of conversation between servers and guests. Diners, bistros, family-style places, and white tablecloth restaurants all have different ways of treating guests, but all are concerned with providing the kind of comfort that guests expect from the type of establishment they have selected.

Remarkable servers are adept at recognizing nonverbal clues in guests' behavior. When guests need something—water, a new napkin, additional wine—their body language is more eloquent than speech, at least to servers who have learned how to read it. Good servers are always reading the table for clues about what the guests might need next, or reading the room to monitor (and be prepared to adjust) the flow of service.

Communication takes other forms as well. For example, the use of appropriate uniforms (i.e., long French aprons, matching polo shirts and khakis, Hawaiian shirts) makes it easy for guests to recognize the service staff and their job responsibilities. Uniforms spare the guests even momentary uncertainty about the location and identity of servers.

REMARKABLE SERVICE IS PERFORMED EFFICIENTLY

Efficiency is obviously important to the servers and the restaurant. More work can be done (and more money made) with less effort when it is done efficiently. The absence of efficiency, while costly in itself, can also seriously affect the comfort level of the guests. Disorganization and unseemly haste are contagious—guests are made to feel just as harried as their servers.

Inefficient technique wastes the guests' time as well as that of the servers. It interrupts the flow of the meal and erodes the environment of trust that is essential to a relaxed dining experience. However, when guests see the server's work being done quickly, smoothly, and easily, they are put at ease. They do not feel that they have put the server to any "trouble."

A general rule for a fast-paced restaurant is "never enter or leave the dining area with empty hands." There is almost always something to be taken to or removed from a table.

Careful attention to mise en place (having everything in its place), an intelligent economy of motion, and a cooperative attitude make the server's job easier to perform, and the resulting ease sends a strong signal to the guests that responsibility for their comfort is in good hands.

REMARKABLE SERVICE IS WELL-TIMED

Remarkable servers anticipate the dining needs of the guests. By providing just the right items or services before the guests realize they need them, servers spare their guests the anxiety of having to ask for them. Here are a few examples of how remarkable service can be properly timed:

- Guests never have to ask for refills on water, iced tea, coffee, bread, or butter.

- Orders are taken promptly.

- Proper flatware is always in place before the guest needs it.

- Coffee never sits cooling in front of the guests while they wait for cream and sugar to be brought to their table.

- The guest's check is processed promptly.

By properly timing the delivery of each course, a server guarantees that guests experience the food while it is fresh and at its ideal temperature. When the meal is over and the guests want their check, a remarkable server already has the check in order, and delivers it smoothly, quietly, and unobtrusively—but only when it is clear that the guests have finished. The guests must never be made to feel rushed. However, when guests are in a hurry, a server should do whatever is needed to pace the meal so that they can enjoy their meal in the allotted time.

REMARKABLE SERVICE IS FLEXIBLE

A good server recognizes that sometimes the rules must be bent a little in the interest of the overall quality of the guests' dining experience. For example, if two guests are deeply involved in conversation, common sense suggests that one should be served from the right and one from the left. Interrupting their conversation would be a more significant violation than deviating from a house rule that states that all guests are to be served from the left. Sound judgment and the willingness to consider what one would prefer if the roles of server and guest were reversed provide the best guides to when and where the server needs to be flexible.

REMARKABLE SERVICE IS CONSISTENT

Guests visit a restaurant the first time for many different reasons. They come back for only one: they like the restaurant, its food, and its service. Making good use of all of the principles of hospitality and service can persuade a guest to come back to the restaurant, and the consistent delivery of high-quality food and service will bring their repeat business.

The key to achieving long-term success is the consistent delivery of the best possible service to every guest—every day, every week, every month, and every year.

REMARKABLE SERVICE EXCEEDS EXPECTATIONS

While repeat customers expect the same level of service each time they visit, they will be less impressed each time. This may seem unfair, but it's a fact of human nature. What is exceptional today will be expected tomorrow, and be barely adequate the day after tomorrow. Remarkable servers are constantly seeking ways to better their performance—finding new ways to delight the guests through the use of the principles already discussed, and incorporating them into this last principle: The best service is constantly improving service.

Personal Qualities of the Professional Server

IF A SINGLE WORD were to describe the sum of personal characteristics that define a professional server, it would be *caring*. Obviously, caring is not, by itself, enough. In addition to possessing the characteristics described, a professional server must master the skills described in the next chapters. In a very real sense, all of the employees of a restaurant are serving their guests. Every task, no matter how small, is carried out for one reason: to make the guest's stay as pleasant as possible. In order to succeed in this pursuit, a professional server must have certain characteristics, both physical (professional appearance and good personal hygiene) and behavioral (appropriate personality traits).

PHYSICAL

We are often told not to judge a book by its cover. However, people base important decisions about any business on their first impressions, especially in the food-service industry. If the servers do not have good aesthetic skills—if they are not neat, clean, and professional-looking—the guests will choose to eat elsewhere. You must always remember that the first (and possibly most lasting) impression one can make is through your appearance. Make it a positive one. The uniform you wear at work—be it a waitress's dress, a tuxedo, or a stylized costume—is a badge of professionalism and should be worn with pride. Uniforms give each employee a recognizably similar appearance that helps the guests distinguish between servers and other guests. Keeping an extra uniform or shirt on hand for emergencies is also a good idea.

Good grooming is a must for anyone working in the front of the house. Well-groomed people always look clean because they *are* clean. Professional servers apply these principles to their everyday grooming habits:

- Hair neatly cut and combed

- Hands and fingernails clean

- Clothing that fits properly, is clean, and is wrinkle free

- Shoes shined and in good condition (including the heels)

Beyond being in the appropriate uniform, every server must have impeccable personal hygiene. Since servers are in close proximity with so many people, they should wash their hands about every half hour, when possible. Fingernails should be clean but free of nail polish, since it can peel off and get into the food.

The scent of food encourages food sales. The scent of colognes and perfumes can conflict with the aromas the guests have come to smell, so they should be avoided. Likewise, since servers work in very close proximity to the guests, daily showers and unscented or subtly scented deodorants are essential.

BEHAVIORAL

The most important behavioral characteristic a truly professional server can possess is an ability to deal with people. No amount of polish or knowledge can replace sincere concern for the customers' enjoyment of their dining experience. Maintaining a high level of this personal concern is not always easy. Most servers are familiar with cranky, demanding restaurant customers who aggravate service personnel while expecting them to be pleasant and efficient in return. Everyone has bad days occasionally, but professional servers should never let this be observed by the guests. It is important to remember that if you can see the guests, the guests can see you.

In addition to being adept with the public, a person in the front of the house must have characteristics possessed by any individual of integrity, particularly as they relate to conducting business.

The following discussion lists desirable traits that professionals working in the service of foods and beverages should possess.

ATTENTIVENESS

Professional servers do not daydream at work, nor are they absentminded. They must always be alert to the needs of the guests. No guest should ever have to work to attract a service person's attention. The station must never be left unattended. The ability to recognize the current state of the dining room while keeping track of what is about to occur calls for more skill than most realize. The professional server must have an ongoing knowledge of what is happening at each of the tables. This is accomplished by reading the table. It is necessary to keep a discreet watch on the diners' progress throughout their meals. Anticipating when more wine should be poured, when the table needs to be cleared, and how orders should be coordinated requires that one's attention stay on the job at hand. A server's eyes should constantly be surveying the tabletop with the five areas of table maintenance (covered in chapter 6) in mind and glancing at the guests' eyes, in case they have a request.

POLITENESS

The professional server must do more than anticipate the food and beverage needs of the guest. The professional server should be happy to assist in any area that relates to the customer's comfort. This includes such tasks as opening doors; helping guests with chairs, packages, coats, and dropped items; correcting glare from lights or the sun; eliminating drafts; and adjusting the sound level of music, if necessary. The magic words, *please, thank you, you're welcome,* and *pardon me* are essential to the vocabulary of food-service personnel. Polite words and considerate actions indicate a sincere regard for others' well-being—for fellow employees as well as for guests. A polite server avoids the use of crude, but commonly used, expressions such as *Behind!, Coming through!* or *Watch your back!*

When a guest asks for directions (i.e., to the bar, coatroom, or rest room) it is both rude and insufficient to point. A professional server should offer to show the guest the way, personally. The guest may prefer simple directions, but one should never assume that to be the case.

PROFICIENCY

In order to advance in one's career, the professional server must be willing to work constantly at the expansion of their technical skills and multitasking abilities. A skill is the development of proficiency in an art or craft and is improved by practice. Examples of serving skills that are acquired with practice are moving through crowds with a tray of beverages; opening sparkling and still wines; properly decanting red wines; and executing elegant tableside preparations.

DEPENDABILITY

Dependability is a sign of maturity and is a desirable trait for individuals in any profession. The dependable person can be relied on to accomplish what they promise, to be at work during agreed-upon hours, and to fulfill commitments. Dependability is a major factor that employers consider in hiring, since guests depend upon the server to provide knowledgeable and smooth-flowing service.

ECONOMY

Professionals in any business are responsible for doing their share to keep costs down. Untold amounts of revenue disappear daily in food-service establishments through waste—the largest and most unnecessary expense in the industry. Common sense is an important key to economy in the food-service industry; a rational person does not deliberately destroy or dispose of someone else's personal or business property. The professional server avoids waste by

- Carefully handling and stacking china and glassware.
- Using glass racks of the correct size.
- Carrying no more than can be handled safely (ask another server to assist you, or make two safe trips, rather than one risky trip).
- Being careful not to discard silverware with refuse or to put them in the dirty linen baskets.
- Avoiding unnecessary soiling of linen.
- Placing linens that were received in a soiled or damaged condition in a separate area so they can be returned to the linen company for credit.
- Serving standard-size portions (serve appropriate portions of items such as butter, replenishing only if required).
- Making sure that all items served are included on the bill, especially coffee.
- Using the recommended amount and type of cleansing chemicals (not only is overuse wasteful, but it can damage the item being cleaned or worse, cause illness).

EFFICIENCY

Economy of motion is essential to a server's success. Acting efficiently means getting the same work done, but with less effort and better results. The ability to catalog orders and plan trips to the kitchen and service area saves steps. The time saved by being organized can be spent on better serving the customer. There should be very few empty-handed trips between the dining room and the kitchen.

POSITIVITY

A professional server maintains a happy and positive disposition, even amid chaos. A positive attitude makes one see all problems as opportunities to improve quality. Working with positive people is a pleasure—they create an environment that is pleasant for everyone, including the guests.

HONESTY

Honesty is an important trait for anyone, particularly an individual who is dealing with the public. During the course of a regular business day, each member of the dining room staff has innumerable opportunities to deceive both the restaurant and the guest. By being, and appearing to be, totally honest in all aspects of the day-to-day routine, the professional server permits the guests to let down their guard a little, thereby allowing them to fully enjoy the time spent in the establishment.

KNOWLEDGE

The professional server must be prepared to answer any questions asked by guests, and to do so without continually making inquiries of busy fellow employees. A good server is a good salesperson—and good salespeople always know their product line. A good server would never ask a chef to leave something off a plate that was never there in the first place. It is essential for the server to take the time to become familiar with the menu and beverage list, to know their ingredients, their preparation time, their proper service temperature and their garnishes. This information can be helpful in dealing with special requests, such as substitutions for, or allergies to, certain ingredients. Awareness of the physical features of the dining room and kitchen can help the server to speedily solve any problems that arise.

The professional server's knowledge of the establishment's special services, hours of operation, history and background, and special facilities can be a real help to new customers and, consequently, is good for business. Community news, future and current events in the region, and local places of interest are all topics on which the professional server should be informed.

By reading books and periodicals about wines and foods, the professional server becomes more knowledgeable, and thereby reassuring in discussions with guests, and learns to appreciate the complexities of the culinary field. Winning the confidence of guests by being knowledgeable generates goodwill and increases tips. The successful server takes the time, on and off the job, to work at being well informed by attending wine tastings and cooking demonstrations or by taking service classes.

LOYALTY

Professional servers make an effort to obey regulations and behave positively toward the firm for which they are working. Loyalty is also demonstrated by maintaining high standards of quality. Part of loyalty is a sense of proprietorship—of belonging to, and ownership of, one's job. Professional servers who see themselves as proprietors of their business work together for the common good, helping their fellow employees to consistently achieve the highest standards of service. Loyalty to the guest is also important to the development of repeat business.

Servers must never blame the kitchen for delays. The servers and the kitchen staff are both working to achieve the same goal: pleasing the guests. The server is the most visible representative of a unified effort to provide good service to the guest. Showing loyalty to, and working together with, all of the restaurant's staff presents the restaurant as a competent and confident entity dedicated to providing remarkable service to the guests.

PREPAREDNESS

The food-service hospitality industry is not a business for procrastinators. Always think ahead; it is the only sensible way to work. Have everything ready before service begins. Putting off work that can be done in advance, such as stocking side stands and folding napkins, usually means having to do it later when time should be spent on the customer. Having all required equipment on hand (a corkscrew, matches or a lighter, an extra pencil or pen, or a small flashlight to aid in reading the menu in dim light) helps to make service personnel more useful and more professional in the eyes of the guest.

PRODUCTIVITY

While grace and showmanship contribute to the making of a successful front-of-the-house staff member, the ability to get the job done is no less important. The best combination of these traits is a balanced one. One should enjoy a certain amount of performing, particularly if doing tableside cookery. At the same time, a server must be a real worker—one who always remembers that excellent service is the first goal.

Feelings You Want a Guest to Have and Ways to Evoke those Feelings

WELCOMED Offer a smile and a warm, genuine welcome at the front door, such as "Good evening. How may I help you?" Make sure the host's desk faces the door, not the back wall.

PAMPERED Provide valet parking and someone to hold the door. Make sure guests' coats and umbrellas are taken and stored securely. Pull out chairs for guests as you seat a party.

IMPORTANT Remember and use returning guests' names, and greet them with "Welcome back." Keep track of regular guests' preferences and important dates.

COMFORTABLE Make sure the dining room's heat, lighting levels, and music are appropriate and consistent. Ensure that the dining room is spotlessly clean and that furniture is attractive and in good repair.

ENTERTAINED Offer entertaining tableside preparations or live music, if appropriate. Know about all of the menu and beverage items you offer, especially novel items unique to your restaurant, and describe them in an enticing way.

RELAXED, AT EASE Make sure the reservations process is clear and efficient. Provide waiters with enough knowledge about menu items so that they can answer questions and make suggestions with confidence, and train them in how to read guests' body language so that they can address needs that the guests may not feel comfortable expressing. Offer diners choosing wine the expert assistance of a sommelier, if possible.

SATIATED Know whether your establishment's portion sizes are considered too big or too small, and help guests by offering guidance if they seem to be ordering too much or too little food.

APPRECIATED Ask guests for their opinions, and listen carefully to the responses.

The key to all of the elements in the list above is that each specific action can be learned. For example, you can train yourself to say "May I put you on hold?" and then wait for the caller to answer before doing so, so that the potential guest does not feel as if they have been dismissed or treated rudely. This is the essence of service— doing things that will lead to a guest's satisfaction.

COMPOSURE

The front of the house is not a place for employees to indulge in unrestrained chattiness. Service personnel should only speak concerning business, limiting their conversations with fellow workers to the job at hand. Using a foreign language while speaking with other employees might give the guest the impression you are talking about them. Service staff should always speak in the language normally used in the restaurant's location, although the ability to converse in the language of the guests (or one appropriate to the cuisine of the restaurant) is an asset. Unless the customer initiates a conversation, the only subjects of discussion with guests should be the meal and its service. Speak in a clear voice with pleasant intonation, and never be loud. A good server is unobtrusive.

SENSITIVITY

The server must be sensitive to the needs of the guest, and adjust the pace of the meal accordingly. For many guests, a meal is a time to linger, engage in conversation, and eat slowly. For others, particularly at breakfast or lunch, a meal is only an interruption in a series of other events, and not an event in itself. Even the devoted gastronome occasionally has a train to catch or a theater engagement scheduled immediately after mealtime. It is important to be sensitive to the guest's desire for quick, efficient service in these cases. While the customer should never be rushed, the professional server can expedite the meal in pleasant ways, such as suggesting menu items with minimal preparation times that enable speedy service.

Waiters should know how long each dish on the menu takes to cook, and use that information when the guest is ordering. This same knowledge can come in handy when a guest sends back a dish that they didn't like, and the waiter needs to offer a replacement.

TACT

The ability to say or do the right thing at the right time without offense to others is important for anyone dealing with the public. The professional server takes care in correcting a misinformed guest and always steers the conversation into safe, agreeable channels.

PERSUASIVENESS

Even before the actual service of the meal begins, the professional server must "sell" the guest on what to order. Selling increases the check average. This, in turn, increases the restaurant's profits and the gratuities, as well. Subtly, a good server will steer guests away from choosing certain menu items (if the circumstances are appropriate) and induce them to order others. Incremental sales in areas such as drink specials, shared appetizers, or desserts not only enhance the guest's experience, they can increase the check average, thus increasing gratuities as well.

As the guests enter the dining room, the professional server can begin to determine whether to try selling them expensive items or extras, or whether to suggest items that are more of a bargain. It helps to be able to sense whether the guests are likely to want a simply prepared, standard dish or a more elaborate and unusual one. Guests may not be familiar with all of the menu items or how they may be combined for maximum enjoyment. Therefore the server is uniquely qualified to increase the guests' pleasure throughout their dining experience. If done properly, the guests will actually appreciate this selling.

WILLINGNESS

A willing server routinely does more than is expected—helping coworkers, carrying an umbrella for guests as they walk back to their car, volunteering valuable feedback to management—without being asked. Remarkable service exceeds expectations.

Good servers cultivate these behavioral traits, recognizing them as the essential tools of their trade. Good servers also know that they do not work alone; they are part of a team, which is an integrated staff of restaurant personnel.

Conclusion

HOSPITALITY WITHOUT SERVICE SKILLS to back it up is nothing more than a series of platitudes and pleasantries. Service without hospitality is impersonal and cold. When you use service skills to deliver on the promise of hospitality and hospitality skills to make service personal, you are practicing remarkable service.

While most of the details of this book involve developing the skills you must cultivate in order to provide a great dining experience for your guests, we must not lose sight of the importance of a remarkable server's behavior. Think of it in these terms: A musician studies the notes and chords on the page and develops the skills necessary to play them. But the sounds are not truly music until the musician puts some passion into playing notes. It is the same in table service; the skills of serving do not qualify as hospitality without a sincere desire to provide for the guests. While it is often argued that a musician must play for himself or herself in order to become an artist, a server's passion for remarkable service is developed by keeping the guest's satisfaction with the total dining experience as a goal.

2

The History and Traditions of Professional Table Service

THE HOSPITALITY AND SERVICE INDUSTRY is a noble profession with a long and varied history. What servers do today is the result of a thousand generations of servers who came before them, struggling with the same issues faced today—and coming up with new and creative ways of dealing with them.

The kinds of table service in use today evolved along with the foods that are served. Foods and service are always reflective of the societies around them. By looking at the way the ancients dined at their banquets, dining habits in modern bistros and family restaurants can be better understood. Even the sometimes bizarre jargon used in today's kitchens and dining rooms can, by examining the past, begin to make sense.

"Those who cannot remember the past are condemned to repeat it."
GEORGE SANTAYANA

The Ancient World

THE EARLIEST WRITTEN DESCRIPTIONS of recognizably Western dining scenes are found in the Old Testament of the Bible and in the *Iliad* and *Odyssey* of Homer. In reading these texts, it's obvious that the status of the diners was a major concern. Cyrus H. Gordon, in his book *The Common Background of Greek and Hebrew Civilizations,* noted that "...each man got a portion commensurate with his station." Who received which portions, and how much, was based entirely upon status. Generally, the host was the ranking personage; he received the largest and choicest portions, the "proportionate feast."

Formal dining, as we know it today, was reserved for wealthy men. These banquets were generally held in private homes, as the Greeks had very few public eating places. Their dining rooms contained couches for the guests, rather than the tables and chairs we see in formal Western dining rooms today. A small table with a basket containing a selection of breads made of wheat or barley was placed in front of each couch. The items served, and the manner in which they were to be served, was well established. Servants brought large dishes from the kitchen and each guest chose his favorite portion, tossing scraps, shells, and bones onto his table.

The meal was divided into three sections. The first course might include fruit, poultry, salted seafood, and small savory meat dishes, much like Spanish tapas today. These light dishes were followed by heartier fare—fresh seafood and roasted meats, such as lamb or baby goat. After the second course, the tables were whisked away with all of the scraps and shells and new tables were brought out. Servants circulated with towels and basins of warm water, scented with essential oils so the guests could clean their hands (much like the finger bowls provided when proper finger foods, such as asparagus or artichokes, are served in fine dining rooms today).

Desserts were then served: dried and fresh fruits, cheeses, nuts, and small pastries or other confections. Wine mixed with water, tableside in kraters (large clay pots shaped like wide-mouthed, handled vases) was served with the desserts. Diluted wine was considered healthier than water alone, and drunken behavior (during the early stages of the meal, at least) was discouraged. After the dessert course, again, the soiled tables were removed, signaling the end of the meal and the beginning of the symposium (a curious mixture of literary and philosophical discussions, music, acrobats, and female dancers—all accompanied by the drinking of undiluted wine).

The Romans adopted a great deal of Greek culture, including the culinary arts, but took Greek ideas about the meal as mere starting points. A Roman dining room was called a "triclinium" because it contained three couches, each accommodating three diners. The three couches were arranged in a U-shaped pattern. Diners rested on their left sides, their left elbows propped up on cushions. This left their right hands free to choose from the sumptuous foods, each carried from the kitchen on a large platter called a "discus." Each guest ate individually from a red pottery bowl or dish, such as the famous Samian ware.

Unlike the Greeks, Roman families often dined together. However, they still used the dining room as a means of indicating rank and power. There was a strict set of rules governing the positions of each diner, based upon status. The head of the household always had the most prestigious position.

Being invited to dine signaled social recognition that was much sought after. Whom one invited, who accepted an invitation, and to whom one appealed to for an invitation, said much about one's power in ancient Rome. Guests had their positions assigned according to status. This behavior is echoed today in the tradition of seating the guest of honor to the right of the host.

A Roman dinner, like its Greek predecessor, consisted of three courses. The first, the gustum, gustatio, or promulsis, was similar to our hors d'oeuvre or first entrée. It was served with mulsum, a light wine mixed with honey. Gustum was followed by the mensae primae, or "first table." A red wine, mixed with water, accompanied the mensae primae. The next course was the mensae secundae. This "second table" included a dessert of fruits and other sweets—and the first unwatered wines of the meal. As in the Greek symposium, this was the time for serious drinking to begin.

The Middle Ages and the Renaissance

THE HIERARCHY OF POWER and status continued to be reflected in upper-class medieval meals. In Anglo-Saxon times, these meals were large-scale affairs, taking place in the main hall of a castle; there were no rooms reserved solely for dining. The tables consisted of immense boards laid across heavy trestles (the origin of the modern sense of board, as in "room and board").

The first thing placed on the table was the salt cellar. It determined the status of everyone in attendance (salt was second only to spices as a valued food commodity in the Middle Ages). High-status diners ate "above the salt," the rest were placed below; only those above the salt were seated on chairs. Diners brought along their own flatware. Knives were used to cut foods into pieces small enough to be conveniently eaten with their hands. Spoons were the primary table utensils. Silver was reserved for the wealthy, which in those times tended to mean nobility. Lesser folk owned spoons of tin-plated iron or, if they were truly poor, wood. The material of which one's spoon was made determined where, relative to the salt cellar, one got to sit.

Typically the only implement on the table was a carving knife. Carving was a manly art and was, at first, reserved for the person of highest status—the host. Later, this task was given over to the "officer of the mouth," the highest-ranking servant. A new concern with courtliness and manners, if not sanitation, demanded that the officer of the mouth "set never on fish, beast, or fowl more than two fingers and a thumb."(*The Boke of Keruynge: The Book of Carving* by Wynken De Worde, Peter Brears,1508, a book of manners and etiquette for young boys at court.)

Food was served from common bowls, called "messes"—an apt term. Food was scooped, or dragged, to large dishes or trenchers (slabs of stale bread used as plates), which were shared by two or three diners. Wealthy European households had a large number and variety of silver bowls, basins, pitchers, and other serving vessels. Ordinary folk might have no more than a pewter mug and a black bread trencher. The display of wealth, through serviceware, was only one of the ways that status could be expressed through meals.

In the late fourteenth century, people began to think of food and its service as art forms, worthy of study and respect. Taillevent, the famous royal cook (real name Guillaume Tirel, 1312–1395), collected and codified the best of medieval cooking in his books, *Le Viander* and *Ménagier de Paris*. In 1475, Platina of Cremona's *De Honesta Voluptate* ("On Decent Enjoyment and Good Health"), appeared in Europe as the first printed food book. In it, Platina discussed proper manners, table etiquette, table settings, and more. This book altered the way the wealthy, who still ate with their hands, thought about eating and manners.

During the Renaissance in the fifteenth century, dining and service became more elaborate, just as art and music did at that time. Professional guilds to regulate the production of goods included those for meat roasters, caterers, and pastry chefs. As more people gained financial security, the demand for better service and food increased, particularly in Italy.

A new taste for cleanliness throughout Western Europe and England required that the boards used as tables in banquets be covered with a large cloth called the "nappe." Its top surface was kept scrupulously clean, but the sides, where it hung down, were used for wiping of hands (made especially greasy by the absence of forks). Occasionally hand towels, known as manuturgia, would be available.

Some historians trace the origins of classic fine dining to a single aristocratic family of the sixteenth century, the Medicis of Florence. It is said that when Caterina de' Medici (1519–1589) married the future King Henri II of France in 1533, she brought, as part of her trousseau, a small army of Italian cooks, chefs, servants, and wine experts.

If Caterina introduced fine dining and its appropriate service to France, her cousin, Marie de' Medici (1573–1642), wife of Henri IV, certainly continued that culinary mission. François La Varenne, the first great chef of France, is reputed to have received his training in the kitchen of Henri IV. While Taillevent looked to the past for inspiration, La Varenne's book, *Le Cuisinier François* (1651), marks the beginning of a more modern approach to cooking, foreshadowing *Le Guide Culinaire* of Escoffier, still 250 years in the future.

New table manners, beginning with Platina, were expanded during the reigns of both Medici cousins. Among the table refinements allegedly brought to France (and later the rest of Europe) by the Medicis were:

- The ritual of washing the hands before sitting down at the table (hand washing before meals seems to have been a forgotten, then restored, practice from classical antiquity).

- Using a spoon for soups and other liquids.

- Using a fork to select food from a platter.

- Passing the best morsels of food to others at the table.

- Blowing on hot food was discouraged.

- Filching extra dessert by hiding it in a napkin (some evidently felt unsated after thirteen or more courses) was also discouraged.

Henry VIII (1491–1547) initiated formal, luxurious dining in England, but it was his daughter Elizabeth I (1533–1603) under whom the practice flourished. Table manners came to be expected of refined folk. Forks were recommended for the serving of meat (which, by the way, was beginning to be carved by women at the table), although their use as eating implements was still not mentioned. Men and women were seated alternately at the table. Husbands and wives shared a plate—but it was a plate, not a trencher (guests might still be given trenchers, because the immediate family outranked guests, and social status still governed courtesy). Today, trenchers survive only in our term *trencherman,* for enthusiastically big eaters.

Books about table manners and the right way to serve became popular. Braithwaite's *Rules for the Governance of the House of an Earl* (1617) listed spoons and knives as essentials, but did not mention forks. During the reign of Queen Anne (1665–1714), napkins and the increased use of forks made it possible to use finer napery. Table setting began to be seen as an art in itself. Books on the subject, including the first titles about napkin folding, began to appear.

Thomas Coryate

Thomas Coryate (1577–1617) was a traveler and one-time court jester in the court of James I of England. He had traveled to Italy, where he became convinced of the usefulness of the fork. Coryate wrote:

> *For while with their knife which they hold in one hand they cut the meat out of the dish, they fasten their fork, which they hold in their other hand upon the same dish, so that whatsoever he be that sitting in the company of any others at meal, should unadvisedly touch the dish of meat with his fingers, from which all at the table do cut, he will give occasion of offense unto the company, as having transgressed the laws of good manners, in so much that for his error he shall be at the least brow-beaten, if not reprehended in words. Hereupon I myself thought good to imitate the Italian fashion not only when I was in Italy but in England since I came home.*

His English countrymen remained unconvinced and, for his efforts to win acceptance of the new device, mocked him with the nickname "Furcifer," a newly coined word combining the Latin word for fork with Lucifer. Indeed, as late as 1897, sailors in the British navy were not permitted to use forks, as their use was considered an affectation.

The dining room began to be a place of pomp and protocol. A brigade system of officers of the household, complete with uniforms (which even included swords for the highest-ranking servants) was created, not to wait in the trenches, but to wait on trenchermen. This brigade is still observed in the hierarchy of the dining room (see chapter 3).The first service manual of this brigade, *L'Escole Parfaite des Officiers de Bouche* ("The Perfect School of Private Chefs," 1662), explained, "Give the best portions to the most esteemed guests, and if they are of great importance, give them an extra portion." It signaled the beginning of a shift of emphasis from meals for the sake of promoting the status of the host, to one of providing the most pleasurable dining experience possible for the guests.

Service à la française ("French service") found its roots in the grand court of Louis XIV, grandson of Marie de' Medici and Henri IV (1638–1715). The meal was divided into three separate parts, or services. The first and second services consisted of the soups, game, and roasts that were listed on the menu. The third service was dessert. The sequence was much the same as it had been in ancient Greece and Rome. As guests entered the dining room, they found the first course, the entrée, already in place. Hot items were kept warm on réchauds or heating units. After the courses in the first setting were finished, the guests left the table while it was cleaned and reset for the second service.

Service à la française had some distinct disadvantages. The tables were overloaded, and not merely with food. Réchauds, centerpieces, flower baskets, and candelabra seemed to fill every available inch. Despite the use of réchauds, the last items served were generally cold or had, at the very least, lost their freshness. With so many dishes served, most guests limited themselves to one or two items and rarely had an opportunity to sample others.

The Eighteenth Century and the Rise of the Modern Restaurant

THE FRENCH REVOLUTION, the rise of democracy, new conceptions of the role of the individual in society, and the ascendancy of capitalism in Europe made possible the restaurant as we know it today. Great chefs, no longer the exclusive perquisite of nobility, began to see themselves not only as artists (in the same larger-than-life sense that painters, poets, and composers began to see themselves), but as entrepreneurs. They were participants in, and chroniclers of, societal changes.

The French Revolution was not, of course, the sole cause of the development of restaurants in France. Rather, both were products of the same democratizing spirit; the first real restaurants in France appeared about twenty years before the revolution began in 1789. It may be that the rise of popular public eating places aided and abetted the rise of democratic and revolutionary zeal.

The term *restaurant* already existed in France, but it previously referred only to small establishments that sold broth or bouillon, that is, "restoratives." Even before that, there was a tradition of food and beverage service in establishments outside the home. The Romans had small restaurant-type businesses called "taberna vinaria," from which we get the word *tavern*. These establishments served a lot of wine, as well as food that was kept warm in stone counters. Cooks' shops of medieval Europe were often little more than booths set up in the market and offered a very limited menu for the common classes. Inns and taverns were more established places of business, serving table d'hôte (literally, "the host's table," the ancestor of our prix fixe menus): these were fixed menus, at a set price, often served at set times.

Coffeehouses began as places for businessmen to meet both in France and in England in the second half of the seventeenth century, serving coffee as well as other beverages and light food. In 1687, Lloyd's of London, the mighty insurance firm, was originally Lloyd's Coffeehouse—a place where the captains and owners of ships, merchants, and insurance brokers could meet and discuss the day's events, art, literature, and politics as well as gamble on the chances of ships reaching their destinations safely. In Paris, the Café Procope was a popular meeting place for intellectuals. It opened at its current address, across the street from La Comédie Française, in 1686, and is today the oldest surviving coffeehouse in Paris.

In 1782, A. B. Beauvilliers opened the first modern restaurant, Le Grand Taverne de Londres in Paris. Beauvilliers and other chefs, notably the famous Antonin Carême, discussed below, had spent time working in England during the French Revolution, when association with the nobility might have endangered their lives. Beauvilliers contributed the à la carte (literally, "from the card") menu to restaurants as we know them. Offering his guests the opportunity to choose from a number of menu items was a marked change from the table d'hôte of the past, signaling a greater interest in the pleasure of the guests.

Marie-Antoine (Antonin) Carême (1784–1833) lived on the crest of the social changes characterized by the French Revolution. He represented the grandest statement of the old, court-based cuisine, but was inspired by the vigor of a new society creating itself. Carême was one of the last hold-outs in favor of service à la française. It was a perfect frame for the exhibition of his art.

However, Carême's preference for the grandeur of service à la française could not slow the shift to a more guest-centered form of service. In 1808, Grimod de la Reynière published his *Manuel des Amphitryons,* a guidebook for table service. The term *amphitryon* is used in place of the old term *officer of the mouth* or *carver* (the person in charge of the dining room), and is henceforth known as the "host." The motto for service staff, according to Reynière, is, "The host whose guest is obliged to ask for anything is a dishonored man." This is a far cry from the kind of host-centered service seen in the courts of the past.

This change in focus was echoed in 1825, in Anthelme Brillat-Savarin's (1755–1826) *La Physiologie du Gout* ("The Physiology of Taste"). Félix Urbain Dubois's *La Cuisine Classique* (1856) took this approach to service another step forward. It introduced service à la russe ("Russian service") to European dining rooms. Food was served hot from the kitchen, in individual portions, rather than from an immense display where all of the dishes, prepared well ahead of time, had been sitting for maximum visual effect.

If service à la française expected diners to be impressed by the host's largesse (even if it was served lukewarm), service à la russe assured that each guest's meal was served at its best. The burden of assuring the guest's enjoyment was shifted to the host (or the host's staff), while attracting as little attention as possible. In a sense, Dubois had rediscovered the best aspect of classic Roman table service: piping hot dishes rushed out for the guests' delectation.

From this point on, the development of European, especially French, cuisine became a series of small refinements. The evolution of table service slowed to a crawl, as the needs of fine dining were met by fine-tuning the formats of table d'hôte, service à la française, and service à la russe. Significant change, for better or worse, would have to come from somewhere else.

The Nineteenth Century

IN 1900, the first edition of *Le Guide Michelin* in France reflected the changes in modern society—a society now characterized by mobility, a desire for freedom of choice, and disposable incomes with which to exercise that freedom. It also reflected the food-service industry's increasing awareness that the guest's satisfaction was paramount. These modern concepts did not originate in France, the world capital of fine dining. They came from the New World, and they were generated by forces that could never have been imagined by the likes of Taillevent, La Varenne, or Carême.

There were two profound differences between the development of dining habits in the two hemispheres. North American culture evolved together with the Industrial Revolution. The combination made efficiency an almost religious virtue. In the nineteenth century, technological changes shaped America's rise to power. While European cuisines developed slowly from ancient historical roots, American cuisine evolved from the sudden need to feed vast numbers of people, spread out over an entire continent, as quickly and cheaply as possible.

Rapidly developing technologies in the nineteenth century enabled this change. Almost simultaneously, the agricultural, transportation, and food-processing industries were transformed. Companies were suddenly manufacturing millions of units of food items and could not afford to make their products according to the specific tastes of just one or two people. By the early twentieth century, marketing science, with tasting panels, focus groups, and surveys of public opinion began to be used first to understand and then define the "American taste."

Dining Room Personnel

AS MENUS AND STYLES OF SERVICE have changed over the years, so has the structure of the dining room staff. The medieval position of officer of the mouth has been replaced by the maître d'hôtel, which in many modern establishments has been replaced by general manager, floor manager, dining room manager, or, simply, host. The titles may change, but the responsibilities continue—altered, perhaps, in some details, but constant in the sense that the entire dining room staff is always functioning as host for the guest. The more expensive and elaborate the menu, the more service staff is required and expected.

It is important that everyone understands the nature of their jobs and the characteristics that must be developed in order to advance in the hospitality industry. One employee often must fill in for another: a captain may work one day a week as maître d'hôtel when she has the day off, a chef de rang will work as the captain if he must attend to a special function, and so on.

Conclusion

THE HISTORY OF TABLE SERVICE consists of a set of parallel developments:

- There has been a general increase in the sophistication of the food served, and a concomitant rise in sophistication of the manner in which it is served. While there have been occasional detours, the trend has been toward a more subtle understanding and integration of the parts of the meal.

- The importance of sanitation has received increasing emphasis. The development, and gradual acceptance, of the fork and of table manners were indicators of that change. Pristine cleanliness is regarded as a sign of quality.

In the past forty years, fine dining restaurant service has changed as dramatically as has the food served. During the first half of the twentieth century, American fine dining restaurants tried to emulate European custom. French service was considered the most elegant, followed by Russian and English. American service evolved from these European forms of service, utilizing aspects of all three styles in varying combinations and customizing them to work in the dining rooms of today (a concept known as "house style," further discussed in chapter 3). Today's dining is less stratified and formal; it exemplifies the democratic shift that has characterized the history of table service. In less than a century, fine food service has gone from being the province of the wealthy and powerful to being much more egalitarian. Remarkable service has evolved with the times, while keeping the guests and the quality of their experience as the most important goal.

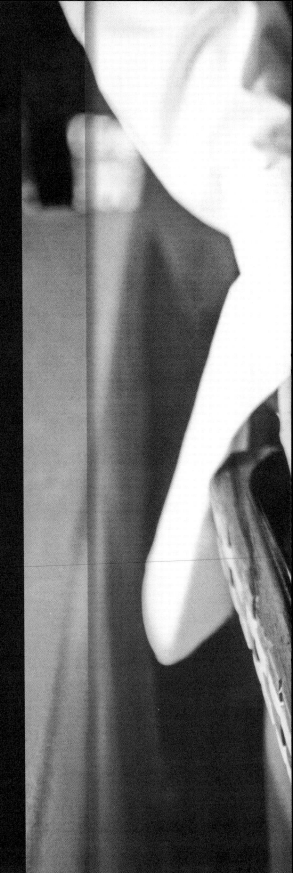

3

Styles of Table Service

THERE ARE MANY STYLES OF
SERVICE, including French, Russian, and
American, as well as English, guéridon,
voiture, butler, and buffet. The type of
service offered at a restaurant is determined
by the menu, the skill and training of
personnel, the ambience, and, ultimately,
the market the restaurant is trying to
reach. No one style of service is better than
another. Each form of service is designed
to meet the specific needs and demands of
distinct circumstances. Any combination of
these styles may be used at different times
if consistent with the restaurant's concept.

Menu and Sequence of Courses

REGARDLESS OF THE TYPE OF MENU, meals have a basic structure that reflects the way foods are experienced by the diner. The basic sequence of courses in most Western menus is based on that of the ancient Greeks, developed to match the sensory requirements of the diners. The Greeks believed that in order for each course to be enjoyed, it must not be overpowered by the preceding course. The meal should build to a climax at the main course, then gradually relax to lighter foods. Even today's simplified sequence of menu items follows the basic pattern established nearly three thousand years ago.

The general sequence of dishes (with certain exceptions, as we shall see) is:

◻ Cold foods before warm

◻ Light foods before heavy

Written menus were often prepared for banquet dinners in France dating from around the 1550s. They show us that a banquet consisted of three courses: the entrée was the first course, and may have included anywhere from ten to forty types of food. The relevés, or removes, was the second course, and it, too, included an astounding number of dishes; this course replaced the "removed" items of the first course. And the final course of the meal was called the "entremets," which corresponds to our dessert course. It included not just sweets, but fruits, a savory item, and a cheese selection. The written menu listed the dishes to be presented in the second course, giving guests a graceful way to pace their consumption while maintaining their appetites.

It is from the French classic sequence of courses that most contemporary Western menus are derived, thus it is essential that servers be familiar with it in order to understand many of today's dining and menu trends. Often, the "latest thing" is simply a rediscovery of a classic tradition.

Today, the menu gives guests at a restaurant a list of options. There are distinct types of menus, described below, including table d'hote, prix fixe, à la carte, and dégustation.

THE CLASSIC MENU

A full classic menu includes seventeen courses, described below:

1. **Hors d'oeuvre (appetizer):** Designed to stimulate the appetite, an hors d'oeuvre could be a small cold tomato salad, or crudité, possibly presented on

a rolling cart from which several items are served on a small plate by the waiter and set in front of the guest. Special utensils such as caviar spoons (of gold, horn, or mother-of-pearl), oyster forks, or snail tongs may be needed.

2. **Potage (soup):** This could be a clear soup, such as bouillon or consommé, served in a two-handled bouillon cup, accompanied by a bouillon spoon (see below). The guests may sip from the cup using the handles or use the spoon. Thicker soups should be served in a soup plate with a soupspoon. The larger, oval-shaped spoon better fits the shape of the soup plate (see below).

3. **Oeufs (eggs):** A small omelet or poached or scrambled eggs.

Bouillon cup and bouillon spoon.

Soup bowl and soupspoon.

4. **Farineaux (starches):** Generally a pasta, such as ravioli, gnocchi, spaghetti, or, sometimes, a risotto (if not served as an entrée). In Italy, "string" pastas are served in a bowl with a fork set on the right. In America, they are usually served on a plate, with a fork on the left and a tablespoon on the right.

5. **Poisson (fish):** Usually soft and easily digestible, meant to prepare the appetite for the following courses. A fish fork and knife may be supplied to assist in boning the fish.

6. **Entrée (light meat):** The first meat dish: a small portion of fowl, beef, pork, or lamb, garnished but served without vegetables when followed by a relevé.

7. **Sorbet (ice):** Sorbets (sometimes fruit- or liquor-based, often with egg whites added after setting to create more volume) are served between main courses to cleanse the palate and to prepare the stomach for the next course. The sorbet

course is sometimes used as an intermezzo ("intermission"), during which the first speech could be given. In Normandy, this course is a trou normande, traditionally a glass of Calvados (a dry brandy made from apples), which is meant to aid digestion and refresh the appetite before the relevé.

8. **Relevé or remove (light meat):** This larger course follows, or replaces, the entrée. Traditionally, it is a joint of meat that is carved and served with sauce or gravy, potatoes, and vegetables.

9. **Rôti (roast):** Together with the relevé, this course is the main event. Usually roasted game, often served with a small green salad. The salad is served from the left, with the left hand, and set above the fork.

10. **Légumes (vegetables):** The winding down of the meal, these vegetables are usually served with a sauce.

11. **Salat (salad):** Aids in digestion after the heavy meal and cleanses the palate.

12. **Buffet froid (cold buffet):** A small portion of a cold meat (i.e., ham, roast chicken) or fish.

13. **Entremets (sweet):** In America, this is dessert, the service of which might require forks, spoons, parfait spoons, and so forth.

14. **Savoureaux (savories):** This course is usually served hot on toast; items include Welsh rarebit, grilled chicken livers and bacon, or an unsweetened soufflé.

15. **Fromage (cheese):** A cheese cart or a platter, brought from table to table, bearing an assortment from which the guests may choose. It should include at least one cheese in each of the following categories: hard, semisoft, soft/cream, and blue-veined. One ounce of each type of cheese is an appropriate portion size for a selection of three or four cheese; for selections of more than four cheeses, serve about ½ ounce each.

16. **Fruit:** Fresh, dried, or candied.

17. **Digestif/tabac (beverages/tobacco):** Coffee, tea, cordials, brandies, cigars, and so on.

Modifying the Classic Menu

A COMMON APPROACH TODAY is to adjust the order of the classic menu, serving the sweets after the savory and cheese courses for example. Also, while European menus treat coffee service as a separate course after dessert, most Americans prefer coffee during the dessert course. Depending on the style of service, it may be appropriate to ask the guests about when in the course of the meal they would prefer to have their coffee served.

COMPARING MENUS

A Current "Classic" Menu (17 Courses)	A Present-Day American Variation	Common Full Meal in American Restaurants
Appetizer (hors d'œuvre)	Cold appetizer	Appetizer (cold or hot)
Soup (potage)	Soup	Salad
Eggs (oeufs)	Fish	Main course
Starch (farineux)	Sorbet	Dessert/coffee
Fish (poisson)	Meat	
Light meat (entrée)	Salad	
Sherbet (sorbet)	Dessert/coffee	
Light meat (relevé)		
Roast (rôti)		
Vegetables (légumes)		
Salads (salats)		
Cold buffet (buffet froid)		
Sweets (entremets)		
Savories (savoureaux)		
Cheese (fromage)		
Fresh fruit (fruit)		
Beverages/tobacco (digestif/tabac)		

Modern Menus

CHANGES RESULTING FROM SOCIAL MOVEMENTS (such as the French and Industrial revolutions) and the need for more efficient use of time have led to a reduction in the number of courses in modern meals.

In most restaurants, guests create their own meal from the items offered on the à la carte menu (à *la carte* literally means "from the card"). With an à la carte menu (shown on page 37), guests order individually priced items, and have the ability to structure their meal in any way they choose.

The table d'hôte menu (see page 38) offers a complete multicourse meal for a set price and may offer a choice within each category. For example, there may be three options for the main course and three options for the dessert course.

The most common type of table d'hôte is the prix fixe menu—a set meal at a set price, usually with no additional choices (see page 39). Since the meal is predetermined, the kitchen can operate more efficiently, and therefore, offer the meal at a lower price. A prix fixe menu may be offered in addition to the à la carte menu. Restaurants may have several different prix fixe menus at the same or different price; some may have more courses than others, but there are usually no substitutions allowed and the total price is charged whether or not the guests want the entire menu.

For both table d'hôte and the prix fixe menu there may be a supplemental charge for a higher cost item, such as lobster or caviar. Coffee or tea is usually included with prix fixe and table d'hôte menus. Espresso or cappuccino may be offered for an additional charge. A variant of the traditional prix fixe table d'hôte menu is one in which, for an additional charge, appropriate wines are paired with each of the courses.

Some fine restaurants may offer a menu dégustation ("tasting menu"), consisting of small portions of numerous items to compose a five- to ten-course meal, sometimes accompanied by paired wines, following the basic classical structure. The menu dégustation allows chefs to exhibit their skills creating an extensive and varied meal. This elaborate meal is served to everyone at the table, thereby eliminating a situation in which some guests have to wait with no food in front of them while the other guests enjoy the multiple courses. The meal follows classic guidelines, but provides small portions of each of the items the chef chooses. If advertised, a menu dégustation may be offered at only one seating, as the time required to enjoy such a dinner makes it impossible to turn the tables. It is not unusual for the chef of a fine restaurant to receive a special request in advance for a menu dégustation—often with recommended wines to accompany the dishes.

Á LA CARTE MENU

WOOD-FIRED PIZZAS   Small 4.50   Large 6.75
  *Mediterranean-Style Vegetable pizza

STARTERS
  Grilled Chicken Skewer With Soy-lime Sauce   5.00
  Smoked Shrimp with Horseradish and Dill-Yogurt Sauce   6.000
  Wood Oven-Roasted Clams in "Casino"-Style Broth   5.50
  Seafood Sausage with Tomato and Leek Sauce   5.50
  *Morel Risotto with White Truffle Oil   6.00
  *Crispy Potato and Vegetable Napoleon   4.50

SOUPS AND SALADS
  Potato-Olive Soup Garnished with Tomato Marmalade   4.00
  Shrimp and Chicken Gumbo   4.50
  Curried Carrot Soup with Ginger Cream   4.00
  A Taste of Each—Our Soup Sampler   4.50
  *Local Organic Mesclun with Choice of Creamy Blue Cheese,
  Lemon-Thyme Vinaigrette, or Balsamic Vinaigrette   4.00
  *Salad of Baby Lettuces with Apples, Walnuts, and Coach Farm
  Goat Cheese Dressing   4.50
  Italian-Style Pancake with Fresh and Roasted Vegetable Salad   5.00

MAIN COURSES
  *"Pho"—Vietnamese-Style Beef Consommé Full of Noodles, Herbs
  and Chilies   9.50
  Monkfish Bouillabaise with Local Potatoes and Braised Fennel   12.00
  *Roasted Pork Tenderloin with Black Bean Sauce, Mango-Tomatillo Salsa
  and Grilled Vegetables   11.50
  Salmon and Potato Rösti with a White Wine-Vegetable Demi-glace   14.50
  Grilled Prosciutto-Wraped Quail with Roasted Shallots and Figs   12.00
  *Braised Celery Hearts with Herbed Risotto—Sauce of Roasted Shallots
  and Chanterelle Mushrooms   10.00
  Grilled Beef Tenderloin with Mushroom Ragout   16.50

  * INDICATES VEGETARIAN SELECTION

À la carte menu.

TABLE D'HÔTE MENU

TERRINA RUSTICA DI MONTAGNA
"Pork Terrine from the Mountains"—Pork, Veal, and Pistachios Served with Salsa,
Salsa Verde, and Seasonal Greens

ANTIPASTO FREDDO ASSORTITO
Assorted Seasonal Cold Antipasti

CARPACCIO DI MANSO CON RUCOLA E PARMIGIANO REGGIANO
Thin-Sliced Raw Sirloin of Beef with a Zesty Lemon Dressing, Saved Parmigiano,
and Arugula

ZUPPETTA DI COSSE CON ROSMARINO
Mussels Steamed in Olive Oil, Garlic, White Wine, and Rosemary

RISOTTO DEL GIORNO
Risotto of the Day

STRACCIATELLA ALLA ROMANA
Egg Drop Soup—Roman-Style

TORTELLI CON LA ZUCCHA
Large Tortelli Filled with Butternut Squash, Amaretti, Mostarda di Frutta, Parmigiano
Reggiano and Sage Butter

RAVIOLI CON FONDUTA E SALSA DI FUNGHI
Small Ravioli Filled with Piemontese-style Fontina Fondue in a Sauce of Mushrooms
and Parmigiano Reggiano

LINGUINE CARBONARA
Linguine in a Traditional Roman Sauce of Eggs, Pancetta, Black Pepper, and Parsley

SECONDI PIATTI

OSSOBUCO CON PORCINI   28.00
Veal Shank Braised with Porcini Mushrooms, Tomatoes, and Marsala Wine

MANZO ALL PIZZAIOLA   28.00
Pan-Fried Steaks "Pizza-maker's Style" with a Sauce of Tomatoes,
Garlic, and Fresh Oregano

QUAGLIE RIPIENE AL FORNO   29.50
Quail with Sausage, Herb, Pine Nut, and Raisin Stuffing with Oven-Roasted Potatoes

MERLUZZO IN CROSTA DI PANGRATTATO SU LETTO DI PATATE   27.00
Fresh Atlantic Cod Marinated in Virgin Olive Oil, Rosemary, and Garlic,
Roasted on a Bed of Thin-Sliced Potatoes with a Crust of Bread Crumbs

APOLPETTINI DI VITELLO CON SALSA D'AGLIO E PEPERONI   27.50
Veal and Pork Patties with a Garlic and Roasted Red Pepper Sauce

MAIALE FARCITO CON SALVIA E FONTINA IN CROSTE DI ERBE   26.00
Pork Filets Stuffed with Fontina, Eggplant, and Sage with an Herb Crust

Table d'hôte menu.

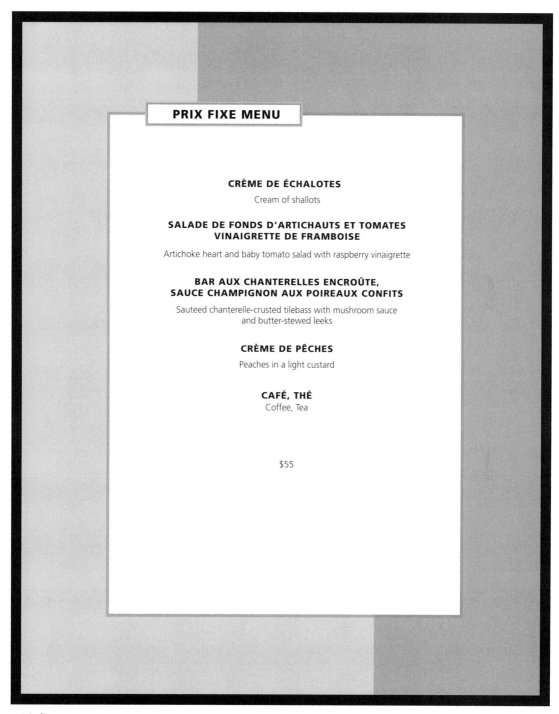

PRIX FIXE MENU

CRÈME DE ÉCHALOTES

Cream of shallots

**SALADE DE FONDS D'ARTICHAUTS ET TOMATES
VINAIGRETTE DE FRAMBOISE**

Artichoke heart and baby tomato salad with raspberry vinaigrette

**BAR AUX CHANTERELLES ENCROÛTE,
SAUCE CHAMPIGNON AUX POIREAUX CONFITS**

Sauteed chanterelle-crusted tilebass with mushroom sauce
and butter-stewed leeks

CRÈME DE PÊCHES

Peaches in a light custard

CAFÉ, THÉ

Coffee, Tea

$55

Prix fixe menu.

Types of Restaurants

THE TECHNIQUES A RESTAURANT MAY USE in order to achieve the two main goals of good service are based on variations of the classic styles, adjusted and adapted to suit the style of restaurant. To facilitate comparison, restaurants can be divided into three basic styles:

FINE DINING	Upscale, luxury, three-, four-, and five-star, "white-tablecloth" restaurants. Examples: An American Place, Charlie Trotter's, Jean-Georges, Nobu, Nora's, The French Laundry, The Inn at Little Washington
BISTRO/TRATTORIA	Grills, cafés. All have less ceremonious approaches to food service. Examples: Da Silvano, Lulu, Fog City Diner, Spago, Tra Vigne, Wild Ginger
CASUAL/FAMILY	Family-style restaurants Examples: Olive Garden, Applebee's, T.G.I. Friday's, Red Lobster, Ruby Tuesday

FINE DINING

Fine dining establishments offer luxurious and comfortable surroundings, usually including tabletop silver, china, linen, and crystal. A maître d'hôtel directs the dining room and the staff of captains, waiters, and bus persons.

A fine dining restaurant.

A typical menu usually offers many choices as well as specials, plus a table d'hôte or prix fixe meal. The wine list is appropriately extensive and well paired to the food. A sommelier may be on hand to help guests.

The service staff attends to every detail of the guests' experience in a fine dining restaurant. The pace of service is leisurely, which befits the elegance of a meal that may last three hours or more (shown at right).

BISTRO/TRATTORIA

The most common type of dining in American cities today, bistros and trattorias range from white-tablecloth establishments, with a range of food styles, to animated and bustling bare-bones places serving simple fare and beverages. The strict definition of a bistro—a family-run establishment, serving foods with a wine theme—has all but been abandoned in the United States. The term *bistro* now refers to any simple, cozy restaurant.

Service should be polite, attentive, and efficient in this level of restaurant, though not as grand as in fine dining venues (shown at right).

Bistros and trattorias.

CASUAL/FAMILY

This category encompasses family-style restaurants, diners, many theme restaurants, and the like. The principles of good service apply here as well, although servers may be less experienced than in the other classifications of restaurants (shown at right).

Family and casual dining.

Guidelines for Serving

IMAGINE a line that extends from the guest's nose across the middle of the plate. The server should never reach across that line.

WHEN the server is on the guest's left, the server should always try to use the left hand.

WHEN the server is on the guest's right, the server should always try to use the right hand.

ALWAYS move counter-clockwise around the table when serving platter (Russian) style, or clearing from the guest's left side.

ALWAYS move clockwise around the table when serving, setting-in, or clearing from the guests' right side.

Styles of Service

BEFORE DESCRIBING THE VARIOUS FORMS OF SERVICE, a little clarification may be helpful. *Serving* to a classically trained server means transferring food with utensils from one surface to another, for example serving food from a platter to a plate as in Russian service (as shown at right). *Setting-in* means to set a plate in front of the guest (onto which food will be served from a platter, or upon which the food has already been arranged). It has become commonplace to call setting a plate of food in front of someone "serving." For the purposes of explaining the reasoning behind the procedures of different styles of service, *setting-in* and *serving* will used in the classical sense in this chapter.

Serving.

Serving food onto a preset plate should be done from the guest's left and setting-in preplated food should be from the guest's right. To provide more fluid service and avoid having to back up, the server moves around the table counterclockwise when serving from the guest's left, and when setting-in from the right, the server movesclockwise around the table.

FRENCH SERVICE

Based upon the banquet styles of the sixteenth century, service à la française is the most elaborate and labor intensive of all serving styles. Traditionally, French service at small banquets in large private homes divided a meal into three separate courses, with much of the food cooked or finished tableside, from a rolling cart or guéridon, in the dining room. (Tableside cooking first began in Russia and was then further developed into a flourishing service style in France. Consequently, there has been confusion over the correct use of the terms French or Russian as a descriptor for this style of service, especially since tableside service equipment is referred to by its French name.)

As guests entered the dining room, the first course was already set up (the origin of the word *entrée* for the first course can be traced to this "entering" of the dining room). Hot items were brought to the dining room on silver platters and placed on the guéridon, or covered warmer. After the guests finished a service, they got up and left the table while it was cleaned and reset for the next service. This second course was the relevé or remove. The first two services consisted of between ten and forty items, including soups, game, and roasts. Many of these items were placed on the table on platters with serving utensils for what might be referred to as family-style service today. The third service, the entremets, included a variety of desserts, savories, puddings, fruits, and nuts.

Today's formal service generally requires two servers (front and back waiters, or chef de rang and commis de rang) to deliver and prepare the food, plus perhaps a captain to seat guests and take orders, a busser (commis de débarrasseur) or guard, and usually a sommelier to assist in wine selection and to serve the wine. The front waiter prepares, plates, and garnishes the food, then the back waiter serves it. The traditional outfit for the servers is black tie and white gloves, with the addition of an apron for the front waiter while cooking. Since white gloves must be changed frequently during serving, it is imperative that servers have enough pairs to change them as necessary throughout the service of the meal. The captain may perform more difficult preparations such as flambéing and may debone or carve meats.

This courtly style of service can be entertaining for guests, but it has some distinct drawbacks in today's more cost-conscious (and less decorous) era. For one, the additional cost of equipment, staff, and space required to serve at tableside is prohibitively expensive for most establishments. The prices have to be high enough that all of the members of the team can make enough money to live on. Thus, this style has been relegated to the formal dining rooms of a few restaurants and hotels around the world.

THE GUÉRIDON

In formal service, the guéridon is center stage in the service act. It is often equipped with a réchaud (a heating element) and a large silver dome or cloche for covering food. The guéridon should contain all of the tools and equipment needed for the menu items. It might be used for mixing salads, deboning fish, or carving meat. The fuel is usually alcohol, bottled butane, or Sterno. Guéridon service is very similar to formal service, except that all items are fully prepared tableside from the guéridon and immediately plated and served. Some fine dining establishments employ a modified form of formal service in which food is fully or partially cooked in the kitchen, placed on a platter, and carried to the dining room by a waiter. The platter is then placed on a guéridon or heating table and plated. This allows some tableside showmanship with less labor for the server. One example of tableside service you may see in some establishments is the preparation and presentation of a cheese plate. For a more detailed discussion of guéridon (tableside) service, see chapter 10.

Setting-in.

Advantages of Formal Tableside Service	Disadvantages of Formal Tableside Service
Elegant	Requires highly skilled servers
Personalized service	Requires expensive equipment
Showcases the food and preparation	Higher labor cost
Entertaining (flambéing, carving)	Less seating capacity (need guéridon space)
Leisurely dining	Less turnover
Higher check average	Can be too formal for some guests

VOITURE AND TROLLEY SERVICE

The meaning of *voiture* loses something in translation. Literally, "a carriage or car," a voiture is generally a decorative cart, also known as a "trolley," equipped with a heating unit and a hinged cover, to maintain the warmth of prepared hot foods—although cold foods can also be served from a voiture. A voiture differs from a guéridon in that it is large enough to hold an entire roast. In practice, *voiture service* refers to the plating of a precooked main course, at the guest's table, from a voiture.

RUSSIAN OR PLATTER SERVICE

Russian service, which is mostly used for banquets, is less showy than French service, but it is quicker and no less elegant. Speed replaces showmanship, though there is skill involved. The main goal of Russian or platter service is to assure the guest recieves fully cooked, hot food served in a swift and tasteful fashion. It is especially expedient for banquets or wherever it is necessary to serve many people attractively presented food quickly but without sacrificing elegance and a personal touch.

In Russian service, all food is fully cooked and artfully arranged and garnished on large platters in the kitchen. With the server's right hand, empty plates are set-in from the guest's right, beginning with the first woman seated at the host's left. The server moves clockwise around the table. The platters of food are carried to the dining room by a server and presented to the table. The server then begins with the first woman seated at the host's right, displays the food from the left, and serves the desired portion. The server transfers the food from the platter to the guest's plate by the skillful manipulation of a fork on top of a spoon. The server then continues around the table counterclockwise. Sauces and garnishes are served either by that same waiter or by another one following right behind. The platter is held in the left hand and food is served with the right hand. Note that service and setting-in are done from the opposite sides of the guest, as compared with French and other service styles.

Even though the entire meal may not be served in the Russian service style, it remains common for waiters to use Russian service to place bread on guests' plates. Additionally, the same skills required for Russian service can be helpful when splitting menu items into two plates for guests, either on the guéridon, on the side stand, or at the table. (There are additional discussions of Russian service in chapter 9.)

Advantages of Russian Service	Disadvantages of Russian Service
Personalized service	Requires space between chairs for wide platters
Grand style	Requires skilled (and physically capable) servers
Entertaining	Less portion control and may run out of items
Guests may choose portion size	Food can become cold and ragged while serving
Guests may choose quantity of sauces	Dangers of spilling soups or sauces
Server can exhibit skills	

BUTLER SERVICE

The procedures for butler service are the same as those for Russian service, except that the guests serve themselves with provided utensils from the platter held by the waiter as shown in figure at right. Beginning with the first woman to the host's right, the butler offers from the left, moving counterclockwise around the table, holding the platter in both hands. During the service of hors d'oeuvre, however, a smaller-size platter may be held in the left hand alone. This frees the right hand to offer napkins from a small plate.

Butler service.

Advantages of Butler Service	Disadvantages of Butler Service
Personalized service	Requires space between chairs for wide platters
Grand style	Less portion control and may run out of items
Guests may choose portion size	Food can become cold while serving
Guests may choose quantity of sauces	Dangers of spilling soups or sauces

ENGLISH AND FAMILY SERVICE

English and family service conjures nostalgic images of families gathered around a steaming roast on Sunday afternoon, with Father carving the meat and passing plates around the table. In restaurants or country clubs, this style of service is usually reserved for private rooms or special group dinners, where guests want to mimic a home-style setting while still being waited on. Plates are preset and the server moves clockwise around the table when clearing used plates.

As with Russian and butler service, all food is fully cooked in the kitchen. The host, or perhaps the maître d'hôtel, carves the meat (or whatever the main dish happens to be), and passes it to the nearest diner who in turn passes it along the table. This carver should be skilled in plating in an attractive and appetizing manner. The host generally serves soup into bowls, which are then passed around the table. Side dishes arrive from the kitchen in large serving platters and guests help themselves, or the host may plate the side dishes before passing the plates. Alternatively, serving dishes can be placed on a sideboard, from which the server plates all of the food, and then presents it to the guests.

Variations on this less formal style of serving are becoming popular in the United States, especially at new American restaurants and grills that want to create a more family-like ambience. It is also seen on tours, resorts, small cruise ships, and in the Pennsylvania Dutch area.

Family style is similar to English style, except that all of the foods are placed on the table in large serving dishes, and guests help themselves. It is quite popular in some value-oriented restaurants, and also in places where the style fits with the theme. It is a remarkably efficient style of service that can make a lot of sense (and money) in the right situation. Customers enjoy the chance to serve themselves, it can lighten the burden in both the dining room and kitchen, and it can lower labor costs.

Advantages of English Service	Disadvantages of English Service
Very casual	Not elegant
Creates a communal atmosphere	Large portions (no portion control)
Guests can have second helpings	No plate presentation
Guests can easily share menu items	
Requires friendly but not necessarily skilled servers	

AMERICAN SERVICE

The common style of setting-in plates in the United States is from the guest's left with the left hand. This is believed to have its origins in American homes with limited service staff. The maid would clear a dirty plate from the right with the right hand, and immediately set-in the filled plate from the sideboard for the next course with the left. It was considered a breach of etiquette for a guest to sit at your table without a plate in front of them.

American service.

Among the least formal styles of service, and by far the most widespread, American service (shown at right) is usually found in bistros, trattorias, and casual restaurants. In American service, all cooking and plating of food is completed in the kitchen. A waiter picks up the plated food, carries it to the dining room, and sets-in the plates in front of the guests from the right with the right hand (although some restaurants prefer service to be from the left, with the left hand). This allows two or three plates to be held in the left hand and arm while serving with the right.

For small parties (less than six guests), women are served first, moving clockwise around the table, then men. For larger parties, the woman to the left of the host is served first. The server then proceeds, serving each guest in turn, moving clockwise around the table, finishing with the host. If there is no obvious host, the server may begin with any woman and proceed as usual. When serving from the left, the server moves around the table counterclockwise.

American service is usually employed in fast turnover, high-volume operations. It can be used in more stylish types of dining operations with procedures varying depending on the service needs. Some chefs prefer American service because plating the food in the kitchen allows them to showcase their creativity in food presentation. American service is frequently used for banquets because large numbers of guests can be handled quickly by a limited number of service personnel.

Advantages of American Service	Disadvantages of American Service
Portion control and lower food costs	Less personalized service
Plate presentation	Informal
Consistency	Guests cannot choose portion size
Fast service	Servers merely set-in plates
Fewer servers required	
Less formal and more accessible	
Limited skill required	

House Style

SUMMARY OF SERVING STYLES

Style	Activity	From Guest's	With Waiter's	Move Around Table	Begin With
FRENCH	Set	Right	Right hand	Clockwise	Woman at host's left
RUSSIAN PLATED	Set	Right	Right hand	Clockwise	Woman at host's left
RUSSIAN PLATTERED	Serve	Left	Right hand	Counter-clockwise	Woman at host's right
AMERICAN	Set	Right (or left, according to individual house standard)	Right hand (or left, according to individual house standard)	Clockwise (or counterclockwise if serving from left)	Woman at host's left

THE MAIN POINTS OF GOOD SERVICE, regardless of the style of service, are

- All foods served at their appropriate temperatures; hot foods served hot on hot plates, cold foods served cold on cold plates.

- All foods and beverages served in a timely, courteous, sanitary manner.

The way any establishment goes about achieving these points can vary dramatically, depending upon the type of service that is practiced in that establishment—in other words, the restaurant's house style. The kind of food to be served is an important deciding factor, but it is not the only one. Certainly the price range, ambience of the room, and the demographics of the market one wishes to attract must be considered. Other considerations go into determining a restaurant's house style as we have already seen, including the type of restaurant (fine dining, bistro, or family-style); the restaurant's personality (formal versus casual); and the type of menu.

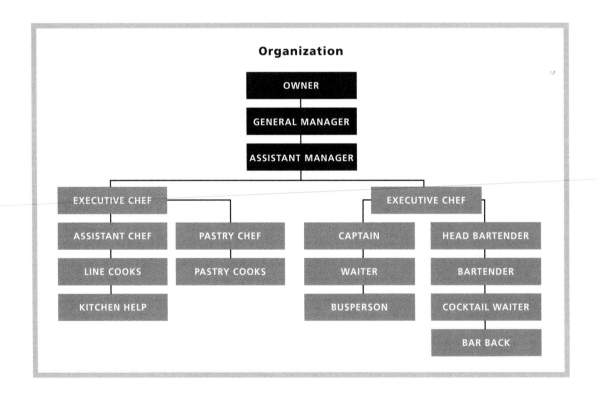

Dining Room Brigade

EVERY ESTABLISHMENT will have some variation on the classic dining room brigade derived from the type and price level of the menu, style of service, and physical structure of the restaurant. In any size organization, it is important that everyone know to whom they report, and to whom their supervisors report. This is the essence of a brigade system, which organizes job functions into a clear hierarchy. To understand some of the hundreds of variations on the classic brigade, it is important to first understand the brigade system itself. Unfortunately, there are various interpretations of the classic brigade titles. So it is most important to understand the job descriptions and responsibilities, regardless of job title.

MAÎTRE D'HÔTEL

The maître d'hôtel is traditionally the manager of the house or the entire operation. This position would be considered the general manager in modern terms. *Hôtel* and *hôte* are both derived from the French word for "host." Fundamentally, that is what the job of maître d'hôtel is about: hosting.

Informally referred to as the "maître d'," today's maître d'hôtel is responsible for the overall management of the dining room: station assignments, public relations, and the physical maintenance of the room itself. In modern bistros or casual restaurants, this position is filled by either the manager or host.

CHEF DE SALLE

The chef de salle is, traditionally, the manager of the dining room, though the French term is rarely used today. The maître d'hôtel is in charge of the dining room service in today's restaurants.

HEAD WAITER

Depending on the establishment, the head waiter may have the responsibilities of the maître d'hôtel, or act as the captain of a dining room or of a primary station in the dining room.

CHEF DE RANG

The chef de rang ("chief of the station"), also known as the "captain," is usually in charge of service in a particular station of tables, takes the order from the guests, and assists the front waiter in serving the food. The captain, as host of his station, should rarely leave it. If necessary, the front waiter can leave the floor to check the status of an order in the kitchen or retrieve drinks from the bar. The captain must have a profound knowledge of food and wine and be able to translate that knowledge into language that is understandable to each and every guest. In some facilities this used to be called "chef d'étage" (literally "chief of the stage" or "floor"), but this term has not been used in many years. In hotels, the chef d'étage was the room service waiter. The captain has more interaction with the guests than any other service staff position.

RÉCEPTIONNISTE

The réceptionniste ("receptionist") is the person who greets (and occasionally seats) the guests, takes phone reservations, and looks after the needs of the front desk area. In casual restaurants, this position often replaces all of the previously mentioned positions, and may be called "the host(ess)."

TRANCHEUR

The trancheur (carver, literally "slicer") rolls a cart or voiture, or works at a chilled station to prepare plates with the meat and accompaniments. Items might include smoked salmon or joint meats such as hams from the voiture. In a modern fine dining restaurant, these functions would probably be performed by the captain.

SOMMELIER

The sommelier (or wine steward) is responsible for the creation of the wine list, the purchasing and storage of wines (maintenance of the wine inventory), the recommendation of wines to guests, and the wine service itself.

COMMIS DE RANG

In some dining rooms the commis de rang is known as the "demi-chef de rang," or "front waiter." Second-in-command of the station, the front waiter takes the order from the captain; relays it to the kitchen through the point of sale system or with a hand dupe; and serves the food with assistance from the captain. The front waiter often assists the captain in taking some orders, or assists the commis de suite in bringing the food from the kitchen. The front waiter's position may not be as glamorous as that of the captain, but the captain relies heavily on the front waiter's efficiency.

COMMIS DE SUITE

The commis de suite (also known as the "back waiter" or "food runner," although the terms aren't exactly equivalent) brings drinks and food to the commis de rang, sets up the guéridon as needed, gets all food and beverage for the assigned station, helps clear, and generally assists the commis de rang.

COMMIS DE DÉBARRASSEUR

The débarrasseur, or "bus person," is often an apprentice or trainee to become a commis de suite or room service waiter and may work the way up the ranks. The bus person is responsible for stocking side stands and guéridon, and cleaning during the preparation time prior to service. While used primarily to clear the tables of soiled items, bus people are often utilized in assisting with bread and water service. Some people, unfortunately, look down on the busser. However, the busser is an extremely valuable member of the service team and can be integral to that team's success. A great busser can lighten the burden on the rest of the service team, enabling them to concentrate more on serving the guests.

Front-of-the-House Position	Duties
MAÎTRE D'HÔTEL	Manages all aspects of the service in the dining room; the host
CHEF DE SALLE	Manages the dining room
HEAD WAITER	May have the responsibilities of the maître d'hôtel, or the captain of a station
RÉCEPTIONNISTE	Greets and occasionally seats the guests; takes phone reservations and maintains the front desk area
CHEF DE RANG (CAPTAIN)	In charge of service in a particular station of tables
CHEF D'ÉTAGE	Responsible for room service in hotels
TRANCHEUR	Rolls a cart, or works at a chilled station, to prepare plates with the meat and accompaniments
SOMMELIER (WINE STEWARD)	Creates the wine list, purchases and stores wines, recommends and serves wine
COMMIS DE RANG OR DEMI-CHEF DE RANG (FRONT WAITER)	Takes the order from the captain and relays it to the kitchen; serves the food with assistance from the captain; assists the commis de suite in bringing the food from the kitchen
COMMIS DE SUITE (BACK WAITER)	Brings the food from the kitchen to the dining room
COMMIS DE DÉBARRASSEUR (BUS PERSON)	Clears the tables of soiled items; an apprentice

One way to better understand the hierarchy of the restaurant as a total unit is to use an organization chart. Charts on the following pages show examples of the possibilities for each of the restaurant styles discussed in this book. It should be noted that the chef or maître d'hôtel may be a part owner and therefore higher in the organizational chart.

Organization Chart

THE MORE CASUAL THE RESTAURANT, the fewer staff members are needed to provide good service. If there is no sommelier, either the captain or maître d'hôtel would provide the wine service. In a casual restaurant, the server would do the duties of the captain and front and back waiters, but of course there would be fewer duties to perform and less expectation of services.

Traditional	Fine Dining	Bistro	Casual
MAÎTRE D'HÔTEL	Owner or general manager	Owner or general manager	Owner or general manager
CHEF DE SALLE	Maître d'hôtel	Floor managers	Floor managers
SOMMELIER	Sommelier		
RÉCEPTIONNISTE	Host	Host	Host
CHEF DE RANG	Captain		
CHEF D'ÉTAGE	Room service waiter		
TRANCHEUR			
COMMIS DE RANG	Front waiter	Waiter	Server
COMMIS DE SUITE	Back waiter		
COMMIS DE SUITE	Runner	Runner	
COMMIS DÉBARRASSEUR	Bus person	Bus person	Bus person

Fine dining restaurants have staff to fill most, if not all, of the traditional dining room brigade positions.

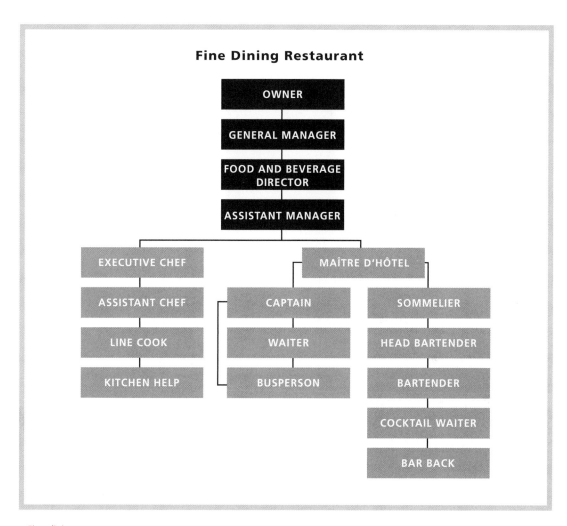

Fine Dining Restaurant

- OWNER
- GENERAL MANAGER
- FOOD AND BEVERAGE DIRECTOR
- ASSISTANT MANAGER
  - EXECUTIVE CHEF
    - ASSISTANT CHEF
    - LINE COOK
    - KITCHEN HELP
  - MAÎTRE D'HÔTEL
    - CAPTAIN
      - WAITER
      - BUSPERSON
    - SOMMELIER
    - HEAD BARTENDER
    - BARTENDER
    - COCKTAIL WAITER
    - BAR BACK

Fine dining restaurant.

BISTRO

In France, a typical bistro would have no captains. Service positions would include, however, chef de rang, commis de rang, or demi-chef de rang.

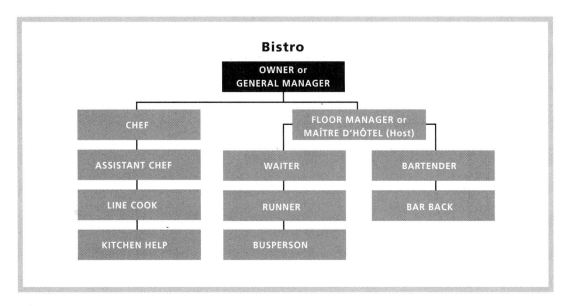

Bistro.

CASUAL (CHAIN)

Chain restaurants may have fewer positions as part of their overall dining room brigade as food service is generally more relaxed than in a fine dining restaurant.

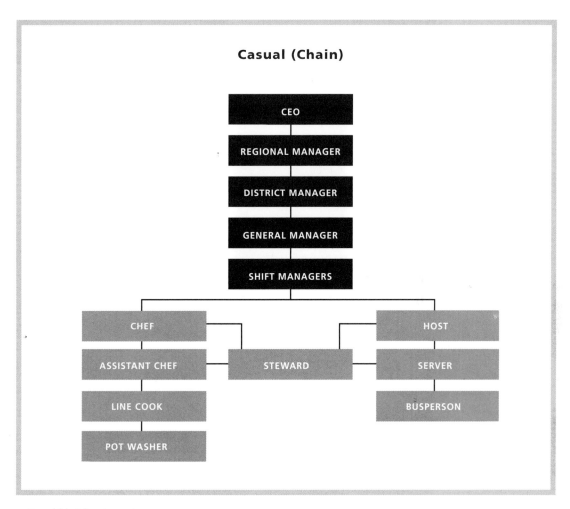

Casual (Chain)

- CEO
- REGIONAL MANAGER
- DISTRICT MANAGER
- GENERAL MANAGER
- SHIFT MANAGERS
  - CHEF
  - ASSISTANT CHEF
  - LINE COOK
  - POT WASHER
  - STEWARD
  - HOST
  - SERVER
  - BUSPERSON

Casual (chain) restaurant.

Conclusion

THERE IS NO SINGLE STYLE OF SERVICE that works for all restaurants or in all situations. Remarkable service occurs when the demands of the menu, the expectations of the management and the guests, and the skills of the dining room's personnel are taken into account. As we will see in chapter 9, there are some further modifications to service styles for special circumstances such as buffets and receptions.

4

Reservations, Greeting, and Seating the Guest

RESERVATIONS, GREETING, AND SEATING THE GUEST are the first opportunity you have to deliver remarkable service. Reservations are often a part of a truly outstanding experience in a restaurant; however, not all restaurants require them. And even restaurants that do ask for reservations can occasionally handle guests who arrive without them. Deciding how to handle reservations is a management decision, but if it is the policy of the restaurant, it is important that the reservation experience be on par with the rest of the dining experience. From the moment guests arrive at the door, the professional server strives to maintain the caliber of the experience. The way you greet a guest, the table you seat them at, even the direction their chairs face can be a matter of concern to the guest, and therefore, to you.

Reservations

IN AN IDEAL WORLD, all restaurants would be so busy every day that they could operate on a first-come, first-served basis and do away with reservations altogether. In that same ideal world, considerate customers would happily call restaurants in advance to ask what time would be convenient to arrive so as not to overburden the chef and service staff.

We do not, alas, work in an ideal world. It often seems that everyone on the planet wants to dine between 8:00 and 8:30 on Saturday evening. Consequently, the vast majority of fine dining and bistro establishments must grapple with the issues of taking reservations.

The question of whether or not to accept reservations is not a simple one to answer, but it's likely you'll have to deal with it sooner or later. The factors that you have to consider when making this decision are as follows:

- **STYLE OF RESTAURANT.** Is the style of your place formal or casual? The fancier the restaurant, the more likely it is that you will need to accept reservations. A couple planning their anniversary dinner will often choose a more formal restaurant, and they almost certainly won't be interested in waiting an hour for their table to open up. Conversely, when you and your friends are going out for Mexican food as a group, it's usually fine if you wind up waiting in the bar of the cantina, drinking margaritas and eating chips and salsa.

- **NUMBER OF SEATS.** The number of seats in the dining room is usually decided early in the planning stages of a restaurant and is integral to the type of service offered. A casual restaurant tends to have more seats with tables closer together; the opposite is true for more formal restaurants. A large casual restaurant tends to turn tables faster, and usually has a table coming available soon; thus, reservations might not be necessary. However, in a formal restaurant where people usually take more time to eat and the number of seats is limited, tables don't free up as quickly—this might be the right place to take reservations.

- **PROJECTED NUMBER OF COVERS PER NIGHT.** Like the number of seats, the number of reservations (or covers) you're anticipating for the shift is important. A high volume of tables that turn over quickly might not require a reservation policy.

- **HOW POPULAR IS YOUR RESTAURANT?** The more famous or visible a restaurant or restaurateur, the higher the demand for tables. For instance, if John Besh opens a restaurant in your neighborhood, you would definitely check out the reservations policy before getting your hopes up for a table. Meanwhile, a restaurant with a talented but as yet unknown chef might open on a first-come, first-served basis, then start taking reservations as the place gets more popular and the host finds it necessary to spread the diners across the period of service rather than taking them whenever they want to come in.

- **OTHER FACTORS.** If you're next door to a theater, there might be an entire seating of the restaurant that leaves before eight o'clock, and one that comes after the show. Handled correctly, the restaurant can have the pre-theater, dinner, and post-theater crowds arranged into three seatings. Being near a convention center can make a difference as well, so you should know when a show or group is coming into town and be ready for more business than usual.

Most restaurants want to have a reasonable estimate of how many diners to expect on a given day. A reservations system can help with staffing, purchasing provisions, planning the menu, and general estimation of costs. Of course, it is often impossible to be exact—some customers, inexplicably and without notice, fail to appear (or show up late), while spur-of-the moment arrivals can increase numbers at unexpected times.

Different establishments have different reservation systems. Many restaurants continue to use a physical reservation book either exclusively or as a supplement and backup for computerized systems in case of crashes.

One step up from the pencil-and-paper method is to input the information into a spreadsheet program. You could also link a spreadsheet to your database in order to keep track of regular customers' birthdays, anniversaries, likes, dislikes, and dietary restrictions. The more information you have at your fingertips, the higher the level of hospitality that you can provide for your guests.

There are computer programs that are specifically designed to accept and keep track of restaurant and hotel reservations. Some of them can be maintained by your own staff. In addition, there are Web-based companies that can manage your reservations while maintaining a database of your guests' pertinent information, such as mailing addresses, birthdays, allergies, personal preferences, and so on. The downside of such systems is lack of complete control and privacy.

Advantages of Accepting Reservations	Disadvantages of Accepting Reservations
Helps an establishment estimate customer flow. Better for kitchen and dining room staffs, as well as guests.	Extra staff needed to work the reservation desk and make reconfirmation calls.
Some guests feel more comfortable when they have a "guaranteed" table.	No-show problem skews customer estimates.
Allows more efficient table assignments.	Requires effort on part of customers who might rather just drop into an establishment at the last minute.
Allows restaurant to become familiar with customers' names and eating preferences.	
Easier to deal with special requests (birthdays, special menus, allergies) at the time of reservation rather than after the customer walks in.	
Phone numbers and e-mail addresses available for future promotions, in case guests leave something, etc.	

It is not necessary to make a firm commitment to either the taking of reservations or of not taking reservations. Some restaurants use both methods. Reservations may only be required for large groups—for example, Carmine's in New York City only takes reservations for parties of six or more.

WHEN RESERVATIONS ARE UNNECESSARY

If a restaurant is so successful that it can't be bothered with such trivialities, its staff may not have to think about reservations. Most of us are not in that situation. However, there are some cases where reservations may not be needed.

Some restaurants take customers in the order in which they arrive at the front door. These restaurants are so busy that reservations are unnecessary. This works for bistro/trattoria places like P.F. Chang's, The Cheesecake Factory, and Carnegie Deli in New York City and Le Bar Lyonnais in Philadelphia. In addition, many casual and ethnic restaurants dispense with the formality of a reservations system. This approach sometimes forces guests to wait for an available table (see Waiting Lists on page 94).

WHEN RESERVATIONS MIGHT BE NECESSARY

Fine dining and bistro restaurants need to weigh the advantages and disadvantages of taking reservations. Some fine dining "destination restaurants" are thirty minutes or more by car or public transportation from residential areas, for example. Their managers cannot expect guests to travel such distances on the off chance they may find a table. Reservations are a must in such cases. Also, the exigencies of a fine dining restaurant require knowing in advance roughly how many guests to expect.

Advantages of a No Reservations Policy	Disadvantages of a No Reservations Policy
Reduces personnel needed to staff the phones.	Susceptibility to the Yogi Berra syndrome: "Nobody goes there anymore, it's too crowded." That is, crowds can scare away newcomers.
Maximizes table use through constant turnover. Tables do not sit empty between seatings.	An establishment can reach the decibel level of a sheet metal plant with all of the voracious cocktail-sipping folks waiting at the bar.
Eliminates dreaded and costly no-show problem.	Customers may get tired of waiting and leave—or worse, tell friends not to bother.
May increase bar sales. Even if guests waiting for tables do not buy an extra drink, a busy bar creates a lively ambience and attracts more bar business.	Some customers will not patronize a restaurant if they are not guaranteed a table.
In some cases lends a more casual and spontaneous aura to an establishment.	The service staff may feel compelled to rush diners to free up tables.
It is a more democratic system; fewer complaints about favoritism.	Need additional space for people to wait, especially in cold weather.
Hordes of people anxiously standing outside of your establishment gives passersby the impression that you must be "a find."	

Taking Reservations

IF A RESTAURANT ACCEPTS RESERVATIONS, the customer's first contact may be with a reservationist. In many restaurants, reservations are handled just inside the front door (at the reception desk, the maître d's podium, or the front desk), either in person or over the phone. In some places, reservations are made by phone to a reservations department that is not even a part of the dining room. Indeed, it might not even be in the same building—they could just as easily be made over the Internet. No matter how the reservation process is managed physically, one must never forget that it is the first opportunity to impress the guest with first-class service.

It is management's responsibility to make sure that everyone who might be called upon to take a reservation is trained, not only in the use of the reservations system and all of the policies and procedures involved, but also in proper telephone technique and etiquette.

RESERVATIONS FOR EFFICIENCY

The primary goal of the reservationist is to fill the dining room to capacity, while staggering the timing of the seatings to ensure the best service from the kitchen and dining room staff. In many restaurants, several people may take reservations, but they may not all understand the intricacies involved in attaining this goal. It is as important to count chairs as it is to count tables. On a busy night you don't want to book all deuces at four tops (except on nights like Valentine's Day when it becomes necessary).

The reservationist has a responsibility to accommodate as much business as the staff can efficiently serve. To assist the reservationists in understanding the maximum seating capacity, it can be helpful to print the times and number of covers in the reservation book in advance (see example on the facing page). It also may be helpful to indicate whether tables can be moved to accommodate different-size groups.

If this information is written in advance, then any reservationist knows if they take a reservation for three people at a table for four, they have lost revenue for the restaurant. If, however, they know they can comfortably seat three people at a deuce, and take the reservation in a slot for two to three guests, they have increased revenue.

Computer systems can be programmed in a similar manner. But the reservationist needs to be aware of the room's flexibility.

Restaurants often have a range of table sizes, some for two, four—even eight and ten. When planning the reservations for an evening, the reservationist takes into account that larger tables almost always take longer to dine than smaller groups. So a certain table for eight might only be booked for two seatings while deuces right next to that big table will be turned four or five times. Large parties, especially those taking up an entire room in the restaurant, will often be in for the night. It depends, of course, on the speed of service, but there is often table-hopping and socializing that doesn't happen when there's just one table for the party. Take advantage of this, though, and suggest a cocktail hour with hors d'oeuvre and perhaps some live music. Since you won't be turning the tables, sell them more food and beverages to compensate.

RESERVATION LOG

Time	Number	Name	Phone	Table
5:30	2–3			
5:30	2			
5:30	4			
5:30	4			
6:00	2–3			
6:00	2			
6:00	4			
6:00	4			
6:00	6			
6:30	2–3			

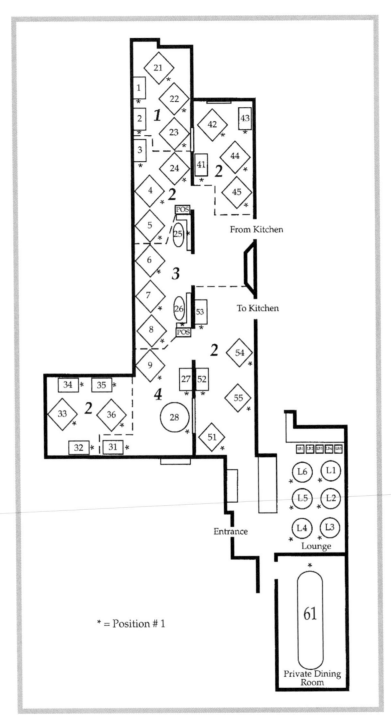

Dining room floor plan showing sections (or stations).

TRAFFIC CHART

	deuce	3	4	5	6	7-10	TOTAL
6.00	卌		||	||||				34
6:30	卌 ||||			卌 ||||			||	1-10, 1-7	91
7:00							0
7:30	||							8
8:00	||							14
8:30	|||			||				22
9:00							4
9:30									2
10:00	卌							12
10:30	|||		||				14
11:00	|||		卌				26
11:30	||		||				1-8	26
						TOTAL	253

Combining the covers list with a floor plan of the room (on facing page), and writing in the times the tables are reserved or seated, will help in keeping track of which tables are available (and at what times) for a second or third seating.

Informing the chef of the total number of guests expected does not provide enough information to prepare for the evening's business. For example: A restaurant seats 130, and has 253 reservations. The chef might think that means two seatings—and send part of the staff home early. However, if the restaurant has a theater crowd, there might be 125 guests between 6:00 and 6:30, 50 between 8:00 and 9:30, and 78 between 10:00 and 11:30. A traffic chart like the example shown above tells the kitchen to allow for some prep time before the late-night rush.

Reservation Procedure

THE RESERVATIONS PROCEDURE SHOULD BE standardized to eliminate confusion and overlooked items. Use of a reservation checklist guarantees that all essential information is secured.

NUMBER OF GUESTS	How many in the party? This allows you to consider tables that are available before taking the caller's name, permitting the most efficient use of available seating and making maximum use of the dining room's capacity.
DATE AND TIME	Note the date and time. If their request is not available discuss alternatives. If your restaurant has a waiting list, offer that to the client. Explain the procedure to the caller, saying that if a cancellation arises during the reconfirmation process they will be called.
SMOKING OR NONSMOKING	The number of seats available in each section is limited, and most guests have very strong preferences for one or the other.
SPECIAL REQUESTS	Some guests prefer certain tables or servers, or may wish to order a special dessert (such as a birthday cake) or wine. When such requests can be honored, they should be noted here.
GUEST NAME	Last name, first initial.
GUEST TELEPHONE	Ask for a daytime number when you can call to confirm. Some restaurants ask guests to call to confirm (see page 78).
RESERVATION NUMBER	If using a computerized system, make sure that the guest notes this number in case any changes are needed later on. These numbers can help in finding solutions when seating errors have been made.
DATE RESERVATION TAKEN	This can be useful in reconstructing details that the guest or restaurant may have confused. It can also be useful when you have to decide which of two reservations should get the window table that both requested. The guests who called first should get it.
YOUR NAME	The reservationist should leave their initials next to the party's name in case questions arise.

If there are no available tables, always mention that guests sometimes cancel their reservations. The reservationist should ask for a number where the caller may be reached if a table becomes open.

TIMING RESERVATIONS

As a rule, restaurants want to seat to full capacity. Achieving this goal can be difficult if one accepts reservations based on the time requested by the party without considering the number in the party. For example, a guest calls asking for a reservation for this evening. The reservationist asks, "For what time?" and the guest answers "Seven P.M." The reservationist then asks, "How many in your party?", which implies that a table is available at seven o'clock. The guest says that there will be two guests. The reservationist sees that only tables for four are available at seven o'clock. But it's too late—there is no graceful way to try to move the time. The party of two winds up seated at a table for four, thereby costing the restaurant 50 percent of the table's potential income.

Once the date of the reservation was established, the reservationist's next question should have been, "How many in your party?", followed by, "For what time?" This sequence would have given the reservationist the flexibility to suggest a time when a table for two would be available, if necessary.

FIXED SEATINGS

This system is generally used by restaurants that have relatively long seatings, say one and a half to two hours or more. Fixed seatings at this type of establishment, for example, could be at 6 p.m., 8 p.m., and 10 p.m. This is ideal for prix fixe menus because the kitchen is able to calculate the serving time with more precision. This kind of slower-paced meal has less turnover in the dining room but often yields higher check averages. Fixed seatings also allow the kitchen to pace itself better, especially if the menu is extensive or complex.

CONTINUOUS SEATING

This system tends to work best for fluid, high-volume establishments, such as bistros, where meals are shorter. Reservations might be taken for one table in each station every fifteen minutes—which prevents orders from crashing down on any one server (or the kitchen) all at once. Of course, this assumes that customers respect reservation times and orders are taken promptly and accurately. Lower check averages can be compensated for by higher volume.

The continuous seating system allows restaurants to accept walk-ins provided there are empty tables.

Try to Seat the Most Desirable Tables in the House First, Gradually Moving to the Least Desirable

Best can mean great view, quietest, or most visible, and *worst* can mean terrible view, nearest the kitchen, or in the back where no one can see you—it all depends on the restaurant. For example, in waterside restaurants, the window tables should go first, then the next row in, and so on. If the best tables are turned over earlier, guests arriving later can also enjoy them. When the dining room manager is dividing up the sections, he or she tries to divvy up assignments to the best tables to avoid a slam. If several good tables are available, try to offer the guests a choice: "Would you like to sit where you can watch the chef in our open kitchen, or would you prefer to be by the window?"

While many cities and towns have adopted no-smoking policies for restaurants, others still allow smoking indoors. In these locales, it's important to determine smoking preference when the reservation is taken. Sometimes, of course, there is only one table that will work, in which case the host brings the guests to that table and says a little prayer.

TIMING IN THE DINING ROOM

Restaurants of every type need to have an idea about how long the average customer stays in order to stagger seatings to achieve a smooth flow in the dining room and kitchen, whether or not they take reservations. They need to take into consideration many factors: the menu, the number of courses offered, the style of service, the type of client attracted (at lunch and at dinner, pre-theater or pre-movie crowd), the ambience of the restaurant, and so on.

How long does it take for a couple to dine? A larger group? One and a half hours? Two hours? Three hours? Dining time varies with the type of restaurant. For example, at casual grills, bistros, and establishments catering to a business lunch crowd, guests could easily be in and out in forty-five to ninety minutes. However, at some renowned fine dining shrines around the country, dinner could last all evening.

Fine dining establishments like Spice Market and Nobu, both in Manhattan, allow about two hours per seating. If the party is larger—say six or eight or more—you can be sure they will stay a lot longer than a smaller group. Everything takes longer with large parties: the ordering, the service, and the cooking. Some primarily prix fixe restaurants like Alinea or Per Se rarely turn the tables, since the meal often takes four hours.

Although it may sound somewhat counterintuitive, the dining room manager should not strive to fill the place up the minute the doors are opened. Although the full dining room may look great, service will be far from perfect because the entire staff is in the weeds—drinks take too long, bread never shows up, the waiters are rushed, and the kitchen is physically incapable of sending out all of the food that was ordered in that initial fifteen-minute period. Some food will come out earlier than guests want, some later, making the diners unhappy. And there's a downside financially, as well—those guests who get their food late will therefore be leaving later, and longer stay times result in fewer table turns, which in turn means lower sales.

If the number of new tables is managed so that they are introduced every fifteen minutes (instead of all at once), the waiters have time to get each table started, the bartender is working at a steady if busy rate, and the dinner orders are going into the kitchen in a nice, steady flow. The restaurant machine works more efficiently.

Menu and staffing changes (including training) can increase the dining room's efficiency, so it is important to remain flexible. After adding additional touches such as tablecloths and candles, the management may watch for signs of service slowing down. They may not necessarily find the slighter slower service a bad thing, though, because they may be able to raise prices a little to counter the loss of revenue from reduced covers.

PHONE ETIQUETTE

The reservationist's demeanor on the telephone is every bit as important as that of the maître d' in the dining room. If the receptionist has all of the charm of a disgruntled badger, the caller is likely to be left with negative feelings about the establishment. On the other hand, if the receptionist sounds welcoming, helpful, and intelligent, the guest will look forward to a pleasant experience.

The first way a reservationist can make a guest feel welcome is by answering within the first three rings of the phone.

To minimize the chances of an error, every restaurant should have a written, standardized greeting for anyone who may answer the phone, acknowledging the time of the day and stating the name of the establishment and the first name of the person speaking. For example: "Good morning, Restaurant Z—Adam speaking."

Repeat information back to the guest when you're taking a reservation: "So, that's five people for dinner at seven-thirty on Friday, December fifth, for Marian Evans; is that correct?" And whenever a credit card number is involved, the entire number should be confirmed, including expiration date.

If the caller wishes to speak with a particular employee, ask, "May I say who is calling?" It is essential that reservationists be familiar with the names of important or repeat customers (see below). If a name is not familiar, the name should be written down and used while speaking with the guest. Courtesy is always important, as everyone is a potential repeat customer.

Putting people on hold can be annoying, but if it is unavoidable; always ask politely, "May I put you on hold?" It is extremely rude to cut guests off before they have a chance to reply to that question. If it looks as if it might be a long wait, ask callers if it is all right to call them back. When picking up a line on hold, say "Thank you for holding, how may I help you?"

VIP GUESTS

The best guests deserve special treatment, and there is no excuse for greeting a regular guest with, "And how do you spell your name, sir?" The maître d' should meet periodically with the receptionists to go over the names of important clients so they can be welcomed on the phone. Caller ID can help identify guests before they identify themselves. This allows the reservationist to search through a computerized customer database for preferences and be prepared for the guest's requests (this process does not absolutely require a computerized database; a simple card file system can also be used to keep track of birthdays, anniversaries, special preferences, allergies, and so on). With a customer database, the reservationist can see all relevant information about the caller.

For these reasons it is advisable that as few people as possible take reservations. If someone else books a table, the regular reservationist should be informed so nothing (or no one) falls through the cracks.

SPECIAL REQUESTS

Guests at all kinds of restaurants may ask for a particular table, a high chair, flowers, a cake, joy buzzers, Champagne, and so on. A diner may have dietary restrictions or allergies. Note this clearly and inform management.

These extra efforts often mean a great deal to customers, so every effort should be made to accommodate them cheerfully. Some restaurants add a special touch to the reservations system by putting out a table card with the customer's name on it.

If the request seems especially unusual or difficult, the reservationist should explain to the guest that it will be noted as a request, and that every effort will be made to honor it.

An inexpensive but effective way to make a birthday presentation (especially at the last minute) is to pipe "Happy Birthday" and the guest's name in meringue on the rim of a plate, then brown lightly in the salamander. Tempered chocolate can be used instead of browned meringue. The guest can order any dessert, which is served with a candle, on the specially prepared plate. Sparklers should never be used indoors—they are toxic, smelly, messy; the ashes may drop onto food, and they can pose a serious risk of fire or burns.

SPECIAL SERVER REQUESTS

Guests sometimes prefer to be served by a particular waiter. While this is not always possible due to scheduling or station assignments, a good host will try to accommodate them. Professional servers can develop their stations as if they were their own businesses—acting as entrepreneurs in promoting their own repeat customers.

SPECIAL TABLE REQUESTS

At fine dining restaurants and bistros, one of the most common requests, especially from regular customers, is for a special table. In most cases the reservation desk cannot make guarantees on the spot, but the person on duty can note the request for the maître d'. When such a table request is made, the reservationist should immediately check to see if that table has been booked already within a certain seating time frame. A good host will try to fulfill these requests whenever possible (especially if given sufficient notice), because of the personal bond it can create between the guest and the restaurant.

Sometimes a particular table has a better view, or has some other distinguishing and desirable feature. Some restaurant managers, finding that these specific tables are always in demand, have taken to adding a surcharge when those tables are reserved. In order to defuse any resentment a guest might feel at being charged an extra fee, the restaurant generally offers some special service—perhaps a card, or unusual dessert or bottle of wine, to make the evening more memorable.

Gift Certificates

Very often, someone will call reservations with a request for something special to be given to another guest. Unless the customer is well known to the establishment, there are many opportunities for misunderstandings in such transactions. A safer approach is to recommend a gift certificate. A sample order form is shown below.

GIFT CERTIFICATE ORDER FORM

Manager's initials:_____

Restaurant name: _____

Telephone number: (___) _____ Fax number: (   ) _____

Name of recipient/reservation:_____

Description of gift: _____ Amount: $ _____

Special comment or occasion:_____

From: _____

Bill to credit card holder: _____

Telephone number: (___) _____ Fax number: (   ) _____

Would you like us to mail you a receipt? (circle) Yes No   _____

Address: _____

Credit card: (circle) Amex Visa MC Other: _____

Credit card number: _____ Expiration date:_____

Signature: _____

Please mail the gift certificate to (circle) Purchaser Recipient

Address:_____

Please fax or send this form to: _____ when completed.
                                    (restaurant name)
Thank you.

GROUP RESERVATIONS

In sizable restaurants, a banquet manager may be on staff to book all large parties; this position would be a luxury for most medium-size establishments. Large groups (10 to 20 percent of a restaurant's seating capacity) require meticulous handling. In order to allow smooth flow in the dining room and kitchen, consider the following suggestions:

- Recommend that the party arrive early, before the bulk of the other customers, or later, when the crowds are dwindling.

- Large groups make special demands upon the kitchen and dining room staff, so try to establish a set menu in advance—one that is satisfactory for both the guests and the staff. If the group is small (5 to 10 percent of seating capacity), a select menu could offer two or more options per course, but not the entire menu.

- If the group is large (greater than 15 percent of seating capacity), it is best to offer a fixed banquet menu. Kitchens can handle set menus more quickly and efficiently than à la carte for groups. Guests, on the other hand, don't have to deal with the delays and confusion that result when many people attempt to make decisions simultaneously. Guests will enjoy faster service, too.

- Consult with the host to preselect wines that complement the meal. This way you ensure there will be an adequate quantity of wines, readily available at the correct temperature, at the correct time.

- Print the menus for each guest in advance to alert the kitchen about any allergies or other problems.

- Before the group arrives, establish a plan for gratuities and payment of the check. Gratuities for large groups range from 15 to 20 percent.

It is advisable to take a deposit of 25 to 50 percent for large groups. Some restaurants require payment in full, while others divide the bill into three equal payments. This protects restaurants in the event some guests do not show up as the restaurant often loses those covers. The number of guests in the group may need to be guaranteed the day of the party. If fewer show, there could be a per-person charge for each no-show. All of this should be in the contract or written agreement that you should provide each time a special party reserves a table.

Some holidays—notably, Easter, Mother's Day, and New Year's Eve—require some additional planning. Many restaurants resort to a simple prix fixe menu with set seatings, while others require a more detailed reservation, essentially a contract. An example of a holiday reservation request is shown below.

HOLIDAY REGISTRATION FORM

Restaurant name: _____

Address: _____

Telephone number: (___)_____ Fax number: (___)_____

Name of party: _____

Date of party: _____Time of reservation:_____

Party of (number of people): _____

Contact person: _____

Telephone number: (___)_____ Fax number: (___)_____

Menu sent by date: _____Any allergies?_____

Specific dislikes: _____ Special requests:_____

Full names of guests in party (including your own) _____

_____

_____

The price for dinner is $ _____ per person. Deposit _____ per person.

Cancellation must be made 48 hours in advance for refund of deposit.

How would you like us to handle the payment? (check one)

    Present at table

    Hold at front desk for your signature

    Charge to credit card and mail receipt to your address

Name of credit card holder: _____

Credit card: (circle) Amex Visa MC Other: _____

Credit card number: _____ Expiration date: _____

Signature: _____

Please fax or send this form to: _____ when completed.
(restaurant name)
Thank you.

Juggling reservations for a large group along with normal reservations can be a complex matter. The clearer the details before the engagement, the more enjoyable the experience for all. When booking large groups, keep in mind that they tend to linger longer, possibly overlap into a second seating, take a number of tables, can disturb other guests, and generally take longer to be served cocktails, order, and eat. At the same time, they often spend more, often buying additional bottles of dessert wine or port. Groups may also introduce your restaurant to new customers who could become regulars.

Birthdays, Anniversaries, and Special Occasions in the Dining Room

WHETHER THE SERVICE STAFF gathers together to harmonize on "Happy Birthday to You" or not, acknowledging birthdays is an excellent way to engender goodwill with customers. Noting anniversaries and special events is important, too. With computerized reservation systems, it is possible to have birthdays and anniversaries pop up automatically. Reservationists should convey such information to the staff. Moreover, the front desk should be familiar with taking cake orders, quantities needed for different parties, pricing, and so on.

Restaurants should establish a cancellation policy for cakes and special requests. This might include a credit card deposit or a clear written arrangement stating what happens if the reservation is canceled on short notice, such as the day of the party. Some restaurants still charge for the entire cake but suggest the client pick it up. Others may decide to sell the cake to regular customers and charge the party a partial fee of 25 to 50 percent of the original price. A typical order form is shown page 78. It should be written in triplicate copy, with one going to the chef, one to the reservation book, and one to the customer.

No-Shows and Late Arrivals

RESTAURANTS CAN MAKE RESERVATIONS for guests, but they cannot force them show up at the restaurant, nor can they guarantee that the guests will arrive on time. No-shows and late arrivals are frustrating and can be very costly to a restaurant. So what can a restaurant do?

CAKE ORDER FORM

Name of recipient/reservation: _____

Date of reservation: _____Time of reservation:_____

Number of people: _____

Name of person ordering cake: _____

Telephone number: (____)_____ Fax number: (____) _____

Any allergies? _____ Alcohol? (circle) Yes   No

Specific dislikes: _____ Special requests:_____

Any inscription on cake? _____

Total amount ($____ per person) / Deposit ($____ per person)

Should we add this amount to the check? (circle) Yes No

Telephone number: (____)_____ Fax number: (____) _____

Would you like us to mail you a receipt? (circle) Yes No

Address: _____

Name of credit card holder: _____

Credit card: (circle) Amex Visa MC Other: _____

Credit card number:_____ Expiration date: _____

Signature: _____

Please fax or send this form to: _____ when completed.
                                              (restaurant name)
Thank you.

RECONFIRMING RESERVATIONS

Many establishments try to minimize no-shows and latecomers by reconfirming reservations on the appointed day. A staff member might begin working the phones in the afternoon, calling every reserved customer to ask if they still intend to come. This may help somewhat, although even reconfirmed reservations have been known to result in no-shows.

Jean-Jacques Rachou, chef and owner of La Cote Basque in Manhattan, says that on a Saturday night his restaurant could have had a no-show rate of more than 30 percent. "And these are people we had called at home just hours before," he said.

Maître d's contend that many no-shows are caused by inept reservation taking. For example, if a guest wants to come at 8:00 P.M. and you offer only 9:00 P.M. or 9:30 P.M., the chances of a no-show rise dramatically. Some professionals note that a reservationist should feel out the customer to determine if there might be another solution—even dining in the cocktail lounge (if there are tables) or at the bar itself. If a customer reluctantly accepts an unsatisfactory reservation, you can be sure they will start calling other establishments to see if something better is available and they may forget to call back to cancel.

Sometimes, guests may be no-shows without realizing it, through no fault of their own (their reservation might have been written on the wrong day, for instance). If reservations have not been confirmed a day ahead of time, it is good practice to call the no-shows the next day. By asking if the restaurant has made a mistake, the guests are not made to feel guilty, but gain an appreciation for the importance of reservations. Such guests will probably be more considerate about cancellations in the future.

It is not advisable, however, to give away a customer's table if the party is only a few minutes late. It is a good idea to establish a minimum time after which you give away a reserved table, taking into account weather conditions, traffic, difficulty of finding the restaurant, and how well you know the guest. The time might range from twenty minutes to a half hour or more. But it might be preferable to lose a table for a night rather than risk losing a valuable customer.

We're Still Waiting

André Soltner, former owner and chef of the famed Lutèce, maintains that many diners make reservations weeks in advance at four or five top restaurants, then decide at the last minute where they want to go—and without notifying the other restaurants.

"What is really bad," Mr. Soltner says, "is when a customer calls many times trying to get a reservation on a fully booked night only to arrive and see empty tables in the room. The customer gets angry and thinks I am playing games with him, when the empty tables could be a result of latecomers or no-shows. It really makes me feel stupid."

Mr. Soltner's colleagues still chuckle over the time several years ago when he became angered by a man who failed to honor a reservation for 8:00 on a Saturday night. Mr. Soltner called him at 4:00 A.M. and said: "Sir, this is the owner of Lutèce. We are still waiting for you."

DEPOSITS

The best insurance against no-shows is a deposit. Many restaurants now require deposits for major holidays, special events, and large groups. However, aside from the ill will that required deposits might create, they can result in bookkeeping headaches for restaurant operators. Consequently, many managers prefer to persuade diners to cancel reservations at least an hour in advance so restaurants have a chance to fill the vacancy. That takes some finesse.

Another recent approach used by some restaurants is a reservation contract. The guest receives, then fills out and returns (by fax) a contract that includes the date, time, number in party, and all credit card information. Some restaurants even require faxed photocopies of both sides of the guest's credit card.

Other restaurateurs find these practices too confrontational and decline to try them. Gordon Sinclair, of Gordon's in Chicago, used a simpler, less alienating method. He had his reservationists ask, "Will you agree to call us if you change your plans?" when taking reservations. This phrasing involved the guest in the process, rather than threatening some form of retaliation. It still managed the situation, but the guest felt respected, not suspected.

Securing Reservations

Gordon Sinclair suggested that when one asks guests for their credit card numbers to secure a table, precise language is important.

"You can't pause when you are asking because the client might start thinking about it. For example, you say 'We need a credit card to guarantee your table. What credit card would you like to use?' If you pause in the middle of that the client might start asking questions about the policy. Don't give them a chance to demur."

When a restaurant has a no-show rate of about 15%, you need to do your best to confirm reservations. You can't really do much about people who have not put down any kind of deposit. There is something about getting a credit card number from the guest—even if you are not going to use it—that makes people more inclined to call and cancel.

Here is a small, country-restaurant perspective:

Priscilla Martel, who for thirteen years owned and ran the dining room at Restaurant du Village, in Chester, Connecticut, says that her type of establishment had a more personal relationship with customers, and no-shows were far less frequent.

"It can happen, but it is not usual with the local people who are the bulk of our clients. On the other hand, a small restaurant (forty-five seats) does not have the flexibility to protect itself by overbooking even slightly."

While asking guests to secure their reservation with a credit card or to confirm a reservation on the day of their visit may seem a simple matter, it is often perceived as an inconvenience by the guests. A friendlier method is for the restaurant to call on the day of (or the day before) the visit to confirm the reservation. This may not be necessary for regular customers, as they are more likely to call in the event of a cancellation.

No single method for preventing no-shows is ideal for all restaurants or all guests. Each manager must use judgment and tact, and consider the record of no-shows in the particular situation, when deciding on the best approach.

The Front Door

THAT OLD SAYING ABOUT FIRST IMPRESSIONS is true—they're important, and you only have one chance. The initial contact that potential guests have with your place of business must be welcoming and overwhelmingly positive, whether it starts on the phone (or your website) before they've arrived or starts the moment they step through the front door.

Sometimes the restaurant is new to the guests, and sometimes the guests are making a return visit to a favorite place. How guests are treated (i.e., reservation taking, the first greeting, the manner in they are seated, or the handling of special requests) in large part defines the quality of their dining experience. This is the moment when the restaurant and the dining room staff establish a comforting relationship with the guest.

THE FIRST IMPRESSION

The actual front door is the very first physical contact guests have with a restaurant. The sparkling clean glass of the restaurant door may be the initial thing a guest sees. Sometimes the guest just happens to be driving by—so a clean parking lot with well-maintained shrubbery may be their first view. These first impressions may determine whether or not a guest chooses to visit the restaurant.

Therefore, the front of your restaurant should be well maintained and clean. Whether consciously or subliminally, the guest will have a reaction to the condition of your entrance. Make sure you attend to the following:

- Keep hardware (such as door handles) working properly and polished so that they gleam.

- Keep glass on the door sparkling clean.

- Remove any trash from the sidewalk or floor.

- Put down floor mats when it's raining or snowy, and keep them clean.

- If smoking is allowed, keep ashtrays clean (even one cigarette butt qualifies the ashtray as "dirty").

A grungy entrance can cause the guest to wonder about the cleanliness of the entire facility. At the very least, it's not a good way to start off someone's meal at your place. A specific individual should be responsible for the condition of the entry areas both before and during service.

Greeting the Guest

UNLIKE THE PHONE GREETING when you take a reservation, if the greeting at the door is standardized, it can begin to sound insincere (especially if a guest hears the same greeting addressed to other guests). There should be several ways to welcome the customers, usually starting with something along the lines of: "Good evening, Mrs. Kinder, welcome to the House of Chez Maison de la Casa."

While the greeting should vary slightly from guest to guest, it should include the guest's name, if known. If you don't recognize the guests, asking them, "What was the name of the reservation?" is friendlier than "Did you have a reservation?" If no reservation was made and seating is available, it is nice to ask them their names so you can add them to the reservation book.

Since people have names, use them. Referring to customers as "the table of four," is rude, as in "Are you the table of two at nine P.M.?" Take the time to look at a party's name and show that you care. Always make eye contact with the guest; do not stare into the reservations book.

If three people walk up to the reservations desk, one should never assume that they constitute a party of three. They could be three singles, two separate parties, or even the first half of a party of six. It is best to greet them and ask, "How many in your party?"

It is fine to chat a little with arriving customers if they initiate it, but avoid getting into long discourses that could throw off the timing of their meal and that of the dining room.

The Reception Desk

WHEN GUESTS WALK IN THE DOOR, there must be someone there to greet them. One person has to be responsible for the door. If the guests walk into a restaurant that's bustling with activity, but there's nobody at the front desk—it makes them wonder if they should be there at all. Uncertainty is not a good first feeling to give your guests.

A properly set-up reception desk (shown at right) makes it simple for you to greet guests, whether you are greeting them over the phone or in person as they walk in the door. It also makes it possible for you to deal with the wide range of situations that can crop up unexpectedly during the course of a meal, whether you need to replace the twelve menus that got soaked when a wine bucket tipped over or replace the pens that keep disappearing throughout the service. Stained, crumpled, or worn menus send an undesirable signal to the guests: "If the menus look this bad, what must the kitchen look like?" When the check is presented minus a pen to sign the credit card receipt, guests must resort to searching the dining room and trying to catch someone's attention.

As a matter of routine, the reception desk should be equipped with

- A hospitality handbook (page 87)

- A reservations logbook (page 88)

- Clean copies of all menus

- An up-to-date telephone directory (for answering customer questions)

- Public transportation maps and schedules (if applicable)

Food for Thought

Imagine two restaurants across the street from each other. If you went to dinner at both, and found that they had equally good food at similar prices, how would you decide which to revisit?

In all probability, you would choose the one where you had felt most comfortable and were warmly welcomed at the front door. The quality of your experience, based on good service and the attentive skill of the host, makes the difference between being a one-time visitor and becoming a repeat customer.

The front desk.

- Plenty of pens and pencils (they are constantly disappearing in dining rooms)

- Wine lists

- A seating chart

- A backup telephone answering machine

Not essential, but thoughtful things to have at (or near) the reception desk are

- Maps of the area (which can often be obtained at no cost from local real estate firms or the chamber of commerce)

- Inexpensive umbrellas that can be given to guests in the event of an unexpected downpour

- Reading glasses

- Flashlights

- Extra batteries

- A wheelchair

In addition, the front desk should have a list containing the manager's name and the contact numbers for waiters on duty and the kitchen staff. In the event of an emergency, fire departments need to know how many people are in the building.

Restrooms, while not typically located at the front door, are still part of the all-important first impression. They should be checked every half hour by one of the front-door personnel. The cleanliness of restrooms is always a high priority among respondents in restaurant surveys. Judging the quality and cleanliness of the restrooms should not be left to the discretion of a busboy, but rather to the receptionist responsible for hospitality.

MAKING NOTATIONS IN THE RESERVATION BOOK OR SYSTEM

Since situations change so quickly, it is best to use pencil in the actual reservation book. The types of notations made in the book can help make service more efficient. For example, since some parties do not always arrive together, a common practice is to draw a half circle around the number in the party when some arrive, and complete the circle when the full party is seated.

Cancellations in the reservation book should be noted distinctly so any staff member can quickly determine which tables are available. The reservationist simply makes a pencil line through the name (so it is still legible) and writes "cxl" or "cncl" in the table number column. It is best to avoid erasing the names, unless that is the only available method to maximize seating.

Keep a clock at the host stand and write the time next to the name on the reservation sheet or the floor plan. This way you'll know which section got the most recent party of guests, and which should be next.

IF THE SYSTEM CRASHES

Murphy's Law seems to have been written specifically for restaurants, where mishaps are legendary. The introduction of computers gave Murphy yet a more powerful opportunity to wreak havoc. There is a corollary to Murphy's Law called Turnaucka's Law: It states, "The attention span of a computer is only as long as its electrical cord." In the event of a power failure (or any other crash of the restaurant's point-of-sale computer), an emergency backup system should be kept at the reservations desk. This might include a printed copy of the reservations list, a flashlight, sequentially numbered guest checks, a sales tax chart, a battery-powered calculator, backup batteries for flashlight and calculator, extra candles, and a manual credit card machine with a supply of manual forms.

HOSPITALITY HANDBOOK

The hospitality handbook is the resource book that the reservationist can use to answer guests' questions. It should be accessible at the reception desk and placed near any phones used to take reservations. The handbook should be updated on a monthly basis. Information might include:

- A description of the cuisine
- Chef's name
- Maître d'hôtel's name
- A price range of the menu
- Wine and beverage information
- Hours of operation
- Guest dress code
- Accepted methods of payment
- Directions to the restaurant from various areas
- Area hotel accommodations
- Area restaurants
- Parking facilities
- Public transportation
- Emergency phone numbers (police, fire department, EMT)
- Taxi phone numbers
- Special events in the area
- Handicapped facilities
- Children's menu
- Cake order forms
- Incident report forms
- A log of problems encountered, including complaints, accidents, food-borne illness reports, and maintenance problems

LOGBOOK

A valuable tool for comparing business from season to season or from year to year is a written logbook that records number of covers, seating times, and any special problems. This way you can, for example, look at your holiday experiences from the year before to determine volume, peak seating times, and other considerations to plan better the coming year.

The maître d' should make daily entries in the reservation log detailing the manager on duty, expected number of covers, final number of covers, number of waiters and kitchen crew, lost-and-found items, sundry incidents and names of people involved, and even weather conditions. Weather is one of the biggest reasons guests are late or fail to show up.

The previous year's data—number of covers, weather, and any other extenuating circumstances—can be noted in the new logbook for quick comparison. Recaps should be formulated and recommendations made to the following year or similar event.

THINGS TO DO AT THE RECEPTION DESK

- Make a good first and last impression.
- Recognize regular guests.
- Thank the guests for coming.
- Help check guests' coats.
- Look happy.
- Answer the phone within the third ring.
- Greet the guests within 15 seconds of their arrival.
- Make eye contact with the guests.
- Repeat the guests' names.
- Scan the room for problems and alert appropriate staff.
- Continually review the reservation plan and status of tables for the next seating.
- Make every attempt to maximize seating while maintaining even service.
- Become familiar with guests' names, especially repeat customers.
- Pay attention to guests who are waiting for a table. Explain why they are waiting and keep them updated as to the status.

Great First Impressions

Here are a few tips to make a great first impression on guests:

- ANGLE THE RECEPTION DESK SO THAT IT FACES THE DOOR AND THE DINING ROOM. **This alerts guests where to go when they walk in and allows the person manning the front door to see guests as they arrive while keeping tabs on the dining room.**

- STAND FACING THE DOOR. **When a guest walks into a restaurant and sees only someone's back, it does not give the guest a warm feeling of welcome—in fact, it feels forbidding.**

- GREET GUESTS IMMEDIATELY AND MAKE EYE CONTACT. **There's nothing worse than a guest standing awkwardly in the entry while staffers chat among themselves or stare at the reservation book. You may even take a few steps toward the guests to welcome them; this leaves no room for doubt that they have been acknowledged.**

- GREET THE GUEST WITH "GOOD EVENING, HOW MAY I HELP YOU?" **Don't forget to change the greeting depending on the time of day. And never, ever have your first words to the guests be "Do you have a reservation?"**

A seating chart marked with each station's designated tables is a useful tool at the front desk (an example of a seating chart is shown on page 66). This can assist in seating parties in alternate stations so one waiter does not get slammed, followed by the next waiter, and so on. Some managers keep the seating chart covered with clear plastic—marking the tables already assigned with china markers, and erasing as necessary with a wipe of a paper towel.

CHECKING COATS AND BAGS

The guests' reception is more pleasant if it includes an offer to take their coats, hats, umbrellas, or shopping bags (rather than sending them to the coat-check room). They have not come to your restaurant to be sent to the cloakroom. The coats could be handed to the coat-check person in exchange for the coat claim check numbers. This way the guests don't wait for their coats to be hung up. The check numbers should be given to the coat's owner or to the men—unless guests indicate some other preference.

Every establishment should have a policy on checking furs and other valuable items. There are legal implications that vary from state to state. Some restaurants have the guest sign the fur in when checked and require the same signature when the fur is retrieved. The coatroom should never be left unattended.

Taking Coats and Bags

Taking coats and bags, while hospitable, can hold a lot of responsibility for the restaurateur. Laptops, fur coats, important papers in briefcases, and even the lowly raincoat can all be of tremendous value to the guest, and a liability for the restaurant. It might be smart to post a sign at the coat-check stand stating that the staff cannot be held responsible for lost or damaged items. To be certain, managers and owners should talk to a lawyer and insurance agent to make sure they are covered.

Seating

ON THE DAY OF SERVICE, the reservations list becomes a waiting list. As guests arrive, take the customers' names and discreetly note some physical characteristic to help remember them later ("White hair, lapel pin on suit, resembles Steve Martin"). Avoid using judgmental descriptions—and never give the impression of being confused or disorganized.

Each restaurant must have a predetermined method for seating the guests. The benefits of such a plan are efficient distribution of guests throughout the dining room and a balanced workload on servers. By paying attention to the distribution of seated guests in the dining room, guests' perception of the room is that it is nicely filled, while providing a comfortable amount of physical space for their own meal. It also permits the servers to prepare each table for arriving guests with minimal disturbance of nearby guests, and gives servers a balanced workload without getting "slammed."

Assuming that guests have not been kept waiting, the host should ask them if they are ready to be seated—they may want to stop at the bar first. This may not always be desirable, especially if a party is late. The host may politely nudge them toward their table by saying, "We don't want you to be rushed, so perhaps you'd like to have your cocktails at the table?"

Also ask, if applicable, if guests prefer smoking or nonsmoking areas. Different states and municipalities have different laws regarding smoking in restaurants. It is imperative that you know every nuance of the law. Your customers (both smoking and nonsmoking) certainly will.

The host should lead the guests to the table, rather than offering the guests a choice. Actually, it is not all that important who seats guests, as long as there is a host to take care of them from the moment they arrive.

In the more polite past, men always seated women in their party by pulling out their chairs. Today, such courtesy is rare. The task is usually performed by the maître d' in fine dining establishments, and by the floor manager in bistros.

If guests bring their coats to the table, the host should repeat the offer to check the coats for them. This is both gracious and practical—waiters can trip on coats while carrying trays, or accidentally spill on the guests' jackets.

Women are generally seated with their backs to the wall, facing the dining room. Men may face the women, with their backs to the dining room. If you sense that there is a problem with the seating arrangement, ask if the table is satisfactory. Most problems with seating arrangements can be worked out by the guests once they are at the table, but the maître d' should remain nearby to help with reseating. If the guests request another table, they should remain at the table while the maître d' checks the reservation book to determine if another table is available.

Once guests are seated, menu presentation can begin. Some restaurants feel it is a good idea to get something on the table as soon as possible, either a drink, bread, or a complimentary snack (classically known as an "amuse-bouche"). Other restaurants prefer to take the order before any food is offered in order to sell more.

HONORING RESERVATIONS

Just as restaurants expect customers to show up on time for a reserved table, so do diners expect restaurants to have their table ready at the appointed hour. This, unfortunately, is not always the case. The unpredictability of customer flow inevitably leads to occasional log jams, but they should be the exception, not the norm. In general, customers are very understanding about delays if they are treated with respect and straightforwardness. The worst thing a restaurant can do is to manipulate customers with half-truths and obfuscations ("It will just be a minute" when it will be a half hour). It is always better to tell the guests that some of the guests have stayed longer than anticipated, apologize for the situation, and try to offer drinks (where legal) or some sort of snack if they are willing to wait. While a lack of information is annoying, candor can do wonders.

If diners arrive, say, half an hour late for their reservation and you have given away their table, it is best to inform them of the situation and make every effort to seat them as soon as possible. Some guests are content to dine at the bar, especially if that helps them catch a movie or theater curtain. Other situations might call for offering a free cocktail, snacks at the bar, or a bottle of wine with dinner.

What do you do for people who have to stand on line because their tables are not yet ready? The usual practice is to send them to the cocktail lounge, although some places merely leave them standing by the coatroom. Tavern on the Green, in

New York City, built an elaborate and elegant tent for those who sit and wait. The restaurant tried to make the mere act of waiting a pleasurable experience.

According to Disney's precepts, people do not mind waiting on lines if they are entertained and kept informed while they are waiting. Some guests will want to see menus, so they can reduce the time in making decisions once they are seated. Andrea Terry of Lobster Roll, Inc. has a game plan prepared for whenever guests have to wait more than forty-five minutes. The person responsible for the front door goes to the kitchen to "drop the torpedo." Translated, the order means, "prepare some finger food from the appetizer menu to be passed out to the guests in the waiting line." This approach keeps the guests happy, and banishes any thoughts of abandoning their wait in favor of another, less crowded, restaurant. Since Lobster Roll is in a family resort area, Ms. Terry keeps toys and coloring books on hand to distract the children.

Graycliff in Nassau, the Bahamas, provides menus to guests while they wait in the lounge—and they also take the guests' orders there. By the time the guests are seated, their meals are ready, and they are served immediately.

Dominique Simon, formerly of Lespinasse in New York, says the most important thing that a restaurant can do with guests is to establish a sense of trust. Always tell them what is happening, even if it is bad news. If you tell them "ten minute wait," and they wait forty minutes, you could lose them as future customers. Most people understand that things go wrong once in a while.

How long can a restaurant expect customers to wait for a reserved table before making some sort of amends? Ten minutes? Fifteen minutes? We asked a cross section of owners, managers, and maîtres d'hotel the following question:

Customers arrive on time for a reserved table at, say, eight p.m. The table is not ready. How long do you think a customer can wait before management should intervene with a free drink, a personal apology, a song, or maybe a complimentary car wash?

Policy	Restaurant
10 minutes, buy drink	Chez Josephine, New York City
15 minutes, buy Champagne	Lespinasse, New York City
20 minutes, buy drink	Restaurant du Village, Chester, CT
15 minutes, apology; 20 minutes, buy drink	Sign of the Dove, New York City
20 minutes, bring tidbits; intervene every 5 minutes	Gordon's, Chicago
15 minutes, apology; 20 minutes, complimentary food	Lon's at the Hermosa Inn, Phoenix, AZ
15 minutes, apology and tidbit	Patina, Los Angeles

GUESTS WITH NO RESERVATIONS

What if you have a reservation policy, but guests arrive without them? Every restaurant will have guests coming through the front door without reservations. If there's a free table, of course they should be seated and served. If there isn't any unreserved space, they can be offered a seat at the bar to wait for a cancellation or no-show, with the caveat that this might not happen. When that walk-in is a regular customer, it's a good idea to get them a table as soon as possible.

Don't get into the habit of referring out loud to people who arrive unannounced as "walk-ins," as in, "Could you seat these walk-ins at table nine?" How would you like to be called a "walk-in" instead of your real name? It is best to ask the guest's name. You may want to keep track of how much walk-in business you do on any given night, so after you write their name in the reservation book, write "NR" for "no reservation" rather than "WI." This may help avoid referring to guests as "walk-ins."

THE VIP GUEST WITHOUT A RESERVATION

Another time when all of your tact and flexibility are required is when VIP guests— whether regulars, celebrities, or your investors—show up unexpectedly without reservations. It is not easy for a maître d' to tell someone like Donald Trump or Martha Stewart to cool their heels at the bar until a table frees up. Besides, most restaurateurs want to have the likes of Donald Trump in the dining room—celebrities can do wonders for a restaurant's popularity.

So what do you do? Here are some tips:

Rita Jammet, co-owner of the former La Caravelle, New York City: "If a good customer calls two hours before service on Saturday, that is just like walking in the door for us. We simply tried to do everything we could to accommodate them, but when we couldn't, we were honest and did not have them come in and wait."

Dominique Simon, of the former Lespinasse, New York City: "I always kept two tables aside for circumstances like that. You can do that with a big dining room, and it avoids many problems."

Henny Santos, of the former Sign of the Dove, New York City: "That is another event that you can't avoid. We had 145 seats so I could usually juggle things around even on a busy night. But you should always tell the customer that there is a possibility there will be a wait. The worst thing you can do is make a promise to a customer that you can't fill."

John Fischer tells this story about handling regular guests who arrive without a reservation.

"At Campagna, we had a reservation policy, but we also had a lot of regulars who had specific tables that were 'theirs.' We would get calls from them often, saying that they were 'on their way over' and wanted their table. Usually, if it was already taken we would offer another table nearby and they understood because of the late notice. Sometimes, if the table was simply unavailable, we ended up with an unhappy executive standing in the middle of the dining room. For some of these people, we would actually keep 'their' table open when we knew that this person was in town that week. This extra work on our part created an extremely loyal clientele. Was it worth it? We figured out that about two thirds of our business came from one third of our clientele. It was worth it."

SEPARATE ARRIVALS

When several guests are going to be dining together, they commonly arrive separately. This means that someone will be left waiting for someone else to arrive. The reservations book can help to keep track of these split parties (see page 86), but what do you do with them while they wait?

Some establishments have found it necessary—especially on busy nights—to ask guests to wait until the party is complete before being seated. However, the guests often get upset and feel it is inhospitable to wait at the bar. Most people prefer to be seated at the table to wait for the rest of the party. This can be costly to the restaurant when, for example, only six members of a party of eight (who must be seated at two four tops pushed together) arrives at the restaurant. At the last minute, the remaining couple calls to cancel. Now there are only six people, who could easily have been seated at one table for six, thereby saving the restaurant the lost revenue from two covers.

WAITING LISTS

If you have decided to go with a first-come, first-served system, you'll find that it's relatively easy to work with—until the room fills up. Now you have to figure out how to implement a waiting list.

Have you ever wondered how hosts are able to look at a list of names and confidently tell you that it would be twenty minutes for a table? To tell you the truth, they may wonder how they do it, too—it's a skill that comes largely with experience. The more experience the host has in your restaurant, the more accurate those estimates will be. The estimate is based on many factors: average guest stay, number of large parties, how fast the kitchen is sending out plates, and even the unquantifiable factor of how the place simply feels that night. The best hosts will take all of the available criteria, analyze them, come up with an accurate estimate, and then add five minutes to play it safe. The more accurate the estimates are, the more business you will do; people who decide to wait and are able to sit down on time will be happy with the result and will probably return. The ones who decide not to wait might well come back someday to see what the hubbub is about, and they might stay that next time.

If, however, the host consistently underestimates wait times, it will eventually hurt your business. Guests who have to wait an hour instead of twenty minutes will be very upset once they get to the table, and the waiter will be expected to tap dance and juggle to make them happy. Even worse is when people walk out because the wait was longer than they expected—good luck getting them to come back.

Needless to say, if you are going with a no-reservations system, the operative word is, of course, *system*. Maintain the wait list on a legal pad, sure, but next to the guest's name, write the current time and the quoted wait time. When the table is ready for the guest, some hosts will walk through the bar calling the guest's name while other restaurants, like the Hilltop Steakhouse in Saugus, MA, have a public address system. Still other restaurants have electronic pagers that they will hand to the guest once their name has been logged. When the table is ready, the host pushes a button and it sends a signal to the pager. It's not a foolproof system, because guests sometimes misplace the pagers, but it can cut down on the number of annoying announcements.

Conclusion

GREETING AND SEATING THE GUESTS is a critical moment in establishing remarkable service in the guests' mind. It is where first impressions are made, where the nature of the dining experience is first suggested, and where the warmth of their relationship with the restaurant is established.

5

Preparing and Setting Up for Service

THE FIRST STEP TOWARD BECOMING a dining room professional is the application of regular, conscientious attention to mise en place. This French phrase literally means "to put in place." In the food-service industry, mise en place is generally understood to mean the organization and completion of all the duties and tasks one must perform to carry out the job at hand smoothly and efficiently. Some aspects of dining room mise en place are commonly referred to as "side work." These tasks may include cleaning and polishing tableware, restocking condiments, arranging tables, and folding napkins.

When the dining room's mise en place is properly organized, there is no excuse not to have the glassware and flatware required for service instantly and unobtrusively at the ready.

Mise en Place for the Dining Room

KEEP IN MIND THE BOY SCOUT MOTTO: "Be prepared." It characterizes all the activities that servers do behind the scenes to ensure the quality of their guests' dining experiences. Every need of the guest should be considered, from Visa napkins (made from a blend of cotton and polyester) to avoid white lint on dark outfits to simple syrup to sweeten iced tea (instead of granulated sugar, which can take a long time to dissolve), to reading glasses for guests who forget their own. It's the only way one can be ready for the challenge of actual service.

The first step in readying the dining room for service is to clean it: tables and chairs are wiped clean; tables leveled if necessary; rugs and carpets vacuumed; windows cleaned; drapes properly arranged; and restrooms cleaned and stocked with the appropriate supplies. From there, the servers turn their attention to other work areas in the dining room.

SIDE STAND

The side stand is the mise en place station for the dining room. It should be cleaned and well stocked with all necessary materials before service. Proper use of the side stand will minimize the number of trips to the kitchen for stock items. A side stand might include all flatware, wine lists, glassware, Sterno, china, coffee cups and saucers (ideally, coffee cups should be kept warm until service), napkins, tablecloths, perhaps a coffee warmer unit, and a menu rack. Since it holds so many different items, a disorganized side stand will hinder rather than facilitate service.

About Condiments

Some states have sanitation regulations restricting the type of containers in which condiments may be served. Only containers that are specifically designed for serving condiments may be used for that purpose. Never attempt to clean an empty bottle and refill it with a condiment.

For example, in some areas, marrying ketchup bottles can be a violation of health codes. It is wise to write the date on the label when the bottle was opened. Many places use squirt bottles that are washed out on a weekly schedule.

Unused items such as butter and cream must be discarded when the table is cleared—they cannot be given to another guest. Consequently, do not overload the table with these little extras. Replacing them just as they are needed is perceived by the guest as caring service—and is less wasteful of the restaurant's resources.

Other items that might be included on a side stand are:

- Ashtrays

- Bread baskets

- Condiment caddies

- Crumbing plate

- Doilies

- Flatware plate or silverware transport plate (STP)

- Flower vases

- Lobster and escargot utensils

- Matches

- Menus in large print or braille

- Menus without prices

- Oyster sets

- Place mats

- Sugar and sweetener refills

- Wine buckets

Special attention should be given to keeping the side stand stocked with such items as condiments, oil and vinegar cruets, salt and pepper (shakers or peppermills), salt and sugar substitutes, ketchup, bottled sauces, or mustards. Edibles should be handled in the following manner:

- Remove storeroom prices.

- Refill half-emptied containers before service.

- Clean the cover, rim, and body of all jars and containers.

- Soak condiment lids and wipe dry before service.

- Store condiments on a clean rack or tray.

- Refrigerate opened bottles overnight.

TRAY STANDS

Tray stands, or jack stands, are made either of wood or metal, but neither is especially elegant to the eye. They should be cleaned before each shift. Tray stands should be fitted with webbing to make them more secure. Some tray stands are equipped with a small shelf midway between the floor and the top—servers should avoid placing any items on that shelf because they will, invariably, fall off when the tray stand is moved.

Fine dining establishments and bistros often cover tray stands with a sixty-inch tablecloth for a neater appearance.

Setting Up and Breaking Down

A RESTAURANT'S WORKDAY can be very long, so many restaurants schedule opening and closing waiters (helping to maintain energy levels and avoid the cost of overtime pay). This system puts more emphasis on the importance of teamwork. The closing waiters rely on the opening mise en place, and the opening waiters depend on the closing responsibilities having been carried out the night before.

PERSONAL MISE EN PLACE

All personal mise en place must be completed by each server for his or her station before the first guest enters the dining room. A personal list may include any or all of the tasks listed below:

PERSONAL MISE EN PLACE FOR THE MAÎTRE D'HÔTEL/HOST(ESS)

- Check reservation book.

- Communicate cover count and pattern flow with chef.

- Communicate any special requests to chef and staff.

- Communicate seating requirements to floor staff.

- Check special supplies (birthday candles, matches, etc.).

- Adjust temperature, lighting, and music.

PERSONAL MISE EN PLACE FOR SERVERS

- A clean supply of properly folded side towels (serviettes)

- An adequate supply of guest checks in proper number sequence (if a POS is not in use)

- Corkscrew

- Crumber

- Dupe pad

- Matches, preferably in-house matches, or lighter

- Miniature flashlight for dark dining rooms

- Two nondescript pens or pencils in working order

OPENING CREW (EARLY WAITSTAFF)

The mise en place of the opening dining room crew includes setting up the dining room and making sure that everything used for service is clean or polished, readily available, easily accessible, and in ample supply. Menu changes, the addition of tableside preparations, and changes to the interior of the restaurant can create new needs for the setup list, so the list of tasks should be under constant scrutiny.

Once service begins, personnel must be able to devote their full attention to the immediate demands of serving the guests. Time cannot be wasted preparing equipment and supplies that should have been organized and made ready earlier. However, some mise en place will need to be replenished during service as well. It stands to reason that staffers generally handle the setup of the areas that they have primary responsibility for. Particular tasks to be performed by hosts, waiters, and bussers as part of the opening mise en place are

- Arrange tables and chairs according to reservations.

- Maintain proper space between tables.

- Repair any wobbly tables (no matchbooks or wadded napkins).

- Wipe tables and counters clean.

- Set up table-cleaning supplies, including clean towels and proper sanitizing solution in spray bottles.

- Check floors for cleanliness.

- Lay tablecloths or set place mats.

- Fold napkins for tables and resetting.

- Polish any serviceware, hollowware, flatware, china, and glasses.

- Set tables.

- Stock side stands.

- Stock backup paper for printing checks, and dupes in the dining room and the kitchen.

- Stock ample creamers and other condiment containers in the pantry area (to be filled as needed during service just prior to use).

- Fill and wipe any condiments, salt and pepper, etc.

- Cut lemons for hot and iced tea.

- Prepare butter curls or pats for bread service.

- Line breadbaskets with napkins and fill baskets with bread.

- Fill wine buckets (just prior to service).

- Prep any underliners.

- Prep decrumbing plates.

- Prep STP (silverware transport plates).

- Load up side stands with flatware for setting tables for subsequent courses.

- Prep coffee/tea area (stock filters, prepare coffee set ups, but do not pre-grind coffee or open bags of ground coffee until you are ready to brew a pot).

- Check supply of staples (for stapling credit card vouchers, etc.).

- Wipe down menus and replace out-of-date lists.

- Make sure any guest paging systems are charged and working.

CLOSING CREW

The duties of the closing dining room crew should be coordinated with the responsibilities of the opening crew. The opening crew sets up the dining room and relies upon the closing crew to clean up and restock the dining room for the next day.

There are two major parts to consider for the closing crew: cleaning up the mess and leaving the room ready for the next service staff. The manager should do a complete check of side work at the end of the meal period, using a checklist to ensure that one shift doesn't "forget" to do something for the next shift. The mise en place of the closing crew might include

- Clean and freshen floral and wine displays.

- Refrigerate flowers.

- Return perishable foodstuffs to the kitchen.

- Clean, refill, and refrigerate condiment containers.

- Wash and store pitchers.

- Clean and organize reach-in refrigerator.

- Clean and restock coffee station.

- Clean and turn off coffee equipment.

- Clean creamers.

- Empty bread-warming drawers of crumbs and clean.

- Clean pantry area.

- Clean side stands.

- Clean soup cart.

- Clean and stow trays and tray stands.

- Clean trolleys (voitures).

- Clean guéridons or side tables.

- Clear, strip, and clean tables.

- Clean chairs (including high chairs or boosters) and stack or stow as appropriate.

- Store flatware and hollowware.

- Clean and store china.

- Clean and store glasses.

- Store menus.

- Check vases for chips or cracks and store.

- Sweep, vacuum, and mop floors.

- Remove garbage.

- Sort linens and bag for pickup.

- Arrange draperies or curtains.

- Check light fixtures (clean, check bulbs).

- Adjust lighting and temperature.

KEEPING CHECKLISTS RELEVANT

As you may have surmised, having a list is not enough. The administration of these setup and breakdown procedures is what ensures that the work is being done. The management of the process involves constant scrutiny as well. For example, if the pantry is never setup on time for lunch service, no matter who is doing the job, it's likely that there is just too much work for one person to do, and some of the tasks should be shared with other members of the staff.

Serviceware

SERVICEWARE IS A GENERAL TERM for all utensils and wares used in the dining room to serve the guest, in addition to certain kitchen utensils such as carving knives and forks, ladles, and perforated spoons. The main classifications of serviceware are:

China: plates of all sizes, dishes, cups, saucers, underliners

Flatware: knives, forks, and spoons, regardless of style or usage

Glassware: items such as glass decanters, carafes, pitchers, and all drinking vessels used at a table or at the bar for beer, wine, and cocktails

Hollowware: technically, service items of significant depth or volume; more generally, large service items including platters, coffeepots, silver trays, etc.

One of the first things the patron will notice on entering the dining room is the tabletop design. For this reason, serviceware must be compatible with the overall design and motif of the operation. Unless service items are selected with regard to simplicity and completeness of detail, the effect created in the dining room will be one of disarray, confusion, and poor taste. In addition, ensuring the symmetry of the place settings will make for a neat and proper look to the tables.

Other qualities to consider when selecting serviceware, aside from aesthetic concerns, are

Washability: Is the item cleanable using the sanitation capabilities of the operation, without requiring excessive time, equipment, and effort?

Durability: Will the item selected stand up to the wear and tear of daily use?

Economy: Is the item affordable?

CHINA

In the course of history many types of dishware have been developed, each comprised of different mixtures of clay, feldspar, flint, and sometimes bone, and baked in kilns (fired) at different temperatures. (Various styles of china used in restaurants are shown on page 106.) The characteristics of ceramics are determined by their composition and firing temperature. For example, those items fired at the upper temperature range become completely vitrified (a glassy, nonporous, dense, practically nonabsorbent condition). Those fired only enough to harden are porous, with large interstices that permit air or liquids to pass through them.

Bisque: Unglazed ceramic material that has been fired once, at a low temperature.

Porcelain: Glazed and nonporous, with a fine texture that has a ring when tapped. It is a form of stoneware made from special clay that consists almost entirely of kaolin, a soft, white mineral.

Pottery: Low-fired, hence it has large pores, but because it is generally glazed, it does not absorb much liquid.

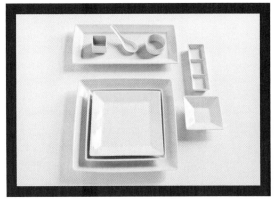

Traditional China.   Contemporary China.

Stoneware: Usually white, somewhat porous, and frequently has a transparent glaze. Stoneware is bisque that has been glazed and refired at a higher temperature.

Terra-cotta: Low-fired (bisque) red clay, usually unglazed, relatively soft, and very porous. A familiar example of terra-cotta is a common flowerpot.

Most restaurant china manufactured today has been vitrified. Fired at very high temperatures, this china becomes more durable, easier to clean, and able to withstand relatively high heat and extreme cold, as long as the temperature change is gradual.

China that has a patterned design should always have a layer of glaze on top of the pattern because the patterns are relatively fragile and can show wear rather quickly if not protected. Chipped or cracked china should be discarded as the more porous interior of the china can harbor germs.

These days, more emphasis is given to china for presentation. There are many shapes, colors, and materials available to help decorate the dining room like artwork. However, care should be taken not to have items that are so heavy that they will become hard for waiters to carry and dishwashers to stack.

FLATWARE

The choice of flatware will vary, depending upon the consideration of several factors:

Balance: Sizes, proportions, and weights should be attractive and comfortable in use. A selection of flatware used in restaurant service is shown on the facing page.

Design: Flatware design should reflect the establishment's ambience.

Durability: Flatware should be chosen with regard to the use and to methods of handling and washing.

Handles: May be made of nylon, compressed wood, solid steel, or hollow plate. Flatware may be one solid piece or have handles fitted with a bolster or rivets. (Note: Some wooden handles do not stand up well to the rigors of commercial dishwashing machines—and may be unsanitary since they must be hand-washed.)

Knife edge: Knives should retain sharpness of edges and serrations; sharp edges require less force in cutting, and therefore result in less accidental cuts and spills.

Longevity: Make sure the pattern will remain in production for replacement purposes. Beware of a pattern offered at a discount price, as the pattern may have been discontinued.

Quality: Composition and finishing plate should be of a quality appropriate to the establishment's overall standards.

Range: The style chosen should be available in all pieces needed for the establishment's menu items, such as cocktail forks, serrated knives, lobster picks, etc.

Stackability: Nesting should be possible with a minimum of scratching.

FLATWARE FOR SERVICE, FROM LEFT TO RIGHT: seafood or cocktail forks, appetizer/salad fork, fish fork, entree fork, dessert fork, butter knife, fish knife, appetizer knife, main course knife, steak knife, dessert spoon, iced tea spoon, entremets spoon, bouillon spoon, sauce spoon, tea spoon, coffee spoon.

CARE OF FLATWARE

Many establishments wash their flatware in sleeves, with all like types of flatware together. This often encourages "spooning," when flatware stacks together so tightly that it does not wash clean. It is best to wash flatware loose in a flat rack and sort it after washing, as long as this is permitted by the health code in your area. If the flatware is washed in a sleeve, it should go into the washing machine with the mouth end of the piece pointing up. Then, to avoid cross-contamination, remove the flatware from the sleeve in a sanitary manner, either by inverting an empty sleeve over the flatware and flipping it so the handles are now exposed, or by laying out a clean napkin on a flat surface and emptying the flatware onto the napkin. Handle flatware as little as possible, only by its handle, regardless of whether or not you are wearing gloves or using a clean cloth.

Stainless steel and silver require distinctly different cleaning methods. To clean stainless flatware, presoak all pieces, especially when stubborn stains occur. Never use an abrasive scrubbing pad, as it will mar the finish. Wash pieces in hot water and detergent, then rinse in hot water that is at least 181°F. It helps to have the different flatware pieces separated before polishing them because it speeds the process. Separator bins at the dish drop make it easier when it is time to polish and restock. A handful of flatware can be dipped into some hot water and then held inside a polishing cloth. Each piece should then be pushed through the fingers holding the cloth and into a clean, dry container or separator that will hold it until needed for use.

Cleaning silver does not have to be a long and tedious job; it can be done simply and quickly. Be sure to wash all silver in sudsy water as soon as possible after use. Silver should only be soaked for a few minutes in the recommended solutions—it should never be soaked for long periods of time. Immediately after washing, rinse thoroughly and wipe dry with a soft, clean cloth. To polish, rub the silver with a high-quality paste or liquid polish, using a soft, clean cloth. For quicker polishing, use a

Tip

If the staff needs to count out large numbers of flatware pieces, they should use a scale. To do this, weigh twenty forks in a container that will fit on a kitchen scale. Do the same with each type of flatware and create a chart that shows what standard numbers of pieces weigh. If you know what a hundred forks weigh and you need four hundred for the banquet, don't count them out one by one—use the scale!

Dangers of Using Ammonia

Some establishments add a few drops of ammonia to the soapy water to cut through residue and add to the brightness of flatware. This is *not* a recommended practice. Ammonia products should be kept out of kitchens because so many of the disinfectants used there are chlorine-based.

When chlorine and ammonia compounds come in contact, toxic gases are released, creating an unsafe workplace. The easiest way to prevent this occurrence is to keep ammonia products out of the kitchen.

treated silver cloth. Buff with a dry, soft cloth. Chemical polishing compounds such as sodium carbonate, sodium hydroxide, and sodium carboxylates are also available. Usually one ounce of the compound in a gallon of warm water (containing a piece of aluminum foil) is a quick-dip solution; rinse and wipe dry with a polishing cloth.

Clean silver should not be touched by bare hands, as oils from skin cause new tarnish spots. Do not bundle silver with elastic or rubber bands; these contain sulfur and will leave dark marks. To prevent tarnish, wrap silver pieces in anti-tarnish cloth and clear film wrap and store in an airtight place. Never use film wrap without completely covering the flatware with the anti-tarnish cloth—if film wrap is left in contact with the silver, the flatware can become marked by any wrinkles in the film.

Detarnishing baths are not to be used for silver pieces with designs in high relief—that is, pieces in which the crevices should remain dark. These baths are only for fast, easy cleaning of smooth-surfaced silver. Use a large aluminum pan with enough water to cover the silver. For each quart of water, add one teaspoon of baking soda. Bring the solution to a boil, then turn off the heat. Add the silver and let stand a few minutes. Remove the silver, wash it in hot sudsy water, rinse, and wipe dry. The aluminum sets up an electrolytic reaction with silver sulfide and removes the tarnish. The aluminum pan will need to be scoured with a soapy steel wool pad, or boiled in a solution of vinegar or cream of tartar and water.

The methods for polishing described so far are all chemical (or electrochemical) in nature. That is, they work by converting the silver oxides and sulfides of the tarnish back into metallic silver. While they work well for tarnish problems, they cannot remove the fine scratches that gradually dull the finish on flatware. A burnishing machine is required to restore the finish on silver plate. The machine pushes a tiny amount of the flatware's silver around, filling the abrasions with this smoothed bright layer of silver. Unfortunately, the use of burnishing machines can cause a gradual loss of the thickness of silver plating on the flatware. The method is only appropriate for wares that possess adequately thick plating—and even then should be done no more than twice a year.

GLASSWARE

Glassware contributes sparkle to the dining room, and tall, stemmed glasses add elegance. Various types of glassware are shown below. Glass is produced by heating sand (silicon dioxide) and other mineral substances to a very high temperature. The molten mass is blown or molded into shape and then allowed to cool and solidify by careful regulation of its temperature. This process is called "annealing." Handles and other parts are attached by welding during this process. The following considerations affect the selection of glassware:

Design: Coordinate glassware with other dining room equipment.

Manufacture: Examine the clarity of glass. Inspect for cracks, faults, bubbles, and distortions.

Marketing: Consider the amount of liquid in the capacity size of the glass. Depending on the style of restaurant, it could appear as though you are offering a "short pour," even though it may be appropriate to pour four to five ounces of wine in a sixteen-ounce glass.

Range: When possible, order multipurpose stock so that pieces may be interchanged.

Replacement: Are additional supplies readily available? Will the patterns continue to be produced?

Serviceability: Durable glasses with smooth, simple shapes are preferable. Consider the width of the opening for proper drinking, washing, draining, drying, pouring and stacking.

Additional information on glasses can be found in chapters 7 and 8.

FROM LEFT TO RIGHT: waterglass, stemmed waterglass, flute for sparkling wines, white wineglass, multi-purpose wine-glass, burgundy/pinot noir glass, bordeaux/cabernet glass

CLEANING GLASSWARE

Glassware for wine must be impeccably clean, because the aroma and taste of wine can be affected by foreign substances such as soap residue. In most establishments, glassware is washed, double-rinsed, steamed, polished, and dried with a cloth. Strong detergents and improper rinsing in industrial machines may leave a residue that can mask the quality of the wine and discourage the effervescence in a sparkling wine.

POLISHING GLASSWARE

Why do glasses and flatware need to be polished if they just came out of the dishwasher? In a perfect world they would be shiny and ready to go, but realistically, water spots may mar their appearance, and occasionally some residues may remain. (You don't want a gentleman guest pointing out to you that the lipstick on the glass isn't his shade.) On top of that, there is nothing like having perfectly polished glasses and flatware on the table—you can almost *feel,* not just see, the difference in the appearance of the whole room. Shiny glasses, individual salt and pepper shakers, knife rests—little things can add up to big impressions for your guests.

Glasses should be steamed and then polished with a polishing cloth. Linen companies will rent these cloths to you, and they should be lint-free. If there are lots of glasses to steam, set up a chafing dish with a small amount of hot water in the hotel pan, then set a shallow perforated pan inside.

Place the glasses upside down on the perforated pan and allow the steam to collect inside the glasses and around the outside (also make sure that the bottom of the glass gets steamy, which can be accomplished by placing a napkin or polishing cloth over the assembled glasses).

When the glasses are steamed up, take the base of the glass in one corner of the polishing cloth. Take the other end of the polishing cloth and stuff it into the bowl of the glass. Hold the base of the glass with one hand, and with the other hand stick your thumb into the bowl of the glass, with your fingers pointed toward the bottom. Only the cloth should be making contact with the glass. Begin to polish the glass by rotating it in the cloth, slowly moving your thumb and fingers up the side of the glass toward the lip. Since the base of the glass stays inside the cloth, the entire glass is now polished and can be placed back into a clean, dry glass rack, ready for use.

For smaller numbers of glasses, a water pitcher or some other vessel can be filled with boiling water to be used as a source of steam. While polishing, special care must be taken to check the glasses before and after for water spots, lipstick, and other foreign substances.

STORING GLASSWARE

Glasses can occupy a large storage area, so give special consideration to requirements for stocking glasses and for service needs in the bar and dining areas. For short-term storage, clean glasses can be placed upright on a side stand, covered with paper towels or a clean cloth.

For longer-term storage, keep glassware upside down in a rack of the correct size that is kept in a low traffic area. To avoid breaking stemware, always place glassware in the correct size rack; the stems should not extend above the lip of the rack.

Specially designed hanging racks and trays can be used for glasses to facilitate storing and handling if they do not violate health codes in your area, since smoking may be allowed at the bar and the smoke can get trapped in the inverted glasses (this may vary according to local smoking laws). Also, the racks can be perceived as unsanitary if the bartender is not tall enough to remove glasses by their stems.

Do not store glasses upside down on a shelf, as each glass will take on the smell of the shelf or rack on which it's resting. The shelf surface may not be sanitary and could be the source of cross-contamination.

HOLLOWWARE

Hollowware pieces used in the dining room are usually specialty items: tea and coffee sets, covered serving dishes, tureens and bowls, ice buckets, oval platters and trays, café diablo sets, chafing dishes, punch bowls, suprême sets, and the like (see below). If plate covers are provided, be sure they fit the plate well and that they are secure to

CLOCKWISE, FROM TOP LEFT: water pitcher, diablo set, table card holder, creamer, gooseneck/sauceboat in stainless steel

CLOCKWISE, FROM TOP LEFT: cake stand trivet, platter, coffee pot, cloche, fingerbowl, candlestick holder in silver

safely stack plates for banquet service. The bottom of the plate must also fit securely into the grooves of the top of the plate cover. It is possible that some plate covers may be interchangeable with other serviceware.

Component pieces may be sold separately or in sets; one example is a soup tureen with or without a cover. In using hollowware, make provisions for the appropriate accompanying serving utensils, such as spoons and ladles.

Often hollowware is made from some form of metal. Metal items are stronger and better able than ceramic items to withstand the impact and stress arising from frequent handling. In addition, the weight of a large metalware dish can be appreciably lighter than ceramic, and a greater variety of shapes is available. Metal food containers can create problems, however. Certain metals can taint foods, and strongly acidic (or, less commonly, alkaline) foods can corrode metals. Difficulties also arise in washing, polishing, and maintaining the appearance of metalware. (Follow the same guidelines as described above for metal flatware.)

Setting the Table

LIKE FIRST IMPRESSIONS OF PEOPLE, the guest's first impression of the dining room—the individual tables and the effect they create together—will dramatically influence the guest's dining experience.

Proper table setting involves a number of elements: the linens, the flatware or silverware, the glassware, and the china. All require the careful attention of the professional server. Whatever the place setting consists of, there should be standards to adhere to. Perhaps in your establishment, water glasses are placed one inch above the dinner knife. With the tables lined up and then all set in this fashion, the room has a satisfying appearance. When the glasses are placed in a haphazard manner, the table setting looks unfinished, even if all of the right pieces are on the table.

DRESSING THE TABLE

Inspect all tablecloths before using them in the dining room. Any cloths found to be soiled, stained, shredded, or torn should be delivered to the supervisor, who will contact the supplier for appropriate credit. Before laying a tablecloth, certain preparations should be made:

- Set up the dining room. Arrange the tables and chairs in an orderly, balanced pattern. Make sure to leave ample aisle space for service. (This rearranging of tables is often needed because tables are often pushed together to accommodate larger parties.)

- Clean the tabletops.

- Level the tables by turning screw glides on the bases of adjustable tables, or by inserting pieces of cork or plastic wedges under legs of nonadjustable tables. Never use matchbooks or wadded napkins—they offer only temporary relief, they are unsightly, and give the dining room an unprofessional appearance. Tighten the center bolt of pedestal tables.

- Make sure there are no loose nails or splinters that might catch or snag the tablecloth.

- Spread and secure the silence cloth (also known as the "underlay" or "undercloth"). Smooth any creases and make sure the cloths are centered.

- Statler tables are square four-tops that can be opened to a round six- to eight-top. These should be clothed with this conversion in mind (the table should always remain covered, even when opened during service). Select a tablecloth that is appropriate for the fully opened size of the table (the drop—the distance the cloth should hang over the edge of the table—should extend to a point just even with the seat of the chair). The tablecloth should be aligned so that the table can be converted back to a four-top if needed, without having to relay the tablecloth

PROPER TABLE ARRANGEMENT

Table arrangements should be neat and symmetrical. Large-scale precision, with everything in its place, starts with the placement of dining tables in the room. They should be in straight lines and evenly spaced. One more thing to do while arranging the tables is to make sure that the waitstaff can get around and between all of the tables, so that every customer in the room can be served. Leaving four feet between tables generally gives enough space for the guest to sit and leaves a foot-wide path between the chairs for service. Chairs should be set square to the table edge, just slightly underneath.

The center crease of all tablecloths in the dining room should point up and run in the same direction, generally toward the entrance. This practice gives an organized look to the room, especially when the tables are not occupied. The linen company should press the tablecloth so the hem is hidden when the crease is up. However, it is more important that the hem face in when the cloth is laid. In that case, the crease may point down. Managers often use the position of the main crease in the table to identify seat number one at the table; seat number one is traditionally the chair with

1. Position yourself so that you have seat number one to your right or left side. Pull the fresh, folded tablecloth open, and lay it across the table. The cloth should be opened upward, toward you, with the hems positioned at the bottom.

2. Hold the top piece of the cloth and the center crease between your middle and index fingers, and the first hem between your index finger and thumb.

3. Raise the two layers of the cloth as previously indicated. There should still be one layer of the cloth on the table unattached.

4. Picking up the cloth by the center crease and first hem, flick the wrist away from you. Place the bottom, unattached layer of cloth so that it is hanging over the opposite side of the table from where you are standing.

5. Pull the remaining hem (bottom) toward you while releasing the center crease.

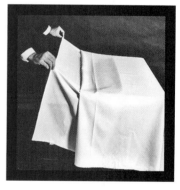

6. The tablecloth will unfold with the center crease pointing upward.

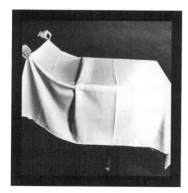

7. Straighten and center the cloth. The cloth should land evenly front to back and side to side; the hem should be rolled under, not exposed.

8. Adjust and straighten to make certain the sides are even.

CHANGING A TABLECLOTH WITH A SILENCE CLOTH

1. Position yourself at the table so that you have seat number one to your left or right side. Hold a clean, folded tablecloth so that the thick rolled edges are on top (hems are on the bottom).

2. Pull the clean cloth open as you would an accordion.

3. Holding the clean cloth between your fourth and fifth fingers, reach down to pick up the corners of the soiled cloth between your thumb, index, and middle finger.

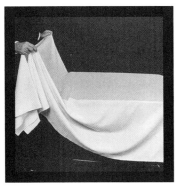 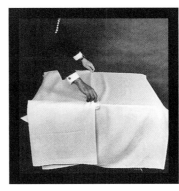 

4. Pull the soiled cloth up and toward you until the far hem (of the soiled cloth) is at the edge of the table.

5. Now lower the partially open clean cloth onto the table. At this point, if the cloths were opened correctly, the hems of the fresh cloth should be on the bottom, center crease on top.

6. Grasp the top layer of cloth (the center crease) with your thumb and index finger; meanwhile, the next layer of cloth is held between your index finger and middle finger.

7. Raise these two layers of clean cloth up and gently flick the bottom layer of the cloth so that it hangs over the far edge of the table. Rest the partially opened cloth on the table so that it covers about one third of the table.

8. Pinch the hem of the clean cloth and soiled cloth together. Pull back both cloths toward you.

9. When the center crease of the fresh cloth reaches the middle, release it and continue to pull the bottom cloth. The clean cloth should be in place—center crease pointing upward, hems rolled under, all sides hanging evenly. The soiled cloth should be in your hands.

Silence Cloth

A silence cloth (molleton) makes the table feel plush, soft, and luxurious. This cloth is placed on the table first and is then covered with a second tablecloth. Silence cloths cushion the noise of plates and cutlery placed on the table during service. Besides preventing noise, a silence cloth protects the tabletop, soaks up spills, and prevents the top cloth from sliding. In addition, the silence cloth keeps the bare tabletop from being exposed when you must change the tablecloth during service.

If there are no spills, the silence cloth can be used for several seatings. However, any linen used in the dining room carries some cost, so its use is more common in fine dining restaurants. As an alternative to a silence cloth, some tables have permanent cushioning on the tabletop to serve as silencer. Another tablecloth or a thin piece of foam rubber or felt can be used as a silence cloth. Some fine dining establishments use padding and an under- or overlay.

its back to the kitchen door. The correct procedure for laying a tablecloth is shown on page 115.

When a tablecloth becomes soiled during service, change it. Never shake out a tablecloth in the dining room. This distracts the guest, is unsanitary, and indicates poor training.

During service, bare tabletops should never be exposed. Some operations use an underlay and a silence cloth to avoid completely stripping the table when it is time to replace the tablecloth—however, an underlay and a silence cloth makes it more difficult to replace the top cloth in a smooth manner. The correct procedure for changing a cloth when the table has a silence cloth is shown on page 116.

LINEN SELECTION

Until modern times, tablecloths and napkins were traditionally made of linen, a natural fiber produced from flax. Today, man-made fibers are often substituted for, or combined, with natural ones. For example, many tablecloths are made of a blend of polyester and cotton. The term *linen* still applies in a general sense to all fabrics used at or on the table.

Several items must be considered in the selection of a fabric for the tabletop. The style and décor of the dining room will dictate the color, pattern, closeness of weave, and texture chosen. The fabric determines the serviceability of the linens. Some fabrics are durable and easy to mend, others are difficult to clean and mend. Some fray or pull, or have a tendency to produce a lot of lint.

Some fabrics are both attractive and economically suitable. Most linen companies can provide samples of linens that have been laundered several times. Poor-quality cotton napkins can leave lint on the guests. Polyester can pill, is less absorbent, and does not have the high-quality feel of cotton, but it is less expensive, more durable, and resists wrinkling.

Colored or patterned cloths are often selected for decorative purposes. While colored cloths generally show less spotting, they are more difficult to launder, repair, and replace than white cloths. In addition, colored cotton cloths may fade and create an uneven look in the dining room. When there is need for color or contrast, a colored or textured tablecloth can be used over a white undercloth. Another alternative is to use placemats or colored napkins on top of a white tablecloth. Restaurants that serve fine wines should avoid colored cloths, though, as the color of the wine is best viewed against a white background.

The laundering of linens is a serious expense for a restaurant. Therefore, it makes sense to take care in the handling and storage of clean linens. A covered shelf set at chest height will help keep the linens from becoming soiled before use. Sorting and labeling them carefully by size will eliminate the need for unnecessary handling. Common sense dictates that liquids should never be stored above clean linens.

Skirting

A large facility that does extensive catering, or a facility that may set-up areas such as a continental breakfast or reception table, may have skirting available. Table skirts are used to hide the table legs and make the table more presentable.

The top edge of the table skirts is usually backed with Velcro clips, with corresponding Velcro tabs, which are placed on the table edge. To prevent the skirt from falling away at the corners of the table, place clips near the corners on each edge of the table.

When not in use, these clips should be kept in a special container; they are the sort of small items that always seem to disappear. Skirts should be kept on special hangers that grasp the Velcro edge, to prevent the creases that result from folding.

Skirt rentals are expensive, as are dry-cleaning bills—consequently, many establishments make inexpensive temporary skirts from tablecloths. Most banquet tables are 30 by 30, so 90-by-90-inch cloths can cover and skirt the table.

STANDARD TABLE AND TABLECLOTH (ALL SIZES IN INCHES)

Table Sizes	Tablecloth Sizes
30 × 26, 30 × 30, 30 round	42 × 42 minimum, 54 × 54 maximum
36 × 36, 36 round	48 × 48 minimum, 60 × 60 maximum
42 × 42, 42 round	52 × 52 minimum, 64 × 64 maximum
44 × 44	56 × 56 minimum, 66 × 66 maximum
48 round	60 × 60 minimum, 66 × 66 maximum
54 round	66 × 66 minimum, 72 × 72 maximum
60 round	72 × 72 minimum, 76 × 76 maximum
66 round	78 × 78 minimum, 84 × 84 maximum
72 round	84 × 84 minimum, 90 × 90 maximum
72 × 30	90 × 54 minimum, 96 × 54 maximum
72 × 36	114 × 54 minimum, 120 × 54 maximum
96 × 30	114 × 120 minimum, 96 × 60 maximum
96 × 36	114 × 60 minimum, 120 × 60 maximum

NAPKINS

Napkins can be arranged in a variety of places, but most often in the middle of the place setting, directly in front of the guest, or to the left of the fork and one inch from the edge of the table.

Each establishment has its own guidelines for the exact placement of napkins and flatware, depending upon the style of service and complexity of settings. Some may have settings placed as close as one finger's width from the edge of the table; others require more space.

Cloth napkins are usually folded in the style of the house. There are countless napkin folds. The choice will depend on the ambience and décor of the dining room, the skill of the staff, labor costs, the time available to actually do the folding, and compatibility with the other tabletop items. A few examples of classic napkin folds are illustrated below. Generally speaking, the trend is toward simple table settings that are not compatible with the involved, archaic, and elaborate folds of the past. Uncomplicated folds take less time and create a mood of simple elegance. Complicated folds involve extra handling by the waiter and may be perceived as being less sanitary (see the video *The Art of Folding Table Napkins,* listed in the appendix).

Napkins are usually delivered to the restaurant already folded in halves or quarters, so the existing creases should be incorporated into the chosen folded design. This will save time and eliminate the need of having to work around the existing crease. After repeated use, the edges of cloth napkins tend to become uneven. Also, the stitching around the edges can be unsightly. If possible, choose a fold that will avoid exposing the edges of the napkin.

Silverware transport fold

Bishop's mitre

Tuxedo fold

Artichoke fold

Bird of Paradise fold

Table linen as we know it represents centuries of evolution. Napkins have been used as early as Roman times. Guests in ancient Rome brought their own napkins, tying one under the chin and keeping another nearby for wiping the fingers. Dining tended to be messy, as forks were not yet used.

By the Middle Ages full tablecloths were common (before that, small tablecloths were used, but only to cover the host's place). At large banquets the tablecloth would be changed several times. It was not long before the runner was introduced—a long, narrow strip of linen laid along the edge of the table. The runner was used by guests to wipe their fingers and mouths. Later came the touaille. This roller-type towel was fixed to the wall and used by several diners.

In the sixteenth century the individual napkin, not seen since Roman times, came back into fashion. The napkin was draped over the left arm, but when large, starched, ruffled collars came into style, the napkin was tied around the neck to prevent soiling the collar. As an insignia of his position, the maître d'hôtel carried a napkin rolled in an epaulet on his left shoulder.

The royal forks (when they came into use) and knives were often wrapped in a napkin and carried in a nef (or "boat"). The serviette, as the napkin was called, was changed at each course of the meal, and was sometimes scented with perfume.

Folded napkins may also be used in the dining room for ornamentation. Napkins can be folded to create a pocket for dinner rolls, bread, or a small bouquet of flowers. This is known as "à la serviette." A common ornamental fold for water pitcher underliners is the artichoke fold.

SALT AND PEPPER

In the 1800s, each guest had their own salt cellar at the top right of their place setting. No ground pepper was served. When salt and pepper shakers began appearing on the table top, the pepper had to go on the left since the salt had established its proper place at the right. Most restaurants today place the salt shaker on the right and the pepper on the left facing seat number 1. Like most condiments, one set for every four guests is customary. If more than two sets are placed on the table, salt should always be on the right side as the guest faces the table. For large round tables such as a 72-inch round for six to ten guests, place the condiments within reach of the guests rather than in the center of the table. For a table this large it might be best to have three or four sets of condiments on the table so they will not have to interrupt the other guests to "pass the salt, please."

The Cover

THE FRENCH TERM *COUVERT* or "cover" has several distinct, and possibly confusing, meanings in the dining room:

- A place setting that is intended for use with a specific type of meal and service is called a "cover." It refers to the flatware, glassware, and china that are set for the guest.

- The minimum charge for a guest who does not order a full meal is also known as a "cover." It is meant to offset the cost of bread, butter, linens, etc. that are not normally included in the bill.

- Since there is one cover in front of each guest, "covers" can also refer to the number of guests in a dining room or at a table. For example, "The dining room will seat 75 covers," or "We did 123 covers for lunch."

Throughout this chapter, the word *cover* refers to a place setting. Except for special occasions, parties, or banquets, the table is not typically preset with every piece of the cover. Knowing what pieces to stock in your side stand or to prepare as setups in the pantry helps ensure smooth, efficient service.

To provide adequate room for each guest, allow a minimum of eighteen inches for each setting. Settings on deuces may be positioned banquette style—side-by-side, or at right angles to allow the guests to face the dining room—or so the guests can face each other. At tables with an even number of guests with the guests are seated facing each other across the table, the flatware should be aligned so one guest's fork is directly across from the opposite guest's knife, whether the table is round or square.

On rectangular or square tables, the bottom edge of all flatware, napkins, and cover plates should be in a straight line, one inch from the edge of the table (see page 114 for placement of linens). On round tables, these items should be placed in a straight line, rather than follow the rim of the table; the outermost pieces of flatware will be closer to the edge of the table than the plate, which is in the center of the setting.

PLACING FLATWARE

Check flatware for spots prior to service, and return any pieces to the dish room that are soiled. Place flatware on the table three-quarters of an inch from the show plate and one inch from the edge of the table. Forks should be placed to the left with the tines facing up or, for a continental touch, with the tines facing down. Oyster or cocktail forks may be placed on the right side or they can be served on the underliner with the food item. Spoons are placed on the right side, faceup. Knives are placed on the right with the cutting edge facing to the left. When a guest picks up the knife with the right hand, it is already in the natural position for proper use.

Whenever possible, set only those pieces that are required for the food to be served. Do not set more than four pieces of flatware at a time except where a cocktail fork is used. If the menu calls for more, it is best to place the utensils just prior to each course. Dessert utensils should be set in after decrumbing and just before the time of dessert service.

Banquet service is an exception to this rule. When setting for a banquet, place the dessert utensils above the cover. The fork's handle should point to the left, the dessert and coffee spoons are placed above the fork with the handles pointing to the right. Flatware positioned above the cover plate should be moved to the correct position by the server before the appropriate course.

Flatware should be positioned in the order in which it is to be used; for example, utensils to be used first are placed on the outside, with flatware for the succeeding courses placed toward the center of the cover.

To ensure adequate space for the china, make certain that the innermost flatware leaves enough space for the largest plate (which usually has a 12-inch diameter) to be served.

Carry all clean flatware to the table on a dinner plate covered with a clean linen napkin (silverware transport plate, or STP). Many restaurants fold a napkin to form a pocket that is placed on a large plate to transport the flatware to the table. The blades of the knives can be inserted into the pocket; other utensils should be placed on top of the pocket. The pocket fold also serves to differentiate the flatware plate from the decrumbing plate.

PLACING CHINA AND GLASSWARE

Place the bread and butter plate half an inch to the left of the cover, or one inch from the edge of the table. On round tables, there may only be room for the bread and butter plate one inch above and to the left of the forks, aligned with the left edge of the outermost fork. Place the bread and butter knife on the right hand edge of the plate, with the cutting edge of the knife facing left

Place the coffee cup and saucer, whether preset (at breakfast and lunch) or added to the service during the meal, to the right of the cover. Position the bottom

Full dinner cover for à la carte service.

Dinner cover with service plate.

Dinner cover with a fish course.

Fish cover (main) with fish knife.

Full dinner cover for banquet service (including soup, salad, main, and dessert).

Pasta main course cover.

Standard dinner cover with seafood cocktail and finger bowl.

Standard dinner cover with escargot appetizer and finger bowl.

Standard cover with string pasta appetizer.

Simple cover.

Caviar setup.

Lobster setup.

edge of the saucer in line with the top of the adjacent piece of flatware. The handle should be pointing to the right and set at a slight angle toward the edge of the table (four o'clock position). This positioning allows the guest to grasp the cup handle with ease. Once the cup and saucer is set, the server should never lift the cup by itself. If a left-handed guest moves the cup and saucer to the left, you should refill from the left side.

When show plates or chargers are decorated with emblems, logos, or names, the decoration should be placed facing the guest, in a way that permits easy readability.

Position glassware to the right of the cover, above the point of the dinner knife. If more than one glass is to be set, such as a white wineglass, a red wineglass, and a Champagne glass, position them at an angle up from the point of the dinner knife in order of service from right to left. If the red wine is to be served after the white wine, place it to the left and slightly above the white wineglass.

If a water glass is to accompany the wineglasses, it is generally placed just above the dinner knife with the wineglasses angled slightly above and to the left. In Europe, it is common to place the water glass to the left and slightly above the wineglasses with Champagne, tulip, or port glasses positioned to the left of the water glass. (For additional information on glassware, see chapters 7 and 8.)

STANDARD COVERS

The following list describes and illustrates some standard covers used in restaurant service (including plated items brought from the kitchen):

À la carte cover: used for French or Russian service; additional serviceware is placed prior to the appropriate course.

Breakfast cover: Fork, knife, spoon, coffee cup and saucer (or mug), napkin.

Dinner cover with service plate: Full cover with a large base plate, show plate, or charger. This plate is used to dress the place setting and may be removed prior to the first course being served, or the amuse-bouche or appetizer course may be served on the service plate. Cocktails may be served on the show plate using a cocktail napkin. If the napkin bears the restaurant's logo, it should be facing the guest. When the service plate is removed, move the cocktail to the right of the setting and remove the cocktail napkin.

Dinner cover with a fish course: A full dinner cover with the addition of a fish fork and knife.

Full dinner cover: Used for banquet service. All serviceware is placed on the table before the guests arrive. Serviceware set will be determined by the menu items.

Simple cover: Includes only the bare essentials.

Standard dinner cover with seafood appetizer: A standard dinner cover with the addition of utensils for shrimp or seafood cocktail, oysters, or clams on the half shell.

Standard dinner cover with escargot appetizer: A standard dinner cover with the addition of snail pinchers (or tongs) and a snail fork.

String pasta cover: A simple setting with the addition of Parmesan cheese. Traditionally, pasta is served as a middle course in a bowl. In an Italian setting, a large fork is placed at the right of the setting, so the pasta can be twirled against the side of the bowl, not with a spoon. It is acceptable in American-style restaurants to preset the fork on the left and a pasta spoon on the right.

SETUPS

These settings may be prepared ahead of time and stored in the side stand. They are referred to as "sets" or "setups." Here are some additional cover suggestions for specific menu items:

Bouillabaisse: large soup plate on a large underliner, soup spoon, and small bone or shell plate for discarded shells, etc.

Caviar: small chilled plate, small mother of pearl, gold, or horn knife, toast basket, butter dish

Cheese: small plate, small fork, small knife

Dessert: dessert fork and spoon, soup spoon or knife for cutting pastry, small plate

Finger bowl: finger bowl filled one third with warm water, slice of lemon in water, underliner, paper doily between underliner and finger bowl

Half grapefruit: citrus spoon, teaspoon, sugar, small bowl on underliner

Hors d'oeuvre (or amuse-bouche): large service plate, small fork, small knife

Melon and prosciutto: small plate, small knife, small fork

Lobster: large fork, large knife, lobster fork, lobster cracker, finger bowl

Melon: dessert spoon (or small fork and small knife), appropriate-size small bowl on an underliner

Pâté: small plate, small knife, small fork, toast

Ambience

THE AMBIENCE OF A DINING ROOM is the result of several elements: the lighting, the décor, the flowers, the temperature of the room, and the music that plays. When these elements are properly combined and balanced, they enhance the guest's experience. If you notice anything wrong, notify the manger if it is a problem you are not authorized to fix on your own.

FLOWERS

Freshly cut flowers can enliven a dining room, but—if not maintained—the effect will be exactly the opposite. A few large arrangements in the room may look better than a vase on every table. In many cases, deuces cannot spare the room for flowers—except for a very small vase, possibly containing a single flower.

In selecting flowers for the dining room, consider fragrance as well as appearance. Highly scented flowers will conflict with the aroma of the foods and for this reason should not be used. When flowers are used on the tables, consider their height (they may block the view of the guest's company).

Avoid potted plants at the table, as they contain soil and sometimes attract small mites or bugs.

Edible flowers are very popular both on the plates and as part of the tabletop, but it is important to note that not all flowers can be safely consumed. Some flowers are inherently toxic (i.e., lily of the valley and foxglove). Some have been sprayed with poisonous compounds or have been treated with systemic poisons, which cannot be washed off. Some have been grown in other countries where untreated human waste may have been used as fertilizer. Only flowers that have been grown specifically for consumption should ever be used as garnishes.

The stamens of some lilies can stain linens, and should be clipped before the flowers are placed on the tables. Peruvian lilies (*alstroemeria*) look good and last a long time—but they contain a sap that can cause severe skin irritation.

CARING FOR CUT FLOWERS

Proper care of cut flowers will extend their beauty and life. Upon delivery, place cut flowers in tepid water in a cool room or refrigerator. Never store flowers near food, especially apples—they give off ethylene gas, a natural ripening agent that causes flowers to fade prematurely. Crush hardwood stems slightly so they can absorb more water. Split soft stems about one-half inch with a knife or scissors. Soft-leafed flowers (such as poppies) are greatly helped if the tips of the stems are dipped a few seconds in boiling water. Be careful to shield the heads and blossoms with paper or cloth. This process also helps to revive wilting flowers and wildflowers. Check arrangements daily and change the water every day or two to keep them smelling fresh. Nightly refrigeration will also help extend the life of most floral arrangements.

Varieties of flowers that offer good lasting qualities (ten to fourteen days, if chilled nightly), are not overpoweringly strong smelling, are relatively inexpensive, and are of a size that is suitable for use on tables, include

- **Alstroemeria** (Peruvian lilies)

- **Smaller chrysanthemums** (home-grown varieties can have unpleasantly strong scents, but commercial varieties generally do not)

- **Miniature carnations**

- **Dwarf anthurium**

- **Smaller haliconias** (such as parakeet)

Everlastings (*limoneas*, such as statice and heather) can be used dry in combination with silk flowers, or simply be allowed to dry in an arrangement—in which case they will last up to three weeks.

A great variety of materials may be used in flower arranging, including branches, berries, leaves, colorful fruit, and even decorative products from the vegetable garden. Properly dried materials can also be used. The charm of an arrangement is a result not only of its composition, but also of the variety of shapes, sizes, colors, and textures of its assorted materials.

LIGHTING

It cannot be denied that light has a great effect on our moods. The desired atmosphere can be achieved in the dining room with the aid of various forms of light (fluorescent or incandescent lights, gas lamps, candles, or natural sunlight). Lighting can be used to

- Attract attention, as with an inviting entrance light.

- Emphasize works of art or food merchandising displays.

- Increase or reduce the impression of space in a room.

- Indicate directions, and project information.

- Indicate exits and warning notices.

- Influence the guests' perceptions of food, alter the pace of the meal, and change the atmosphere or ambience of the dining room.

- Provide color, animation, and contrast.

- Reveal texture and heighten shape and form.

- Be more flattering to guests (skin tones look best in warm-colored light).

Within the dining and associated areas, bright lights should be out of view. Textures and shapes are best emphasized with lighting directed from the side, at an angle (as opposed to lighting from directly overhead or the front) to show the surface in strong relief. Pictures, displays, and other features of interest should be illuminated by directional lighting. When evening dining is in subdued light, the illumination should be concentrated over the tables and service areas. It should be light enough that patrons don't have difficulty reading their menus.

The flicker of candlelight, for creating mood and intensifying atmosphere, is difficult to reproduce with artificial light. Candle lights are often equipped with removable and washable globes and refillable inserts. Small oil lamps require frequent cleaning; at least once a day for proper maintenance.

Refillable candle lights must be cleaned well before the glass portion is run through the dishwashing machine. This is because high washing temperatures will melt any residual wax, eventually causing the machine to malfunction. It is best to spread a thin layer of oil inside the container before installing a new candle, as this makes the removal of excess wax easier. The use of water for this purpose is not recommended, as many of these candleholders are equipped with a small metal base to secure the wick. Water can form unsightly rust on the candleholder. Freezing the candleholder can ease removal of used candles.

Open flames, such as candles or small oil lamps, can pose a fire risk (especially to menus and napkins), and can contribute undesirable odors in the dining room.

It is proper for the candles to be lit just as the guests are seated—but most restaurants prefer the look of a dining room with all of the candles lit.

MUSIC

Music provides a significant part of a restaurant's ambience. It is generally chosen to complement the décor and theme (if any) of the restaurant. The music chosen for a House of Blues franchise will be significantly different from the music used in a Neapolitan-style trattoria, which would also be different from that played in a four-star French restaurant. The type of music chosen, the volume at which it is played and the times of day that it changes must be determined for each specific situation. Whatever the type of music, it should be loud enough to hear and enjoy, but not so loud that guests cannot hear each other or the server. It must be remembered that the music is chosen to enhance the guests' dining experience—it is not intended to provide entertainment for the staff.

Conclusion

TO REPEAT BRILLAT-SAVARIN'S MAXIM, "To entertain a guest is to be answerable for his happiness so long as he is beneath your roof." The professional server can only do that successfully through conscientious attention to mise en place. This means attention to every detail of the dining room, from aesthetics to sanitation, from napkin folding to silver polishing, from table setting to choice of floral arrangements.

6

Serving Guests

PEOPLE VISIT RESTAURANTS to dine in a relaxing, pleasurable, yet stimulating environment. A skilled server, regardless of the type of service offered, must orchestrate the dining experience so that the customer's expectations are not only met, but also surpassed. If not, the server can expect no return business and below-average gratuities.

Before we address the specifics of serving guests, there is one basic consideration for all servers to keep in mind. Anticipating the customer's needs and wishes is the key to good service. The professional server should always be one step ahead of the guest.

The ability to remain confidently in control of the guest's dining experience, without being overbearing, is a skill one learns gradually, practicing with each encounter. Proper table maintenance, reading the table, and taking the order correctly are all critical in any successful dining room. Additional important aspects of remarkable service, such as dealing with delays or mistakes and handling difficult guests and children, are discussed in this chapter.

Steps of Service

WHILE INDIVIDUAL FOOD-SERVICE ESTABLISHMENTS develop house rules to cover all aspects of service, from greeting to actual service to the presentation of the check, all restaurants follow the same basic sequence of activities; in other words, the steps of service:

- Greeting
- Seating
- Bread and water (may occur after taking the order)
- Beverage service
- Menu/wine list presentation (may occur upon being seated)
- Taking the order
- Service
- Clearing
- Check presentation/payment
- Farewell
- Resetting tables

Sequence of Courses

THE SEQUENCE OF COURSES for most Western menus follows the order listed below. The history of this sequence is described in chapter 2.

- Appetizer
- Soup
- First course (may be a combination of the above items; a family restaurant may offer a choice of appetizer, soup, or salad as a starter course, rather than as separate courses)
- Main course
- Salad (traditionally served after the main course in a European-style meal; American restaurants generally serve salad between the first and main courses)

- Fruit and cheese (usually offered only by fine dining establishments and some bistros)

- Dessert

- After-dinner beverages (see chapter 7 for more details)

- Tobacco

Standards of Service

EACH RESTAURANT HAS ITS OWN STYLE and establishes its own standards of service. The following list is a typical example:

- Greet guests within thirty seconds of being seated.

- When serving a table, always look where you are walking. Never walk backward.

- Serve children first, then ladies (eldest first), followed by gentlemen, and the host (when known) last (regardless of gender).

- All courses should be served in the proper sequence, unless otherwise specified or requested by the guest.

- Serve all guests at the table at once; do not serve just one or two guests and leave the others to wait. (An exception is made when the guests do not all order the same number of courses.)

- All foods and beverages are served from the patron's right side with the waiter's right hand.

- If guests request water, ask if they would like tap or bottled water. Serve water for everyone at the table. Serve bottled water chilled with no ice. Offer, but do not assume that the guest desires, a garnish such as lemon or lime.

- All soiled dishes should be removed from the patron's right side with the waiter's right hand and transferred to the left hand—except bread and butter plates, which should be picked up from the left side. Do not scrape dishes in front of the guest.

- Avoid reaching across the front of a guest. Imagine a line that runs down the middle of the guest's face and chest, and plan actions so that line is not crossed. If, because of the seat's location, it is absolutely necessary to reach across the guest—apologize for the breach of protocol.

Everything that happens in the dining room, if done well, should be exactly the same all of the time—except for one variable: the guests. Every guest is different, and has different needs. Some are in a hurry, while some want to enjoy a leisurely dinner. Some want a four-course meal, others would prefer three appetizers, and still others are on restricted diets.

Skilled servers need to be able to read the table in order to control the pace of the meal, suggest additional items, and occasionally even steer the guests away from certain items. A little conversation when the guests are first seated can provide the kind of clues servers need to do their job well. A series of carefully phrased questions can garner some clues about what the waiter can suggest to the table that will both make them feel attended to and generate sales for the restaurant. For example, an initial dialogue might run as follows:

Q: Would you like to see our cocktail menu?

A: No, thanks, we'll just be drinking wine tonight.

Q: How about a wine list, then?

A: Sure, but we're not sure what we're going to be eating yet.

Q: May I suggest, then, a glass of Champagne while you make up your minds?

A: That sounds perfect!

The waiter followed the lead of the customers, guiding them toward a decision that will make them happy and make a nice sale for the house. In addition to the guests' words, servers can make use of nonverbal hints, such as body language, to better serve their guests. When guests peek at their watches, scan the room as if gazing at some distant horizon, pick at their food, or toy with a nearly empty glass, they are sending signals that they are in need of something. If a guest tastes the food, then pushes the plate away, something is wrong. By reading these signs, and acting upon them, servers can exceed the expectations of the guests—and make the guests' dining experience favorably memorable.

Sometimes the waiter can feel conflicted at the table: "Should I tell them that the steak tartare is raw, or will they feel as though I think they're stupid?" There can be clear signs that a guest needs to be clued in. It usually isn't that obvious, though. This is when experience in reading guests comes in handy. A guest who shows the signs of being someone who dines out frequently probably doesn't need to be told that vichyssoise is served cold.

The diner who has less apparent dining experience can be clued in subtly. One way is to repeat back their menu choice in a descriptive manner, such as "So you will start with the cold potato-leek soup, then move on to the chilled raw beef for dinner?"

Without such clear indications, though, the waiter should look for signs of tension or timidity (asking to have the name of a dish pronounced or pointing at their menu selection) or confidence (asking leading questions about dishes and pronouncing the names of more obscure dishes or ingredients correctly). Once you have an idea of what a guest is comfortable with (or worried about) you can work to relieve the tense diner or try taking the confident guest into more adventurous territory by suggesting things they might not have had before.

The Three *T*s of Service

VIEWED BROADLY, service can be broken into three main areas of concern: Technique, Timing, and Teamwork. Attention to these three *T*s can guarantee happy customers—which leads to a happy staff and management.

TECHNIQUE

Guests try new restaurants for many reasons, but they come back for only one: they liked what they found there. They come back because they want to repeat that experience. Consistency, then, is essential to the creation and maintenance of repeat business. Customers expect the same high level of service every time they visit. The professional server reads the table after each course or beverage is served and again at the end of the meal, to make sure that the dining experience is everything the guest would like it to be and that the guest knows that the server cares about their needs.

When speaking to guests, it is important to sound sincere and avoid repeating a few stock phrases and responses. In addition, keep in mind that people have a "zone of privacy"—an invisible boundary around them—that can only be entered by their most intimate friends and relatives. If anyone else (i.e., a server) intrudes into that private space, the person will become uncomfortable. The size of the zone varies from culture to culture, as well as from one situation to another.

Rather than ask "Is everything alright?"—putting guests on the spot, while they mentally review the entire meal—the server should ask a specific question. For example, say, "Isn't the hint of rosemary in the lamb wonderful?" or mention that, "The chef goes to the market every morning to select the fish." These are pleasant openings that give the guests some information with which to respond, as well as something to talk about later.

TIMING

Servers should treat guests as they themselves would like to be treated. The best way for a server to accomplish this is to anticipate the guest's needs before the guest notices them: They should put themselves in the guest's place, and imagine what would be needed at each stage of the meal. Anticipation of need not only impresses the guest, but it makes the server's job easier because it allows the server to control the flow of work, rather than having to try to play catch-up.

Timing in the dining room means always having everything set up before it is needed. The flatware for each course should be in place before the course is served. The wine that is meant to accompany the main course should be poured before that course leaves the kitchen. You should never walk anywhere in the dining room empty-handed, if you can avoid it. There are almost always items to restock in the side stand, or plates or glasses that need to be cleared.

Good timing means that cold food is delivered while it is still cold and crisp. It means that hot food arrives at the table piping hot, at the moment when it is at its best. It means that the server is able to accomplish these feats in a timely, easy, and comfortable manner, without communicating any sense of haste to the guests.

TEAMWORK

The success of the entire restaurant depends on all of the stations running smoothly. In a busy restaurant, there is nothing more frustrating for a server than having to wait: for coffee to brew, for more ice, or for something that was supposed to have been stocked by another waiter before service. If one person in the restaurant fails to complete those jobs, everyone is affected. Bad service in another waiter's station will affect the restaurant's reputation, diminishing everyone's chances of success. It is important for servers to help each other out, assisting in serving a table, starting another pot of coffee, asking the bus person to bring ice before the bin is empty, pouring water at other servers' tables if they are "in the weeds." Even pulling a chair out to seat someone at another table will encourage the other waiters to reciprocate.

This consideration for your colleagues—the regular application of the Golden Rule—creates a more productive environment. It helps everyone be their best, especially when circumstances are most demanding.

Carrying Plates

SIMPLE ACTIVITIES SUCH AS carrying plates or glasses need to be perfected to a point of automation so the waiter does not need to concentrate on them. When basic skills are perfected, they recede into the background and the staff can concentrate on the finer points of service and hospitality.

When picking up the dishes in the kitchen, the server picks up the plates in the reverse order in which they will be served. That is, the last plate to be served in each trip should be picked up first. Either two or three plates can be carried in the left hand.

The ability to carry four plates at the same time (three with one hand and arm and the fourth in the other hand) means that you can serve a four-top without any assistance. The practice is usually not allowed in more formal restaurants, where each server will carry only one or two plates at a time, avoiding anything that resembles plate stacking. Carrying fewer plates is more elegant and it also allows the staff to perform synchronized service described on page 157, where the food is placed in front of all guests at the table at the same time.

TO CARRY THREE PLATES

 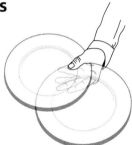 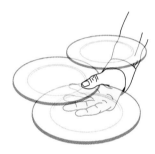

Rest the plate's base on your index finger and grip with your thumb.

Slide a second plate under the first to rest the base on your middle finger. Fan your ring and pinky fingers under the second plate.

Rest a third plate on the wrist, forearm, and outer edge of the second plate.

TO CARRY TWO PLATES

Rest the plate on three fingers and steady it with your thumb and pinky.

Rest the second plate on your wrist and support it with the tips of your thumb and pinky.

The kitchen staff takes extra effort to remove any thumb prints on the rim of the plate, so the servers should be careful not to leave any of their thumb prints on the plates. One way to accomplish this is to hold the plate between the knuckle and the meaty base of the thumb rather than the thumb itself.

It is part of the server's job to present the kitchen's food in the best way possible. The plate should be accurate as it was described to the guest. The chef will determine the actual placement of food on the plate. When setting-in, the server should place the plate in the alignment chosen by the chef. Be sure to find out what that alignment is, if you are unsure. To make service as smooth as possible, the server needs to take an extra second before picking up the plate to make sure their thumbs are in the right area. The plate in the right hand will be served first so the thumb should be placed about three o'clock. The thumb on the plate in the left hand should be placed about seven-thirty so when it is passed to the right hand, the right hand thumb is in its correct position at three o'clock.

TRAY SERVICE

When serving from large trays, covered plates should not be stacked more than three plates high, as shown at left. Never stack cold food on top of hot food when plate covers are used. Heat travels upward and could warm the cold plate to possibly unhealthy temperatures. The last plate to be served is the first one to go on the tray.

If the tray does not have a cork or nonskid surface, you can place a damp cloth napkin on the tray to prevent items from slipping. Place heavy items in the center of the tray and slightly

Using trays in the dining room.

toward the carrier. Place lighter or smaller items toward the outer edge of the tray. Avoid placing filled stemware near the edge of the tray; they are top-heavy and can fall off easily, especially when the waiter is going around a turn.

Place beverage hollowware (coffeepots, water pitchers) toward the center of the tray.

Keep all objects within the boundaries of the tray. Items hanging over the edge can get knocked off more easily. Keep open plates containing food well away from your hair.

Do not overstock or overfill trays. There are no medals for carrying huge, overstacked trays—it's not the Olympics. Accidents are frequently caused by overstacked trays. For their own safety, servers should always use proper lifting and carrying techniques. Get help or make additional trips.

Table Maintenance

THERE ARE SEVERAL ASPECTS of table maintenance that a server must consider, aside from the actual serving of food and drinks:

- Glassware
- Flatware
- Clearing
- Decrumbing

The goal is to always keep the table neat, clean, and running smoothly—and to do so as unobtrusively as possible.

MONITORING GLASSWARE

The monitoring of glassware is a good example of anticipating the customer's needs. A server should always remember, and practice, the Three *R*s.

- **Refill:** If a glass or cup is empty, refill it. (In table service it is not pessimistic to consider a half glass of water empty. It should simply be refilled.)
- **Replace:** If a beverage is finished, sell the guest another, or refill it (coffee or tap water). If a cocktail glass is empty, ask the guest if they would like a fresh cocktail before you remove the glass.
- **Remove:** If the guest does not want a refill or replacement, remove the glass or cup.

CLEARING THE TABLE BY HAND

Depending on the style of the house, clearing of dirty plates may be done only after all of the guests have finished that course. In other operations, it is acceptable to clear plates as each guest finishes. If a guest asks for a dirty plate to be removed, it should be done no matter what the house rules. Cracker wrappers or sugar packets should be cleared whenever possible.

In some restaurants, you can use the same method as described above for carrying plates from the kitchen to the table when you are ready to pick up plates and deliver them to the dish room. There is also a method whereby the plate with the most uneaten food is picked up with the right hand and transferred to the left, then subsequent plates are stacked on the heel of the hand, balanced with the left ring finger or pinky. In formal restaurants, clearing is done the same way as delivery—no more than two plates at a time.

CLEARING THE TABLE WITH TRAYS

Trays should be placed on a stand, not a table when guests are present. Never stack more than one tray on the tray stand (or jack stand), because it is very difficult to separate them when the top one is laden (some establishments get around this problem by inverting all trays except the uppermost tray). The dirty plates should be scraped onto one plate (only when out of the guests' view—and not too close to another table). Never stack more than four plates (and no more than two stacks per tray). Flatware is piled on one side of the tray or separated by type to make it easier to sort in the dish room.

Glassware should be stacked on a separate tray, with the tallest items in the center of the tray. Empty bottles should be laid down so they won't fall over and possibly fall off the tray.

For sanitary reasons, when picking up used glassware it should always be carried upright by the stems, never the rims. Servers should avoid using "the claw," grasping glasses with the fingers inside the glasses. Flatware must never be placed in glasses because it can create invisible hairline fractures that cause the glass to shatter in the heat of the dishwasher.

Improper clearing of glasses.

LIFTING AND CARRYING TRAYS

Trays filled with soiled dishes can be quite heavy. Therefore, it is even more important to use good lifting techniques to avoid strains and accidents. The server should always bend at the knees and keep the back straight while lifting the tray with the left hand above, not resting upon, the left shoulder, as shown at right. This frees the right hand for opening doors (you'll notice that most kitchen doors swing that way) and keeps the tray away from the server's hair.

It may seem counterintuitive, but it is better to use the fingertips to hold the tray rather than the open palm. While the latter may seem a stronger and more stable method, it doesn't permit the finer adjustments possible with the fingers. The weight of the tray should be kept close to the server's center of gravity and the server should squat to set the filled tray onto a jack stand.

A bus tub is easier to use, and there is less chance of breakage, if it is placed on a cart. Separate tubs should be assigned for flatware, china, glassware, and waste. Bus tubs should not be placed on the seats of chairs since they may soil or dampen the seat.

Lifting and carrying trays.

HANDLING GLASSWARE AND FLATWARE

Stemware should be handled by the stem, and other glasses should be handled as close to their bases as possible. Also, fingers should never be placed inside any glass, clean or dirty. The first reason is to avoid putting fingerprints on the sides of the glasses. The second is that carrying dirty glasses with your fingers inside them may imply to the guest that this is how clean glasses are handled as well, which is unsanitary.

Bus tub.

As with plates, how you carry glasses depends on the type of restaurant. It is always safest to carry glasses on a bar tray, whether clean or dirty. Dirty glasses, of course, must be transported on a tray because there is often liquid still in them,

It can be appropriate to carry clean stemware hanging upside down between the fingers of your nondominant hand as shown on page 144. This technique promotes efficiency—at least eight glasses can be carried this way, and there is no tray to dispose of once the glasses have been placed on the table. However, in the most formal dining atmospheres, this practice might be frowned upon and a tray used instead.

CARRYING STEMWARE

1. Turn the left hand palm upward. Place the stem of a glass between the index finger and thumb, so the glass is upside down and the base of the glass is resting on the fingers and palm of the hand.

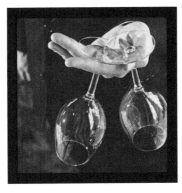

2. Add the second glass between the index and middle fingers.

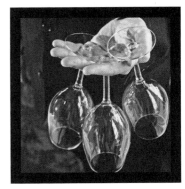

3. Add a third glass by placing it between the ring and pinky fingers.

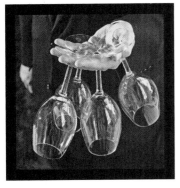

4. Place a fourth glass between the ring and middle fingers.

5. The fifth glass is placed between the thumb and index finger. Be sure the glass already held there is held as far back as it can go. The fifth glass is secured additionally by placing its base under the bases of the first and second glasses.

6. Add a sixth glass between the index and middle fingers. Again, secure the glass by placing its base under the base of the glass already held in this position.

7. A seventh glass is added between the ring and pinky fingers.

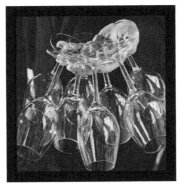

8. An eighth glass is added between the ring and middle fingers. When adding the last few glasses, slightly flex the hand, curling the tips of the fingers slightly upward to better grasp the glasses.

A waiter should touch only the handle of any type of flatware, clean or soiled. Flatware should always be transported on a clean tray or plate, usually on top of a folded, clean napkin. Some form of silverware transport plate (STP) should be used both for setting tables initially and for any replacement of serviceware for subsequent courses.

The use of a tray keeps the noise down and also allows for better organization by keeping the different types of flatware together. Other than aesthetics, delivering flatware from a tray or plate is faster than having to pick through a bundle of forks, knives, and spoons.

DECRUMBING THE TABLE

Before dessert (or whenever necessary), the table should be decrumbed. A special decrumber or brush may be used. An alternate approach is to use a folded linen napkin to brush crumbs onto a six- to ten-inch plate, but this method tends to be less effective. Do not sweep crumbs onto the floor.

Decrumbing the table with a decrumber.

To decrumb a square four-top, imagine a large + on the table running from guest to guest. Begin decrumbing on the left side of one guest, then decrumb the right of the next. Move clockwise around the table repeating this procedure three times to complete the table. The table should not be decrumbed if no crumbs are present, but should be done at other points in the meal if needed. When decrumbing a round table, imagine the surface divided into wedges. Decrumb from the narrow point to the wide edge of each section.

NOTE: If something liquid, like a drink or soup, spills and dampens a large area of the tablecloth, a half cloth or dinner napkin can be temporarily used to cover the area, rather than replacing the entire cloth during the middle of your guests' dinner. For surfaces that are not covered with linen, a simple wipe with a clean cloth is sufficient.

The Role of the Bus Person

After guests are seated, the next person to approach the table is often the bus person. In some operations, the bus person receives an hourly wage as well as a percent of the total gratuities—either of the server with whom they work, or a pool from all of the servers.

The first responsibility is usually to provide water, bread, and butter or other bread condiments. The bus person should always help the servers to anticipate the guests' needs, of course. Other duties can include

- Bringing food from the kitchen
- Refilling water and ice as needed
- Helping to clear dirty dishes and glassware
- Providing any items requested by guests
- Refilling coffee and tea
- Ensuring that all condiments, such as cream, sugar, and ketchup are available
- Helping to maintain side stand supplies
- Resetting tables

The Sequence of Service

ALL DINING ROOM MANAGERS establish a sequence of service that makes sense for each meal period in their particular establishments. For instance, coffee is offered immediately at breakfast, but it might not be at lunch (some restaurants serve coffee after lunch, as most places do for dinner). Of course, if guests request coffee or tea at any time, they must be served immediately, regardless of the established house sequence of service.

The following sequence of service is meant to address the widest possible variety of restaurants. In reality, most restaurants do not offer all of these courses (a cheese course or wine list, for example, may be completely absent). The principle is the same, even if the particulars vary.

GREETING AND SEATING

Guests should be greeted by the host, maître d'hôtel, or manager within thirty seconds of their arrival. A warm smile with good eye contact will help make the reception a success. A timely and appropriate verbal greeting should accompany the smile, such as: "Good morning," "Good afternoon," or "Good evening." Servers may assist guests with wraps, umbrellas, and parcels, checking these items if appropriate. (For more about greeting the guest, see page 82.)

After the reservation has been verified (see chapter 4), the guests are seated at their assigned table. Since the person doing the seating can only seat one guest at a time, the servers should assist by pulling out additional chairs. It is traditional to seat ladies first. (Extra place settings and chairs should be added or removed prior to seating, if there is enough time. This gives guests the impression that the table was set just for them.) If the number of guests is fewer than the number of place settings, the maître d' should indicate this to the captain or waiter with a predetermined signal, such as placing the butter knife on top of the folded napkin, so that the waiter can remove the extra place settings. Remember to reposition the centerpiece when the number at the table changes.

Once they are seated, the server should greet guests as soon as possible, or at least acknowledge them. Allow them to place their napkins on their own laps.

N O T E : Napkins should not be replaced unless they become excessively soiled or if they fall to the floor. If guests leave their seats, do not refold their napkins—folded napkins are always unused napkins. When they return, their chairs should be pulled out to seat them. Napkins should not be touched by servers unless they have become extremely soiled and in need of replacement.

BREAD AND WATER

After all of the guests have been comfortably seated, it is time to offer water or serve bread. A useful phrase is, "Would you care for ice water or bottled water?" When pouring ice water from a pitcher, position it two or three inches above the glass to avoid touching and chipping the glass. It's important to make sure that glasses are refilled frequently.

In some establishments, the house standard of service may specify that bread is to be served after the order has been taken—so the guest will not "fill up" on the bread. As the bread and butter plate is to the left of the cover, bread is served from the left. Note the use of the fork and spoon for serving the roll as shown here. The same technique is used in Russian service. You may hear this style of service referred to as "pincé," the French world for "pinch." To execute this maneuver, rest the spoon on your pinky, ring, and middle fingers and use your pinky finger to grip the handle. Place a fork between the index finger and thumb. The tines of the fork should be up for sliced bread and down to better grasp rolls.

Serving bread using the Russian service technique.

Sometimes a basket of bread and a dish of butter are placed on the table. For tables with six or more guests, two baskets and two butter plates are more convenient.

NOTE: When serving children, it is advisable to bring them something to eat immediately since they are not accustomed to sitting at the dinner table waiting for the food to be ready. Breadsticks are always popular since they become an edible, yet versatile toy. Offering children coloring books and crayons can keep them entertained for a while, but they may soon get bored. Stocking inexpensive, colorful toys is yet another successful ploy. For more about serving children, see page 135.

BEVERAGES

No matter which meal of the day, guests generally want something to drink soon after they arrive at their table. If there is a house specialty beverage or daily special drink, the server should be sure to mention it. Many guests prefer to order wine as an apéritif, so be prepared with a wine list. Chapter 7 gives additional information about beverage order taking and service. Traditional apéritifs are designed to stimulate the appetite, so serving the cocktail before the menu is presented can encourage a more adventuresome, and possibly larger, order.

MENU PRESENTATION AND ORDER TAKING

After the beverages have been served, the menu is presented to the guests, if it was not already presented when the guests were seated. The menu may be presented by the maître d', headwaiter, captain, or server. A conscientious server presents the menus, right-side up, in the most convenient manner for the guest. Since most fine dining establishments take some care with the cover of the menu, it is generally preferable to present the menu closed. Use the same service standard for presenting the menu as you do serving the food or beverage, present from the right with the right hand or from the left with the left hand.

Before the guests begin to read the menu, inform them of any specials that are being offered during the meal period, and any unavailable items or substitutions. This can prevent disappointment. Often, a guest will listen to the server's recitation of the day's specials, then ask, "What was number three, again?" The server should be able to answer the guest's question without having to repeat the entire specials menu. This can be done successfully if the server knows the menu (as opposed to merely memorizing it), and always recites it in the same order. It must be part of the server's mental mise en place.

Servers should provide a full explanation of menu items that might be unclear or foreign to new guests, or new items that might be unfamiliar to regular guests.

THE MENU AND WHAT REMARKABLE SERVERS KNOW

A good server always has a clear idea of the ingredients in the items on the menu, as well as the manner in which they are prepared. Guests have a number of serious concerns that require clear, unequivocal answers. Among them

- Nutritional information (e.g., calories, fat, salt content, etc.)

- Alternative preparations (e.g., substitutions for dairy products, broiling instead of fling, etc.)

- Whether or not a dish contains an allergen (e.g., peanuts, fish, eggs, etc.)

Many people are allergic to dairy, wheat, shellfish, eggs, nuts, and nut oils. Allergens can cause life-threatening situations and should not be taken lightly. If there is any uncertainty whatsoever about the answers to these questions posed by a guest, the server should consult with the chef.

The server has the advantage of having seen and (ideally) tasted the menu items being served, and having observed the needs of previous diners confronting the same meal. Using this knowledge to prevent problems from occurring is vastly preferable to trying to correct problems after they have occurred. For example, if a guest orders a green salad with blue cheese dressing, to be followed by grilled tuna niçoise, an astute server would simply say, "The tuna is served on a bed of greens. Would you prefer some other appetizer?"

Not everyone is an expert on cooking terminology, although a surprising number of diners have become quite sophisticated in recent years. When guests ask about a dish and its preparation, the server should not use technical jargon, but speak clearly, without condescension. Servers should resist the temptation to show off their expertise. Their job is to make the guest comfortable with, not envious of nor humbled by, the server's vast knowledge. (A glossary of frequently used culinary terms can be found in the appendix.)

Servers should be honest, without being negative, in answering pointed questions such as, "How is the soup today?" Establishing a feeling of trust between guest and server is essential to a comfortable dining experience for the guest, increased sales for the restaurant—and a better tip average for the server. The best way to instill trust is to share information with the guest. Describing an item with specific details, such as "The chives came from our own herb garden," "Our oysters are flown in daily," or, "The beef is grass-fed," can make the meal more memorable and give the guests the kind of information they will be likely to share with friends who may be potential customers.

TAKING THE ORDER

The near ubiquity of point-of-sale (POS) systems has changed the way waiters take orders. Handwriting is not as important as it used to be, there is no longer any need for "waiter's shorthand," and waiters don't have to go into the kitchen to place an order. However, the existence of such systems means that communication between front and back is more important than ever, and waiters have to send a lot of clear, accurate information to the cooks. Along with getting solid training on the house computer system, waiters have to realize how important the process of correctly placing the order is. If the order is clear and free of errors, the server can push the send button and then move on to other chores. An unclear or mistake-riddled order, however, will require the attention and talents of the expediter, the waiter (who now has to go into the kitchen), and potentially the chef, manager, bartender, or cashier—none of whom has time to spare on such matters. The irony is that just a few more moments is all it takes to make the order unmistakably clear.

Even with a POS system, you will still need to write the order down in enough detail so that you can complete the order at the computer. All of the data in the information box at the top of the guest check should be filled in before approaching the table, typically including the table number, the number of guests, and the server's initials. Other information may be necessary as well, depending upon the house standards.

Guest check.

The server observes the table for cues—such as closed menus—that the guests might be ready to order, or waits a reasonable amount of time (five to ten minutes), and then asks politely, "Would you care to order?" or "Do you have any questions about the menu?" If the guests need more time, the server withdraws and returns in a few minutes.

Sometimes guests are so rapt in conversation that they don't notice that the server is ready to take their order. While it might seem rude to interrupt (the guests' pleasure is foremost, of course), tables must be served if a restaurant is to stay in business. Since the guests can't be served if they don't order, the server is presented with a dilemma. There are some solutions:

- The server should try to make eye contact with one of the guests, who may inform the rest of the table that they should order.

- The server may be able to find one of the guests who is not actively involved in the conversation. The server can quietly ask if the guest would like to order.

- The server can also offer to come back when they are ready. Very often this will stimulate an urge to order in the talkative guests.

- Finally, the server can explain that a large group is expected shortly, and if they postpone their order it might be further delayed by the impending crush. This little fiction allows the guests to become allies of the server, and feel that they are exercising some control over the timing of their order.

Table and Seat Numbers

The system of numbers for tables and chairs in dining rooms is based upon long experience and has been designed with a great deal of thought. The first row of tables in a room begins with numbers in the teens, the second row in the twenties, and so on. The first table in each row ends with a one, not a zero. The system makes it easier to count (i.e., third row, fourth table is thirty-four—not thirty-three as it would be if the tables in that row start at thirty). It is important for the server to maintain the established table number and seat numbers rather than creating a different system independent of the management's design. Most restaurants have no table thirteen, because some guests believe it to be an unlucky number—just as many buildings have no thirteenth floor.

Seat numbers are usually assigned, by the management, as follows: Seat number one is the one with its back to the door (either the kitchen door or the front door) and subsequent chairs are counted clockwise from that chair. The sample dupe on page 150 shows how to use table and seat numbers effectively.

Often, tables are set at different angles, and a chair may not be in a direct line with the door. In such cases, the chair closest to the number one position, moving clockwise, is designated seat one. Seat numbers remain constant, whether the seats are occupied or not. If three people are seated at a four-top, in seats one, three, and four, those numbers are to be used in ordering. This way, if a fourth person joins them and sits in seat two, there is no need to inform the entire staff of a new numbering system at that table.

Should a server need assistance in serving, it is more specific (and more courteous) to ask, "Please pour some more water at table twenty-three, seat three" than to point and say, "Pour some more water for the dark-haired man at that table over there."

SUGGESTIONS, RECOMMENDATIONS, AND UPSELLING

More often than not, customers will have questions about the menu for the waiter to answer. Indeed, they usually want some advice from the waiter, as well. One of the reasons for going to a restaurant in the first place is that a knowledgeable server can help the guest to order an enjoyable meal, recommending, for example, an appetizer that complements the main course particularly well, or helping diners avoid a combination that will clash, or suggesting a wine that will enhance what's been ordered. When answering the guests' questions, the waiter has two options: *suggest* or *recommend*. Suggesting is the safer of the two. For the most part, it connotes giving information without any personal opinion.

When it comes to food, the act of suggestion can go further than just naming the dishes—the staff's menu knowledge should be good enough that the ingredients and preparation techniques used in each dish can be recited. This can work in a lot of situations at the table, and it is relatively safe.

When the guest asks a question, the answer can be either information or an opinion. To decide which one to use, remember: Suggestion = safe; Recommendation = risky.

Life isn't always safe, though, and at some point the waiter will probably have to wade into the dangerous waters of personal recommendation. When the guest asks, "Which shellfish appetizer should I have?" the waiter can't just keep reciting

Waiter's Shorthand

The purpose of writing dupes is not only to help remember the order, but also to communicate the guests' needs to the kitchen or bar or to another server. Consequently establishments often have their own system of dupe writing with standardized abbreviations. This is true even if the restaurant uses a POS system; you may even see some of them as part of the POS system itself. These are some common abbreviations for food.

- BLK & BLU: **black and blue (a very rare steak)**
- R: **rare**
- MR: **medium rare**
- M: **medium**
- MW: **medium well**
- W: **well**
- SOS: **sauce on the side**
- STK: **steak**
- CX OR CHK: **chicken**
- OM: **over medium**
- OW: **over well**
- OE: **over easy**
- SCR: **scrambled**

the menu offerings over and over. No, the waiter is eventually going to have to offer an opinion, at which point they are vulnerable to blame for recommending something the guest finds less than satisfactory. However, the more time that a staff member spends working with a menu, the more they learn how customers react to different dishes. They can use that accumulated experience to make personal recommendations that almost always pay off. With this knowledge, it's not just the ingredients or even the preparation methods that the staffer can now describe, but the subtleties and even the personality of the dish.

The server's confidence is reassuring to the guest, increasing the level of emotional comfort at the table. One of the tricks to use when coming up with suggestions is to mention a specific item to a guest to see how they react. For instance, you can bring up some unique characteristic of the dish, such as intense spiciness, wild mushrooms, or raw fish, and observe the guest's reaction. If they seem to register abject fear, it's time to pull back to a meat-and-potatoes position.

Servers should make either recommendations or suggestions in order to up-sell, without being pushy. The motivation should be to improve the guests' experience, not to inflate the bill. If everyone else has ordered an appetizer, but one guest has not, the server might ask if that person would like an appetizer as well. Open-ended questions work better than closed-ended questions. For example, "What would you like for dessert?" is an open-ended question that encourages further discussion. "Do you want dessert" is a simple yes or no. Ways to up-sell (and thereby increase the check average), include

- Suggest premium liquors when guests order generic drinks.

- Suggest a fresh fruit plate if the guest hesitates on the desserts.

- Suggest side orders that complement entrées (e.g., "The roasted potatoes are especially good with the steak").

- Suggest definite menu items rather than asking "Will there be anything else?"

- If the entrée takes some time to prepare, suggest an appetizer.

- Use appetizing words, such as steaming, sweet, spicy, juicy, fresh, savory, and refreshing.

- If an item is available for takeout, such as a special cake, salad dressing, or other prepared food, an alert server might note if a guest especially likes something they ordered and then suggest taking home an extra portion.

WRITING THE ORDER

The order is generally taken from the right of each guest, but as with all dining room procedures, it should be taken in whatever manner will least disturb the guests. When requesting the order for a table of two, it is important to establish eye contact to see who will order first. Traditionally, the male used to order for the female and then follow with his own order, but today one should not assume that to be the case. When both guests are of the same gender, the elder is usually first to order, followed by the younger. When there are four or more guests in a party, each one usually orders separately. If there is a host for the party, start with the guest to the left of the host and move clockwise around the table. The host orders last.

The server should stand near each guest as they order so no one has to shout across the table. He or she takes the complete order, getting each person's appetizer, soup, salad, and entrée order, in that sequence, before moving on to the next person. Any guest preferences, such as doneness of meat or sauce on the side, should be noted at this time. If salad is to be served after the entrée, the salad order is written after the entrée order. The waiter should take the menus from each guest after they order.

It is advisable to repeat the names of any order as it is recorded if there is some possibility of confusion to make sure that the information is being interpreted correctly. For example, the guest says, "I'll have the scallop main course." The waiter might then say, "So that will be the sautéed sea scallops," just in case the customer perhaps meant the escalope of veal. Clearing up any potential confusion must be done now, rather than allowing the wrong menu item to be prepared and delivered to the table. One simple question while taking the order can avoid a big problem down the road.

Once all of the orders are taken, the waiter has another chance to clear up any potential confusion. If there is even a glimmer of doubt in the waiter's mind when putting the order in, it is imperative to go back to the table to clear up that doubt before the kitchen starts work on it.

If some guests have ordered two courses while others have ordered three, this should be pointed out to the guests so they can either modify their orders to match each other's or at least be prepared for awkward moments when only a few members of the party will have food in front of them, although there are ways the alert server can minimize those moments by writing the order appropriately. For example, if two of four guests order a salad and main course, and the other two order appetizers, salads, and main courses, it is best to forego classic dining structure and the order should be written so that you can serve the two salads with the two appetizers so all four guests have a first course together. Then the other two salads can be served after the appetizers have been cleared.

WINE LIST PRESENTATION AND THE WINE ORDER

After the food order has been taken, the wine list is presented to the host by the sommelier, maître d', headwaiter, captain, or server. The more special the wine list presentation, the more effective the sale. When the wine list is delivered with the menus, it can be overlooked, but handing it directly to one of the guests will initiate the ordering process. If the restaurant has a wine by the glass program, it is best to offer all guests this wine list. Presenting the wine list separately from the menu is a good way for the captain or waiter to break into the conversation. It helps the staff identify the table's host, and it brings some attention to the list, influencing the guests to look at it and perhaps order from it.

The wine order is usually taken after the food order because the selection of wine will depend on the choice of food—unless, of course, the host wants to select a bottle of wine instead of cocktails.

If only one wine has been ordered, the server could suggest a special wine or a multi-wine meal, such as a split of Champagne, or a half bottle of white and a half bottle of red, with the main course instead of a full bottle of one or the other. This will most certainly enhance the meal by creating a new wine experience for the guests without necessarily increasing the check average. Suggestions might include a light wine for starting the meal, a full-bodied wine for the main course, and possibly Champagne for dessert.

The server should record all pertinent information concerning the wine order—such as name of the wine and bin number. Finally, the server should inquire as to when the host wants the wine served.

(Wine ordering and wine service are covered in greater detail in chapter 8.)

APPETIZER

Before the appetizer is served, all required utensils must be set in place, if they have not been preset. Clean flatware is carried to the table on a clean dinner plate and napkin (STP, the silverware transport plate; see chapter 5) by the server. Several appetizer covers are described in chapter 5 on page 127.

The appetizer fork is placed to the left of the dinner fork, with the left hand. The appetizer knife or spoon is placed to the right of the dinner knife, with the right hand.

If wine is to accompany the appetizer, it must be served before the food; this is usually done by the person who takes the wine order. After the wine has been poured, the appetizer is served from the right with the right hand. All courses are served according to the standards of service of the house, but generally, women are

Show Plates or Chargers

Many operators, especially those using expensive show plates, instruct their staff to remove the show plate before serving the appetizer to avoid having the show plate scratched by the underside of the appetizer plate. Otherwise, the show plate is typically left in place until the appetizer, soup, and salad courses (if served before the main course) have been served and cleared.

served first. Any accompanying sauce may be served by the server from the guest's left. Bread and rolls, water, and wine should be checked and, if necessary, replenished at this time.

SOUP

The appropriate soupspoon is set in place to the right of the dinner knife, with the right hand. A round bouillon spoon is needed for soup served in a cup and an elongated soupspoon, similar to a tablespoon is needed for soup served in a bowl. Once this has been done, the soup is served. As usual, soiled dishes and flatware are removed from the right, with the right hand (proper handling of flatware is discussed in chapter 5).

SALAD

According to custom, most American restaurants serve salad before the main course. American diners generally choose soup, salad, or appetizer—not all three—so, in effect, the salad is a form of appetizer course. After the guests have finished their salads, the table must be prepared for the main course. All dishes and flatware that were set for the salad should be removed whether they were used or not.

As with the appetizer and soup courses, all necessary tableware must be set in place prior to the service of the salad. The salad fork is positioned to the left of the place reserved for the salad plate. The salad knife should be positioned to the guest's right, with the right hand. The salad itself should be served from the right side of the guest, with the right hand. A pepper mill may be offered or left on the table.

N O T E: In Europe, salad greens are served after the main course. This delay in the service of salad allows the guest to better appreciate the main course. Also, greens have a lightening and relaxing effect on the stomach, so their consumption after the main course helps to prepare the guest for dessert. By this point, guests will have consumed a considerable amount of food, so they need a little rest. If salad is to be served after the main course, the bread and butter plates remain on the table and are cleared with the salad plates. When the salad course is finished, the plates should be cleared from the right, salt and pepper removed, and the table reset for the fruit and cheese course.

MAIN COURSE

The main course is the high point of the meal. It usually takes more time to be consumed and a leisurely air at the table ensures optimum enjoyment. By the time diners have reached the main course, their appetites have been appeased and their thirsts quenched. Sometimes, all that is needed to revive the patron's appetite is a simple but well-designed plate, offering pleasing contrasts in color, texture, and contour, and presented with flair and style.

At other times (and other restaurants), special presentations, such as sous cloche, en papillote, and flambé or other forms of tableside cookery help to stimulate the palate. If a guéridon is to be used for preparing, finishing, or plating the main course, the server must check to see that it is equipped with all needed serviceware. (For more about tableside cooking, see chapter 10.)

Synchronized Service

This style of service is efficient, elegant, and much simpler to perform than it is to describe. True synchronized service calls for one waiter for each seated guest. The waiters carry only one plate each. All the plates are set on the table simultaneously upon a signal from the lead waiter. Plate covers, if used, are lifted simultaneously.

As the waiters arrive at the table from the kitchen or the guéridon, the first server walks to the guest farthest away from the kitchen or guéridon. As the succeeding waiters bring a plate or plates to the table, they position themselves to the right of the first guest they will be serving.

When the situation demands it, synchronized service can also be done with one waiter for every two seated guests; in this scenario, the waiters carry two plates. They set the first plate in front of the guest, then walk around the table to the next guest to set down the second plate.

It is possible to perform synchronized service with one waiter for every three guests, if the area is too crowded to accommodate a large number of waiters walking around the table. In this case, waiters carry two plates in the hand they will not use for service, and one more in the hand used to set the plate down.

Russian Service

In Russian service, the main course is presented to the entire table so the guests can view the platter arrangement. When plating the food, the server moves swiftly, yet gracefully, plating first the main course, and then any accompaniments, such as vegetable and potato.

The server should place the food on the plate in a manner that will facilitate cutting and eating by the guest. The main course item should be placed so that the guest does not have to reach over the accompaniments to cut the protein. Generally, the main course is served with the protein in the lower, center portion of the plate (the six o'clock position). If accompaniments are served on separate dishes, they are placed on the table, to the guest's left, after the main course is set.

If wine is to accompany the meal, it should be poured before serving the appropriate course. If, as the meal progresses, the guests require more of the same wine, it might be appropriate to offer the "wine by the glass" list, to permit some of the guests to try a different wine (the details of wine service are covered in chapter 8).

The flatware for the main course should have been set prior to the guests' arrival; there should be no need to set it now unless the guests have used or dropped it, so it is wise to double-check before the food comes out from the kitchen. When the main course calls for a special utensil, such as a lobster pick or steak knife, it should be placed in position before the main course is brought into the dining room. (See Covers, page 126, for more information.) Flatware should only be held by the handle, never by any area that will touch food or the guest's mouth. It should be brought to the table on an STP.

As the main course progresses, bread and butter should be replenished as necessary, and water and wine repoured as needed. After the guests have completed the main course, the table should be cleared in the same manner as in the previous courses. Bread and butter plates and butter knives are left on the table only if they will be used during a salad course that follows that main course or when there is a cheese course.

FRUIT AND CHEESE

In the United States, those restaurants that offer fruit and cheese at the end of a meal generally serve them together. In France, guests typically do not like to mix foods; they prefer to have them "sans mélange," or pure and unblended. Normally, a cheese board of as few as three or four contrasting cheeses (a total of three to five ounces of cheese) is adequate for even the most discriminating diner.

A simple cheese course is offered in some establishments along with the salad, especially if a respectable Stilton or Roquefort is available. This simplifies the cheese course, but does it with style.

There should also be variety in the accompanying fruit. Only fresh, ripe fruit should be offered. Due to seasonal variations and fluctuating market availability, it is not generally a good idea to specify on the menu exactly which fruit or cheese will be served—but the server should always know what is available each day.

Before the cheese and fruit cart is presented to the table, the server should set a knife and fork in the appropriate places. The cart should be arranged in a neat and organized fashion. The mise en place should be checked: knives to portion cheese and carve fruit, a bowl of clean water to wash certain fruits, service forks and spoons, plates, and clean napkins. Each guest makes a selection of fruit and cheese. Carefully slice and plate the desired cheeses.

Some fruits, such as grapes, may be rinsed in the dining room, since washing them too far in advance can affect their quality and flavor. Using a fork to hold a small cluster, the grapes should be dipped into clean water. The server then places them onto a clean linen napkin atop an appropriately sized plate, serving from the right.

Much food has been consumed by this time, so portions should be modest. If, after completing their first serving, guests desire more, they should be accommodated, of course.

Some restaurants have a cheese and fruit course that is plated in the kitchen, in place of tableside service. It is faster, involves less service, and allows better portion control—although it is less elegant.

After the guests have completed the fruit and cheese course, everything that will not be used with dessert should be cleared from the table: bread and butter plates and knives, bread baskets, butter dishes, salt and pepper, empty wineglasses from previous courses, and any other soiled flatware and dishes.

DESSERT

Ending the meal with a superb dessert is as important as beginning it with a quality appetizer. The insatiable sweet tooth of the American public makes dessert a popular course and the profit margin on most desserts makes this sale quite desirable from a management viewpoint.

A simple and effective approach to merchandising dessert is to offer a separate menu listing desserts and after-dinner beverages. The more unique the presentation of dessert, or even the idea of dessert, the greater the likelihood of the sale. Dessert on the main menu reminds the guest of the amount of food, both in terms of calories and cost, they have just consumed. A simple dessert card or separate dessert menu will arouse the patrons' interests and set them up for a sale. A dessert display or cart, which visually stimulates and lures the guest to order, is even more effective. Merely carrying a tray of available desserts to the table can sometimes be an irresistible presentation.

As with any course, the table must be made ready before dessert is presented and served. After the plates, glassware, and condiments are removed, the table is decrumbed and the flatware necessary for dessert set in place. If the original table setting included dessert flatware above the cover (as in a banquet setting), they should be moved down into the appropriate positions. From the guest's left, the fork should be brought down into position; from the guest's right, the dessert and coffee spoons should be moved down. Wine or Champagne to accompany dessert should be served at this time.

All food should be neatly and appetizingly arranged on a dessert cart before presenting it to the guests. Make sure the cart is stocked with all necessary equipment, including serving forks and spoons, napkins, dessert plates, and clean knives for cutting. A container of warm water may prove useful on the dessert cart. Dipping a knife into warm water and then drying it before slicing a cake or pie prevents icing from sticking to the knife.

The dessert cart should be presented and the guests invited to make a selection. Some restaurants offer their guests a sampler plate, so they can try small portions of several different desserts. If the sampler is served family style, bring enough serving utensils to the table. Each dessert order should be plated, and then served with the right hand from the right side of each guest.

AFTER-DINNER BEVERAGES

Guests often enjoy hot beverages, such as tea or coffee, and after-dinner drinks (Cognac, cordials, or dessert wines) at the conclusion of a satisfying meal. A wide selection of coffees and teas can be stocked and controlled in the pantry or cold-food section of the kitchen. A special house blend of American and French roasts can be created by the coffee purveyor. A selection of herbal and regular teas, easily stored in boxes or tins, can also be offered to the guest.

Hot beverages containing liquor, such as café diablo or Irish coffee, can be offered in place of a heavy dessert. This type of selection increases the check average and adds style at the conclusion of the meal.

Before serving after-dinner beverages, all necessary flatware, empty cups, and accompaniments must be delivered to the table. Coffee should be poured at the table from the patron's right side. Orders for after-dinner drinks should be taken in the same manner as before-dinner cocktails. The drinks should be served from the right. (For more detailed information on serving coffee, tea, and after-dinner drinks, see chapter 7).

TOBACCO

In years past, smoking was done—by men only—at the completion of the meal. After a meal, men would gather in a room separate from the women with a waiter stationed in attendance at the door.

Several states and municipalities have passed ordinances making separate smoking sections mandatory, or have prohibited smoking in restaurants entirely. Even in places where smoking is permitted, air purifiers are recommended to minimize the irritation to nonsmokers.

Cigar service, as practiced in some fine dining establishments, deserves special attention. When cigars are offered and served, an ashtray and a book of matches should be placed to the right of each cover, or one ashtray may be conveniently shared by two guests.

Service for cigars is normally performed in a room separate from the dining room—unless it is part of a special cigar dinner. The procedure for cigar service is shown on page 162. Cigar service is usually provided from a cart or guéridon equipped with cigars, cedar strips (from the box of cigars), cigar clipper, ashtray, and nonsulfur matches. For proper cigar service, the server should

- Present the cigars.

- Allow the guest to make a selection.

- Unwrap the cigar.

- Clip the cigar.

- Present the cigar to the guest.

- "Warm" the cigar if the guest requests it.

- Light the cedar strip or non-sulfur match.

Selecting.

Clipping.

Lighting.

- The guest may prefer to light his or her own cigar. Otherwise, light the cigar using the cedar strip (or non-sulfur match), allowing the flame to be drawn to the cigar as the guest turns it to ensure that it is evenly lit.

When changing a soiled ashtray, care must be taken to prevent ashes from spotting the tablecloth. The following is an effective method:

- Take two clean ashtrays to the table.

- With an inverted ashtray, reach for the soiled ashtray.

- Cap it with the clean ashtray.

- Remove both the soiled ashtray and its covering clean ashtray.

- Place the second clean ashtray on the table.

- Keep the soiled ashtray capped until reaching the dish-washing area. This will prevent ashes from flying through the air.

- Clean the soiled ashtray and return the two clean ashtrays to the proper storage area.

CHECK PRESENTATION AND PAYMENT

After the last course has been served, and the meal nears completion, the guests should never be abandoned; a server must be available, for example, to offer additional beverages. Many operations instruct their service personnel to present the check only if the host requests it. However, if it is obvious that the patrons are waiting for their check, the server should approach the table and ask if any further services are required. The totaled guest check should be presented in a book or in a simply folded napkin on a dinner plate.

No matter the type of restaurant, most guests find having to wait for their check especially frustrating. Some of the nonverbal methods a guest might use to "ask" for the check include

- Looking around the room, as if searching for something.

- Making a "checkmark" in the air.

- Writing with an imaginary pen in the air.

- Placing a credit card on the table.

- Reaching for a wallet, or placing it on the table.

- Returning napkins to the table.

- Fidgeting.

- Part of the party getting up to leave (this can be a sign that the guests feel the server has been tardy in presenting the check).

If no one at the table has specifically requested the check (or is hosting the party), or if there is an argument about who is going to pay, it is best to place the check in a neutral zone not too close to anyone. In some restaurants, the guests are expected to take their checks to the front desk or register—if that is the house policy, the server should politely inform the guests. The server does not leave the table immediately after delivering the check. If guests are ready to leave, they may wish to pay immediately. If they do not indicate that they are ready to pay the check, the server withdraws a short distance and waits for a sign that they are ready.

Friands ("dainty tidbits") or mignardises may accompany the check. Like dessert, these lagniappes ("something extra," in Louisiana Creole) are meant to leave a sweet taste in the patron's mouth at the completion of the meal—literally and figuratively.

At this point, the server should thank the guests and tell them to whom the check should be paid, if necessary (i.e., to the server at the table or to the cashier). When picking up the paid check, the server should stand next to the host, write the total amount of monies received from the guest on the check, then excuse themselves. The receipt and any change should be returned in the same manner that the check was presented, either in a book or in a napkin on a plate.

The server should be prompt, but not overly hasty, in retrieving the payment once it is placed with the check. If payment is in cash, the money is discreetly counted before leaving the table. The plate is taken to the cashier, then returned to the table with the change and receipt.

If the payment is not in cash, the server takes the credit card for processing, then returns the voucher and the credit card to the guest, along with a plain pen. Pens should be "click" type—not capped—to eliminate any temptation to remove the cap with the teeth, and should contain no advertising printing—with the possible exception of the restaurant's name or logo.

When the Table Lingers

How should one deal with those diners who never seem to leave? These are usually folks who are having such a good time that, after the meal, they sit and sip endlessly, as if they are in their living room. Meanwhile, the party waiting for that table might be fuming at the bar. What is a restaurateur to do, especially in a fine dining restaurant or bistro/trattoria, where clients are not very forgiving about waiting?

Jean-Claude Baker, of Chez Josephine in New York City, shares some thoughts about dealing with customers who never leave.

A lot has to do with the price of the restaurant. If you are at Le Cirque in New York or maybe Valentino in Los Angeles, where dinner could be $100 or more per person, customers should be able to linger as long as they like. In a more casual place, like Chez Josephine, with a $37 average check and only seventy seats, you have to rotate the tables to survive. We have a payroll of twenty, and we'd starve if we didn't.

Early diners are usually no problem. But the 8:00 to 10:00 p.m. seating is where people can come late, order late, and sit over coffee or after-dinner drinks. Waiters are not usually aware of the timing problem—but managers and owners are, and they start to panic. They have to do something!

If I know the customers I might say, "Please, you have to save my life!" Who doesn't want to save somebody's life? "This table was booked at 10:00 p.m. and I have some people waiting at the bar for twenty minutes. Could I buy you a cognac at the bar so you could save me?" I don't offer cheap dessert wine that comes in tankers; cognac may cost me money but it keeps the customer happy. By sharing my problem with customers they become part of the solution. You will find that most people will be very nice about it. Most have no idea such problems exist.

If I don't know the people, I might have to be more firm and professional. "I'm sorry, but sometimes we have people waiting for tables that they have reserved at a certain time." I might offer them something at the bar. It is a double-edged sword, really. If you approach people in the wrong way, you could destroy the relationship that you have had for the past two or three hours.

The server should never assume that the change is a gratuity, or examine or count the tip in front of the guest. It is unprofessional for a server to comment on or show in any way that a tip is expected or that it was not as much as desired. If the server suspects the guests were displeased based upon the amount of tip, it should be brought to the attention of the manager to approach the guests if necessary.

The service staff should be prepared to provide any general information that might be requested, such as other available facilities and services, the location of the restroom and telephones, and suggestions as to entertainment areas in the city. Guests may wish to take home their leftovers (doggie bags); sanitation laws vary from location to location, and they will determine the policy in particular restaurants.

The service staff should assist with departure of the guests—as it does with their arrival—helping with parcels, wraps, and any personal items left on the table. The final farewell to the guest should be as engaging as the first hello. Establishing a friendly and lasting impression, in a sincere manner, encourages the guests to return.

RESETTING THE TABLE

Each establishment has its own policy concerning the resetting of tables. It is often disconcerting for those guests still in the dining room at the end of a meal period to find themselves in a kind of demolition zone. It is generally better to reset each table as it is vacated than to reset all of the tables for the next shift at one time. At the end of the evening, glasses can be inverted (to avoid gathering dust) if the surface is sanitary.

Handling Complaints and Other Special Situations

ANTICIPATING GUESTS' COMPLAINTS is as important as anticipating their needs. After serving any food or beverage, servers shouldn't disappear. Servers should stay long enough to observe the guests' behavior and reactions and then return after a minute to make sure everything is still satisfactory.

The truth is, it is likely that someone will have a complaint or other concern. When they do, it's somebody's job to fix it. Problems tend to fall into one of several categories, which need to be addressed in different ways.

FOOD AND BEVERAGE PROBLEMS

Either there is something wrong with the product and it needs to be replaced, or the guest does not like it and it has to be replaced.

If an unsanitary foreign object is discovered in a guest's food or beverage, the server must immediately apologize and replace the item. Most people understand that such things can happen—even in the most fastidious establishments—but a mere glimpse of a misplaced hair or insect can spoil the appetite of the most reasonable of people. Some guests may wish to order something different. (Once, a guest found a slug in her salad—and was afraid to order *anything* from the responsible kitchen. The maître d' was able to calm her fears by guaranteeing that he could provide a plate on which there was "no place that anything could hide.") If the server handles a problem like this quickly and calmly, the guest will usually be forgiving. As soon as the problem has been resolved to the guest's satisfaction, the server must inform the chef and manager. Always give the guest whatever replacement is requested—and make sure the offending item is removed from the bill.

When a steak is gristly or the Champagne is flat, anyone can see that the product is not up to standard. Normal guest recovery procedures (see Guest Recovery, page 168) can be followed, getting a replacement for the substandard item and perhaps doing a little something extra for the guest. It's not as easy when the guest is not happy with a perfectly good menu item or bottle of wine. Staff members can feel irritated or even angry when a guest complains about, say, a steak that to most observers is cooked perfectly. Unfortunately, *medium-rare* is a relative term, and the guest's perception is the reality in this case. No matter who explains that the meat is perfectly prepared, the customer will not be happy.

In the vast majority of cases when a guest is unhappy it is because what's on the plate or in the glass is not what they expected. The best solution is to apologize and then bring the guest something pleasing. The truth is, if the customer expects one thing and gets another, it doesn't matter how good the food that arrived at the table is. Part of the solution is a menu that is clear and easy for guests to understand. The other part is the ability to read a guest's uneasiness during the ordering process or spotting the potential problems with certain types of dishes.

Whether real or perceived, guests' disappointment with food that has been served to them must be dealt with swiftly. Disenchantment can turn into annoyance very quickly.

If a guest seems dissatisfied with the food, beverage, or service, or if the server perceives any potential problem with a guest, it is wise to notify the dining room supervisor or manager after handling the problem. When a food item is returned because it is overcooked, undercooked, served at the wrong temperature, or unacceptable in any way, the guest is not usually charged for a fresh item, if the kitchen or dining room is at fault. However, an additional charge may be made if the guest ordered incorrectly in the first place, as when a customer asks that a fresh steak be prepared rare, even though he ordered one well done. In some cases, it may be better to appease the guest by not charging for the item—even if the restaurant was not at fault—in order to keep, or develop, a regular customer.

DINING ROOM CONDITIONS

One guest says it's too hot, but another thinks the same dining room is too cold. One guest says that the room is too noisy, while another says she can't hear the music well enough. Someone complains that the sun is in his eyes, and another person then summons the waiter to ask that the shade be lifted because she can't see the sunset.

Every dining room has its own foibles and listening for certain repeated complaints will help you to pinpoint specific problems that need your attention so that you can address common complaints before they happen. There are some situations that seem constant from restaurant to restaurant. Here are a few:

- Elderly guests tend to feel cold more easily than younger guests. When possible, seat them away from any known drafts, and when that isn't possible, turn down the air-conditioning a bit.

- Most customers don't like to sit next to the swinging kitchen door. Either don't put a table right next to the door or, if you can't afford not to, at least face the table away from the door or make it a four-top; deuces are more easily distracted because fewer people are talking.

- Sitting next to the band or in front of the sound system can be unbearably loud for most guests. Nowadays, audio system designers tend to distribute a larger number of small speakers around the dining room, which allows for lower volume levels but still ensures that the music can be heard throughout the room.

- Dining rooms that are too dark make it hard to read the menu. Well-aimed lights over the tables or raising the overall light level somewhat will not only solve that problem but also make it easier to see the carefully presented food.

SERVICE ISSUES

Many service problems can be avoided if the manager or captain rarely leaves the dining room. The waiters are, because of the nature of their jobs, moving around the restaurant—picking up drinks from the service bar or running into the kitchen to find out if the fried flounder can be broiled. The best solution is to have someone whose main responsibility is to watch the room and the guests within it. In most cases, it should be a dining room manager, but in restaurants where the tip pool is big enough, you may see additional headwaiters or captains. The captains can add to the tip pool by selling wine, up-selling the menu, and providing more immediate service than the waiter is able to.

When a guest has to wait a long time for anything, the waiter is aware of the problem but may yield to the temptation to hide from the guest rather than face them. This, of course, adds to the guest's frustration. If the waiter instead goes directly to the guest and explains the delay, the guest, while still somewhat inconvenienced, usually relaxes a bit. In fact, saying something like "The chef wasn't happy with the quality of your main course and is preparing another one for you" can make the guest feel particularly well taken care of—it's nice to know that the chef is watching over you. The key here is, of course, for the waiter not to avoid the problem—it won't go away by itself.

GUEST RECOVERY

The term *guest recovery* implies that you had the guest at some point but lost them somewhere along the way, and in a sense that's exactly what happens when there is a problem, whether it is with the food, the service, or the dining room environment. You can sense when it happens—everything is going along nicely, but then the guest gets the wrong food, or it's cold, or it takes too long, and the atmosphere at that table suddenly changes. Many waiters will avoid the guest at this point, apparently hoping that the problem will go away if they ignore it, but the only reliable way to get a customer back is to address the problem and the guest directly. Avoidance merely exacerbates the problem. When something has gone wrong, the best time to correct it is at the beginning, before the guest has had a chance to become annoyed or resentful.

So how do you bring the annoyed guest back? You communicate with him honestly. For example, a guest tells you that his steak is overcooked. The kitchen immediately puts another steak on the grill, but it will take ten minutes to reach medium-well, the doneness the guest requested. The waiter could avoid the guest altogether, figuring that the steak will eventually arrive. For the guest, those ten minutes can seem like hours, especially if they are not aware that the kitchen is working on the new steak. The guest spends the next ten minutes darting annoyed glances around the room, wondering when the food is going to arrive. It would be better to let your guest know how long it will be until the steak arrives. The guest might be a little miffed but will at least know what is causing the long wait for dinner, and perhaps will be happy to get a little something free out of the deal.

The basic steps of guest recovery are as follows: apologize, correct the problem, make it up to the guest, and finally, follow up to make sure that the situation is amicably resolved.

APOLOGIZE

Apologizing is one of the easiest things to do, but too often the power of a simple apology is ignored in favor of much more elaborate schemes. When the slipup is not too serious, sometimes an apology is all you need to appease the guest. In the example given above, the waiter could go to the guest, apologize for the anticipated delay, and perhaps bring the guest a little something to munch on during the wait. The foundation of an effective apology is, of course, sincerity. To show sincerity, the server should

- Make eye contact.
- Use the words I'm sorry.
- Avoid blaming others.

Making eye contact is not the easiest thing to do. Eyes are indeed the windows to the soul, but not everybody wants to look in there. Even if you can't muster the courage to look straight into the eyes of someone who doesn't, for the moment, like you very much, saying you're sorry goes a long way.

Having apologized to the guest, blaming someone else for the slipup can instantly bring into question the sincerity of the person who is apologizing. Most guests realize that the waiter is not personally responsible for the undercooked chicken, but a server taking the blame can bolster the reputation of the entire staff.

CORRECT THE PROBLEM

There is a series of basic steps that are key to correcting any problem:

1. **FIND OUT THE GUEST'S VERSION OF THE PROBLEM.** Don't assume you know what the guest is upset about. A veal chop that's still a bit pink in the center is not necessarily the problem—it could be the broccoli rabe that the guest wasn't expecting.

2. **REMOVE THE OFFENDING ITEM.** If there is something on the table, whether it is food, flatware, china, or glassware that is causing a problem, the sight of it will only upset the guest more—get it off the table right away.

3. **TAKE STEPS TO REMEDY THE SITUATION.** Go directly to the person who can accomplish that. For example, if the manager or maître d' is the only person allowed to talk to the chef, then go find him or her—quickly.

4. **GIVE THE GUEST AN ACCURATE TIMEFRAME FOR THE REPLACEMENT.** Don't forget that when everybody else at a table has their food, an extra five minutes to bring a replacement for one of the guests can seem like a lot longer. Once the wheels have been set in motion to correct the problem, you should go to the guest to let them know how long it will take. An honest and accurate estimate will help you to build your credibility. Be conservative, that is, overestimate the time needed. If the replacement item comes out sooner than you said, the guest should be even happier.

5. **BRING THE REPLACEMENT PERSONALLY, IF POSSIBLE.** First, it shows personal concern. Second, it allows the waiter to confirm the guest's satisfaction, or lack thereof, immediately. If a nameless, faceless runner brings the dish to the table, this cannot take place.

MAKE IT UP TO THE GUEST

Here is where professional judgment and experience can really come into play. The most important thing to recognize is that there are different kinds of problems, of varying degrees of seriousness. There is no single answer to the question "What should I do to make the guest happy?" A couple of suggestions:

- Consider each situation on an individual basis.

- Don't always assume that offering a free dessert is the best solution.

The response should match the situation in scale and nature. Before choosing a remedy to the situation, consider both the seriousness of the problem and the type of problem. If the guest is unhappy with a cocktail, a glass of wine chosen by the waiter or sommelier to accompany the guest's next course is both more appropriate in style and closer in proximity to the problem than a free dessert at the end of the meal. Or if the guest complains that their appetizer was lackluster, you ask to have a plate of risotto sent out along with the main courses—the risotto that you overheard all of the guests discussing, though nobody actually ordered it.

When an entire dinner is ruined by interminable delays, the response needs to be different. Sometimes, it takes a grand gesture such as buying the whole dinner and inviting the guests back for another visit on the house, so they can see what the experience is supposed to be like.

FOLLOWUP

Arguably, follow-up is the most important part of the guest recovery process. You could carry out all of the previous steps, but it is for naught if the guest never gets the replacement steak or the drinks that you promised to remove from the check are still there. Any goodwill that you engendered by offering to take care of the guest's bad experience is gone when the guest doesn't get what was promised.

The more often you carry out these steps in guest recovery, the more precise your judgments will be.

Conclusion

REMARKABLE SERVICE MUST BE CONSISTENT AND LOGICAL, yet flexible. There is no single proper way to serve a meal. Actually, there are three ways: the correct way, the wrong way, and the best way.

The correct way is to adhere to the rules as established by management. The wrong way is to disregard house policy for no obvious reason. The best way is to adapt the rules to adjust to unique or unforeseen circumstances. For example, most operations instruct service personnel to clear soiled dishes from the patron's right side; this is the correct way. The wrong way would be to arbitrarily remove the soiled dishes from the left side of the patron. However, if two adjacent guests are leaning toward each other, engaged in conversation, the only way to remove the soiled dishes of one of the speakers without disruption is from the left side.

The prescribed procedures for service should not be taken as gospel. Circumstances will always arise that require service personnel to make instant decisions that alter their customary way of doing things. At first, these exceptional situations might prove unnerving—but with experience, they will be handled as second nature.

This chapter has discussed the basic tasks and processes that comprise the service of a meal. However, certain parts of the meal will need a bit more explanation, for example, beverage service, the subject of the next chapter.

7

Beverage Service

AN EXCEPTIONAL DINING
EXPERIENCE always includes prompt,
knowledgeable, and responsible beverage
service, with or without alcohol. Whether
you are serving cocktails, beer, or water, the
beverages you serve should complement
customers' food selections and lead to a
pleasurable dining experience. (Note: For
information on wine service, see chapter
8.) Beverage service is also one of your best
moneymakers, as beverages sales account
for 25 to 30 percent of gross restaurant
sales, on average.

Cocktail Hour

COCKTAILS—distilled alcohol mixed with other beverages and sometimes garnished with vegetables or fruit—take a variety of forms, depending on the primary liquor. Cocktail hour is a nebulous stretch of time between the end of the workday and dinner, and has been seeing a resurgence in popularity over the last few years. Guests may order one or two cocktails (or other alcoholic beverages) during this time, and specialty cocktail menus can be fun for guests and profitable for the restaurant.

All waiters and dining room staff should know some basic information about cocktails. Most cocktails are mixed in or poured into a special cocktail glass. It is important for you to be able to distinguish one cocktail glass from another.

Most cocktails are served from a cocktail tray, which you balance on the fingertips of your left hand, removing one glass at a time with your right hand. When placing a cocktail on a hard surface, first place a cocktail napkin (with the restaurant logo facing the guest) on the surface to absorb moisture. When drinks are served on a tablecloth, forgo the napkin, as it is a common rule that you should not set paper on linen. Before serving the first course, the cocktail is moved to the right of the first service glass, and the cocktail napkin and any used garnishes are removed. It is more pleasant for all of the guests if children are also served a drink that makes them feel special. To be safe, ask the host or a parent so he or she can help children choose a suitable beverage, rather than asking young children directly what they want to drink.

Making Mixed Drinks

Waiters should know the primary liquor of drinks ordered (to up-sell or offer better quality liquor), possible variations on the drink, proper garnish, and ways in which the drink may be served (i.e., up, on the rocks, frozen). If a guest orders a specific brand that is not carried or is out of stock, it should be brought to the guest's attention, asking if he or she would care to make another selection.

Cocktails are mixed in one of four ways:

- BUILD: Pour each ingredient into the glass, one at a time.

- STIR: Mix ingredients by stirring them with ice in a mixing glass, and then straining the cocktail into a chilled serving glass; this process keeps a drink from becoming diluted by melting ice.

- SHAKE: Use a hand shaker or mechanical shake mixer; this process is used for cocktails with cream, fruit juice, and other difficult-to-mix ingredients.

- BLEND: Mix ingredients in an electric blender to blend fruit chunks, such as with strawberry daiquiris and margaritas.

GLASSWARE FOR COCKTAIL SERVICE. FROM LEFT TO RIGHT: grappa glass, martini glass, Manhattan glass, pony/sherry glass, highball/Collins glass, rocks/old-fashioned glass, brandy snifter, glass for single-malt scotch, pilsner glass.

If there is a house specialty beverage or daily special, the server should be sure to mention it. Many guests prefer to order wine as an apéritif, so be prepared with a wine list. Sometimes the host will order for the entire table, otherwise the server should take orders from women first (beginning with the woman seated to the left of the host, proceeding clockwise around the table, finishing with the host's order). While recording the cocktail order, the server should repeat the name of each cocktail as it is ordered, and write standard abbreviations on the dupe pad.

Shaken and Stirred

Shaking aerates and mixes drinks, often making them taste better—that's why we shake drinks made with fruit juices, as well as cream drinks. Why, then, is it incorrect to shake other drinks? Part of the enjoyment of many alcohol-only cocktails (such as a martini) is the crystal-clear quality of the liquor, and shaking such a drink introduces thousands of tiny bubbles that disrupt that clarity. Second, it is important to keep dilution to a minimum during the preparation of a drink that is made mainly from liquor. Stirring a drink such as a Manhattan or Rob Roy with good-size ice cubes will chill the drink (giving it a noticeable viscosity, which contributes to mouthfeel) without introducing too much water, as shaking could do.

Ice cubes means cubes, not slivers or mini-cubes or mini–ice doughnuts. The quality and size of the ice cubes used can make a huge difference in the final quality of the drinks that the bartender can produce. A good-size ice cube (1¼ to 1½ inches) allows the bartender to make better drinks. If the drink is shaken or stirred, the lower surface area of the larger cubes will allow the drink to be chilled with less dilution. For rocks or highball drinks, the larger cubes will last longer, keeping a scotch on the rocks from turning rapidly into a scotch and water.

BARWARE

Glass Type	Capacity	Typical Use
Beer glass	10–23 ounces	Beer
Carafe	.5–1 liter	Wine, sangria
Cocktail glass	4.5–6 ounces	Martinis, Manhattans
Cordial glass	1–4 ounces	Sherry, liqueurs, cordials
Collins/cooler/iced tea	16–23.5 ounces	Iced tea, Collins
Coupette	7–60 ounces	Margarita
Highball	7–12 ounces	Gin and tonic, rum and Coke, whiskey sour
Mixing glass/ pint	16–20 ounces	Beer (traditional Irish beer glass)
Mug/ stein/tankard	10 ounces–1 liter	Beer
Old-fashioned glass	7.5–10 ounces	Whiskey, scotch cocktails
Pilsner	6–22 ounces	Beer
Pitcher	34–96 ounces	Beer/ soda
Pony	1–3 ounces	Shots, cordials
Port	3–4 ounces	Port
Pub glass /pint	12–19.5 ounces	Beer (traditional English beer glass)
Rocks glass	5.5–10 ounces	Whiskey, scotch
Sherry glass	1–4 ounces	Sherry
Shot/shooter	1–2 ounces	Whiskey
Snifter	5.5–7.0 ounces	Brandy
Sour	4.5 ounces	Whiskey sours
Tequila shooter	1–2 ounces	Tequila

The server should excuse him- or herself from the table by stating to the host, while keeping eye contact with the entire table, "Thank you, I will be right back with your order." It is important that this promise be kept. The guests should have their beverages before them within two to three minutes of the time that they are seated or have ordered. With the advent of PDAs it is possible that the back waiter can bring the drinks to the table while the front waiter is still at the table explaining the specials or answering questions about the menu.

When picking up the beverage order, the drinks are placed on the tray in the order in which they will be served, carefully noting the position of any similar-looking drinks. A gin and tonic and vodka tonic, for example, can be distinguished by placing two stir sticks, or two lime wedges in the vodka tonic, since *vodka* has more letters than *gin*. The tray should be carried on the fingertips of the left hand (it is much less tiring than carrying with the thumb hooked over the edge). Guests must never remove the drinks from the tray themselves, because only the server can feel whether or not the tray is balanced. If guests reach for their own drinks, stabilize the tray by grasping its edge with the right hand.

Mentioning the name of each drink as it is served will eliminate possible misunderstandings with the order. Drinks are served from the right, placing them to the right of each cover or directly on a cocktail napkin on the service plate. If no service plate has been set, the drink is placed directly in front of the guest. Cocktail napkins should only be used when serving the glass on a table with no tablecloth or on the show plate. If the drink is transferred to the tablecloth, the cocktail napkin is removed from the table.

COCKTAIL TERMS

In order to serve your guests, you want to be familiar with a few key cocktail terms:

Apéritif: A dry alcoholic beverage such as Campari, Lillet, or Dubonnet served before a meal, ordered immediately upon seating.

Call: A high-quality, popular name brand of spirits (usually midpriced) that guests will ask for by name.

Cocktail: A spirit or liquor combined with some other beverage and mixed together. All cocktails have specific names and a primary spirit/liquor, although guests may request variations. Most have a particular glass in which they are served, and some also require a garnish. Also called a "mixed drink."

Cordial: *see* liqueur

Digestif: An alcoholic beverage served after a meal.

Liquor: Distilled alcoholic beverage; also called "spirit."

Liqueur: Flavored, sweetened alcoholic beverage that may also have been mixed with milk or cream. Also called a "cordial."

Mixed drink: *see* cocktail

Neat: A liquor poured from the bottle into a glass and served at room temperature, without ice and with nothing else added. Whiskey is commonly served neat (usually in an old-fashioned or rocks glass), and customers may request other spirits this way, such as an unmixed shot, served in a pony glass.

On the rocks: A spirit served over ice in an old-fashioned (or rocks) glass. If the drink is shaken (as are most fruit juice–based cocktails and cream-based spirits), repour the shaken cocktail into a new glass with fresh ice, instead of using the shaken ice, which will be rounded and partially melted from shaking.

Premium: The highest-quality brand of spirits and the most expensive. Also called "top shelf."

Proof: A reference to the amount of alcohol by weight in spirits; the proof is twice the percent of alcohol by weight (100 proof means 50 percent alcohol by weight).

Short: A cocktail served in an old-fashioned or rocks glass, with a smaller amount of mixer.

Spirit: *see* liquor

Straight up: A spirit or mixed drink served chilled but without ice. To chill the drink, place the contents in a cocktail shaker with ice cubes, stir or shake, and then strain the drink into stemmed glassware, making sure to leave the ice behind. The vodka martini is the most popular drink served straight up, and customers may request gin martinis and Manhattans this way, as well.

Tall: A cocktail served in a highball or Collins glass, with a larger amount of mixer.

Top shelf: *see* premium

Up: *see* straight up

Well: The lowest-priced house brand of spirits.

SPIRITS 101

Spirits and liquor are distilled alcoholic beverages made from grains, fruits, sugar, and other plants, that are often used in cocktails (mixed drinks), or served straight up or neat. Five primary spirits—vodka, gin, rum, tequila, and whiskey—are discussed here in the order of their popularity, followed by a discussion of brandy and liqueurs (cordials).

VODKA

Grain-, fruit-, or potato-based vodka, the most popular distilled spirit in the United States, is a favorite in cocktails because of its indistinct flavor, although it is also served neat. (The word *vodka* is Slavic for "water," alluding to its neutral flavor and lack of color.) Vodka is filtered through charcoal, diamond dust, quartz and/or paper before it is bottled, and it is not aged. Despite the common belief that vodka has no flavor, the different ingredients used to make a vodka gives each variety its own distinct flavor profile. Potato vodka generally has a sweet finish; rye-based vodka has a slight spiciness; wheat has a soft flavor profile.

Flavored vodkas, including lemon, raspberry, vanilla, and chocolate, are popular in mixed drinks and on the rocks. Customers may also request additional flavors, such as pepper, lemon, and black currant.

Popular brands of vodka include Absolut, Finlandia, Stolichnaya, and Smirnoff; luxury brands include Ketel One, Belvedere, Chopin, Hangar One, Grey Goose, and Ciroc.

Vodka (flavored or not) can be served neat or straight up, as well as in a number of cocktails, including the following:

Bay breeze: Vodka, pineapple juice, and cranberry juice, served on the rocks in a highball glass.

Bloody Mary: Vodka and tomato juice with many savory spices (or bloody Mary mix), served with a wide variety of garnishes (most notably, celery or olives) in a Collins or hurricane glass.

Cape Codder: Vodka, fresh lime juice, cranberry juice, and sugar, served in a highball glass with a slice of lime.

Cosmopolitan: Vodka, Cointreau, fresh lime juice, and cranberry juice shaken with ice, strained into a cocktail glass, and served with a lime wedge.

Greyhound: Vodka and grapefruit juice served on the rocks in a highball glass.

Madras: Vodka, cranberry juice, and orange juice served on the rocks in a highball glass with a lime wedge.

Salty dog: Vodka and grapefruit juice served on the rocks in a highball glass with a salted rim.

Screwdriver: Vodka and orange juice served on the rocks in a highball glass and garnished with an orange slice.

Sea breeze: Vodka, grapefruit juice, and cranberry juice, served on the rocks in a highball glass with a lime wedge.

Vodka gimlet: Vodka and lime juice (preferably Rose's lime juice), served in a cocktail glass and garnished with a slice of lime.

Vodka martini: Vodka and dry vermouth (see chapter 8 for more on vermouth), either shaken or stirred into a chilled cocktail glass, served straight up, and garnished with cocktail olive or lemon twist (or, occasionally a cocktail onion).

GIN

An unaged spirit made from grains and flavored with juniper berries and other botanicals, gin is used in a number of cocktails. Popular brands of London Dry gin include Beefeater, Bombay, Boodles, Gilbey's, Gordon's, Seagram's, Hendricks, Plymouth, and Tanqueray. Depending on the botanicals used in making the gin, each has a distinctive flavor profile. Some are a more herbaceous while others have a more pronounced juniper flavor.

Holland or genever gin has a different flavor profile than London dry gin. Genever has malty aroma and flavor. Both London dry gin and genever can be used to make cocktails. The type of cocktail determines the correct gin to use. Gin-based cocktails including the following:

Bronx: Gin, dry vermouth, and orange juice shaken with ice, strained into a cocktail glass, and served with an orange slice.

Fitzgerald: Gin, simple syrup, lemon juice, and Angostura bitters shaken with ice, strained into an old-fashioned glass, and garnished with a lemon wedge.

Gibson: Gin and vermouth, stirred with ice, strained into a cocktail glass, and garnished with cocktail onions and onion juice.

Gimlet: Gin and lime juice (preferably Rose's lime juice), served in a cocktail glass and garnished with a slice of lime.

Gin and it: Gin and sweet vermouth, stirred and served neat in a cocktail glass.

Gin and tonic: Gin and tonic water served with a lime wedge in a highball glass on the rocks, and stirred.

Martini: Gin and dry vermouth, either shaken or stirred, strained into a chilled cocktail glass, served straight up, and garnished with a cocktail olive or lemon twist (or, occasionally a cocktail onion).

Negroni: Gin, sweet vermouth, and Campari bitters, stirred with ice, strained into a cocktail glass nearly filled with cracked ice, and garnished with an orange slice.

Singapore sling: Gin, grenadine syrup, sweet-and-sour mix, chilled club soda, and cherry brandy, served in a Collins glass with a cherry.

Tom Collins: Gin, fresh lemon juice, and superfine sugar shaken with ice cubes, strained into a Collins glass nearly filled with ice, and served with club soda, a maraschino cherry, and an orange slice.

RUM

Rum is produced from the fermented juice of sugarcane or sugar beets or molasses. Aged rums tend to have a caramel hue, which may be from the type of barrel in which the rum is aged, although may also be the result of adding some caramel for coloring. Light rums have a light flavor and are clear in color; amber rums are darker in color with a more pronounced flavor; dark rums have the strongest molasses flavor. Rum is made in over 200 different countries and is a source of great national pride. They each claim theirs is the best rum in the world. Premium rums have complex flavor profiles and they should be reserved for serving on the rocks or in a brandy snifter.

Popular brands include Appleton, Bacardi, Gosling's, Mount Gay, Myers's, and Zaya. Rum is used in cocktails such as the following:

Bacardi cocktail: Bacardi light rum, lime juice, simple syrup, and grenadine syrup shaken with ice cubes and strained into a cocktail glass.

Cuba libre: Dark rum and cola, served on the rocks with the juice of a lime rubbed on the edge of a Collins glass and squeezed into the drink and served with a lime slice.

Bitters

The term *bitters* refers to a mixture of herbs and other aromatics (such as citrus) dissolved in spirits, resulting in a bitter or bittersweet flavor. Cynar and Campari are popular bitters that are usually served as an apéritif. Angostura may be mixed with other beverages.

Daiquiri: Light rum, fresh lime juice, and sugar shaken or mixed in a blender, strained into a Collins glass.

Jamaican rum punch: A blend of various types of rum, pineapple, orange, and lime juices, and grenadine syrup, mixed in a blender or punch bowl and served on the rocks.

Mai tai: Light rum, dark rum, orgeat syrup, triple sec, fresh lime juice, and pineapple juice served unstirred in a Collins glass.

Mojito: Mint, lime wedges, and sugar are muddled together in a cocktail shaker, then ice is added, followed by a light rum. The cocktail is shaken to dissolve the sugar, then poured into a Collins glass and topped with chilled seltzer.

Piña colada: Light rum, coconut cream, and pineapple juice blended with crushed ice and poured into a Collins glass.

Rum and Coke: Rum (usually light rum) and Coke (or other cola brand) served neat in a highball glass.

Rum and tonic: Rum and tonic water mixed in a highball glass and served on the rocks with a lime wedge.

TEQUILA

Served in both cocktails and as a shot drink, tequila is a spirit produced in five different areas of Mexico, from the agave plant, the finest of which is made from one-hundred percent blue agave. Premium tequila may be served in a snifter, like brandy. For mixed drinks (including those in the following list), nonaged tequila (called "silver" or "plata" tequila) is best. For shots or sipping, choose aged tequila (called "reposado" or "añejo"). Aged tequilas tend to have a more pronounced, complex flavor than unaged ones. Reposado tequila has an earthy profile and it can be enjoyed both neat and in cocktails. Ultra-premium tequilas should be consumed like fine brandies, either on the rocks or in a brandy snifter. The most popular tequila brands include Jose Cuervo, Sauza, Porfidio, Patrón, Monte Alban, and Herradura. Tequila is used in cocktails, including:

Margarita: Tequila, orange liqueur, and fresh lime juice shaken with ice, and either strained in a cocktail glass or served on the rocks, garnished with a lime slice. Guests may request that the glass be salt-rimmed.

Tequila sunrise: Tequila, orange juice, and grenadine syrup served in a highball glass over ice with a stirrer, straw, and cherry or orange slice garnish.

WHISKEY

Whiskey comes from fermented and distilled grain mash that has been aged in oak barrels. It is the barrel aging that gives whiskeys their color and characteristic flavor, which differentiate them from clear grain spirits. Varieties include bourbon (a type of American whiskey), Canadian whiskey, Irish whiskey, and Scotch whisky (without the e).

Bourbon, a distinctly American whiskey made mostly from sour mash including at least 51 but no more than 80 percent corn, as well as malt, wheat, and/or rye. It is aged for two years or longer in new oak barrels, contains no coloring additives, and traditionally comes from Kentucky; however, bourbon may be produced elsewhere in the United States. It is used in the bourbon Manhattan (bourbon, sweet vermouth, and Angostura bitters served in a cocktail glass with a cherry or orange slice garnish) and the bourbon sour (bourbon, fresh lemon juice, and superfine sugar shaken and served in a whiskey sour glass with an orange slice and cherry), but because of its full-bodied, sweet nutty flavor, it is most often served neat, on the rocks, or with water or soda. Popular brands include Wild Turkey, Jim Beam, Heaven Hill, Maker's Mark, Old Grand-Dad, I.W. Harper, and Evan Williams. Luxury brands include Basil Hayden's, Knob Creek, Booker's, Baker's, Blanton's, and Pappy Van Winkle.

Canadian whiskey is a delicate spirit made from several different grains, including rye, giving it its nickname, "rye whiskey." Rye works best in mixed drinks, including the Manhattan, dry Manhattan (made with dry instead of sweet vermouth), perfect Manhattan (made with sweet and dry vermouth), whiskey sour (whiskey, lemon juice, and powdered sugar served with a cherry and lemon garnish), 7 and 7 (Seagram's 7 and 7Up), and old fashioned (a Manhattan without vermouth but with added sugar). Popular brands include Black Velvet, Canadian Club, Seagram's 7, Seagram's VO, and Seagram's Crown Royal.

Irish whiskey, made from barley and wheat blended with rye, is also delicate, and is served neat, on the rocks, or mixed drinks. Popular brands include Bushmills, Jameson's, John Powers, Tullamore Dew, and Murphy's.

Scotch whisky (always written without the e) is the most distinctive of the four, due to its strong flavor, derived from malted barley that has been dried. Scotch tends to be more of an acquired taste than the others and isn't as adaptable to cocktail recipes. However, it is used in scotch on the rocks (on ice), Scotch and water (mixed with water), Scotch and soda (mixed with soda water), Scotch sour (just like a bourbon sour but with Scotch whisky), blood and sand (Scotch whisky, vermouth, cherry brandy, and orange juice), and Rob Roy (Scotch whisky and sweet vermouth).

Single-malt Scotch whisky is distilled at a single facility and is labeled according to the region of Scotland from where it originates: the Highlands, Campbeltown, Speyside, Islay (pronounced *EYE-luh*), and the Lowlands. Popular brands include Macallan, Oban, Glenfiddich, The Glenlivet, Laphroaig, and Knockando. Blended Scotch whiskies may be distilled at several distilleries and, therefore, may be less expensive. They are known for consistency and relative simplicity compared to single-malt Scotch. Popular brands include Dewar's, White Label, Johnnie Walker, Chivas Regal, Pinch, Cutty Sark, Justerini & Brooks (J&B), and Compass Box.

BRANDY

Brandy is distilled from grapes or other fruit, and then aged in oak barrels from just a few years to as many as forty years. Cognac, the best-known brandy in the world, is double-distilled and produced only in the Cognac region of France; Armagnac is a single-distilled brandy from the Armagnac region of France; and Calvados (an apple brandy) comes from Normandy. Grappa is an Italian brandy, similar to marc from France, which is distilled from the pomace (skins and pits) of grapes.

Brandy is categorized as V.S. (very superior), V.S.P. (very superior pale), V.S.O.P. (very superior old pale), and X.O. (extra old, a luxury category). Popular brands of brandy include Kelt, Clear Creek, Germain-Robin, Courvoisier, Paul Masson, and Hennessy.

Brandy is served neat in a snifter, often as an after-dinner or dessert drink, or it may be mixed into cocktails such as the following:

Brandy Alexander: Brandy, white crème de cacao, and half-and-half, shaken with ice, strained into a cocktail glass, and garnished with nutmeg.

Sidecar: Cognac, triple sec, and lemon juice shaken with ice, strained into a chilled cocktail glass, and garnished with a lemon twist.

Stinger: Brandy and white crème de menthe shaken with ice and strained into a cocktail glass.

CORDIALS (LIQUEURS)

Cordials (also called "liqueurs") are spirits that have been flavored and/or sweetened, and may also be mixed with milk or cream. They are often served as an apéritif or digestif or as a dessert drink, either in very small, stemmed glasses or in brandy snifters. Some restaurants even bring guests a cordial cart, which is much like a dessert cart, but with a variety of cordials.

Cordials are grouped according to their strongest flavors, as follows:

Almond: amaretto

Anise: anesone, anisette, ouzo, Pernod, sambuca

Banana: crème de bananes

Black currant: crème de cassis

Cherry: Chéri-Suisse, Cherry Heering, crème de cerise, kirsch, maraschino

Citrus: Cointreau, curaçao, Grand Marnier, crème de mandarine, Triple Sec

Chocolate: crème de cacao, Sabra

Coffee: Kahlúa, Tía Maria

Hazelnut: Frangelico

Herbals: Bénédictine, Drambuie, Galliano, Goldwasser, Strega

Honey: Irish Mist

Melon: Midori

Raspberry: framboise

Roses: crème de rose

Violets: crème de violette

A few other unique varieties exist, such as advocaat (egg and sugar), rock and rye (orange or lemon essence and rock candy), and crème de noyaux (fruit pits).

A Kir Apéritif

Kir (pronounced "keer") is a popular apéritif that combines chilled white wine with a splash of crème de cassis, while a kir royale combines sparkling wine with crème de cassis.

Beer

BEER IS AMERICA'S MOST POPULAR ALCOHOLIC BEVERAGE, making up more than 50 percent of all alcohol sales. It is made from malt (sweet malted grains such as barley, wheat, and rye), water, yeast, and hops (bitter-tasting flowers that balance the sweetness of the malt and help preserve it). The sweetness of the malt is mostly lost when the naturally occurring sugars convert to carbon dioxide and ethyl alcohol, although some beers (notably, porters and stouts) do retain some sweetness. The flavor is affected mainly by the degree to which the malt is roasted, by the type of yeast used, and by the type and amount of hops added.

Unlike spirits, for which you double the percentage of alcohol by volume to get the proof, beers are labeled simply with their percentage alcohol—generally four percent for a light beer, six or seven percent for most other beers, and up to 14 percent for a few varieties. Microbrews—produced by small breweries—are increasingly popular.

TYPES OF BEERS

Beers are grouped as either lagers or ales, as follows:

Lagers: Lagers are fermented at cooler temperatures than ales, a process known as "bottom fermenting." As a result, they have a crisp, clean taste. The most popular American brands—Budweiser, Miller Genuine Draft, and Coors—fall into this category. Pilsners and bocks are the two varieties of lager that customers prefer most. Lagers usually have an alcohol content of about 4 percent. Serve pale lagers at 45° to 50°F. Dark lagers should be served at 55° to 60°F.

Ales: Ales are fermented at slightly higher temperatures than lagers in a process called "top fermenting." They tend to have a fruity, full, complex taste, although the taste ranges from bitter to almost sweet (as is the case with porters and stouts). The color, too, can vary from blond to almost black. The most popular varieties of ales include India pale ale, stout, porter, and lambic, and all have a slightly higher alcohol content than lagers do—most about 6 percent. Serve light ales at 50° to 55°F; serve dark ales at 55° to 60°F. A general rule is the higher the alcohol content, the higher the serving temperature; however, too high a temperature risks shortening the beer's life span, and too low induces cloudiness.

SERVING BEER

Serve beer in a perfectly clean glass—without any oil or detergent residues—so as not to destroy the flavor of the beer. A pilsner glass has traditionally been the glassware of choice for serving beer, but fine ales are often served in goblets because of their more complex aroma. Steins are popular in some establishments, as well.

Pouring beer while holding the glass.

The size of foam "head" that should result from pouring each type of beer varies. Traditionally, lagers should have a 1-inch head, ales a ¾-inch head, and stouts, only a ¼-inch head. If your hands are free, pour straight down to the bottom of the glass, then tip the glass about 45 degrees to the side, shown at right. As the head forms, move the glass to its full upright position and finish pouring, giving the bottle a slight twist as you finish pouring to stop dribbling. The longer a beer is poured straight down into the center of the glass, the larger the head on the beer. If one of your hands is busy holding a tray, leave the glass flat on the table and pour the beer slowly down the far side of the glass. If the beer has sediment at the bottom—as is the case with some imported beers—do not empty that sediment into the glass. Lambic, a type of ale, can be poured much like Champagne, since it is not known for producing the typical foamy head.

STORING BEER

Beer stock should be rotated to ensure freshness and should always be kept out of direct sunlight; beers that are exposed to sunlight develop an undesirable "skunky" flavor. Draft beer is extremely perishable, so always serve draft beer within thirty seconds of drawing it from the tap.

BEER AND FOOD PAIRINGS

Although beer (lager or ale) is often thought of strictly as the beverage of choice for pizza, hamburgers, and barbecued foods, you can complement the flavor of other foods by pairing them with the right beer. The most important technical aspect of matching beer to food involves taking into account the fact that most beer doesn't have an acid component to counteract the richness of food. The bitterness supplied by hops, however, can help to cut the cloying effect of richness in food. Here are some examples of beer and food pairings that usually work well:

Salads: pilsners

Nonspicy appetizers: lagers

Seafood: lagers

Soup and spicy foods: pale ales

Beef, game, and other meats: porters

Desserts: stouts, bocks

Responsible Beverage Service

ESTABLISHMENTS THAT SERVE ALCOHOL until someone is intoxicated, to someone who is already intoxicated, or to a minor (whether or not that minor gets intoxicated) can face serious legal and criminal action if an accident or improper behavior occurs after the patron leaves the establishment. In other words, both a restaurant and its servers can be held liable for the alcohol-related actions of its patrons.

Your state may require servers to take an alcohol-awareness course, which trains servers to recognize signs of intoxication to keep from overserving guests and to manage guests who have consumed too much alcohol. Even if your state does not require this training, all servers must possess these skills.

The process of telling a guest that they cannot have any more alcohol is rarely, if ever, an easy proposition. One thing that doesn't work is the avoidance method— staying away from a table that has been cut off. The direct approach, with a show of genuine concern for the welfare of the guest, usually works best. Offer the guest a nonalcoholic beverage (perhaps on the house), and discuss with them the fact that you want them to get home safely.

ESTIMATING BLOOD ALCOHOL LEVELS

A person is considered legally intoxicated when his or her blood alcohol concentration (BAC) reaches .08 percent, which equates to roughly four to five drinks per hour for a large person; three drinks per hour for a small person. At .08 percent, a person might have slurred speech and blurred vision. However, driving may be impaired with a BAC as low as .05 percent (three to four drinks per hour for a large person; two drinks per hour for a small person). One drink is defined as one and a half ounces of 80-proof spirits, three ounces of 14-percent wine, six ounces of 6-percent wine (including most white wines), or twelve ounces of 4-percent beer.

Do not allow intoxicated guests to drive away from your establishment. Offer to call a cab for intoxicated patrons; if they attempt to drive on their own, notify the police immediately. Also, do not allow guests to leave the premises with any unconsumed alcohol; it must be left behind. Some states, including New York, make an exception for bottles of wine ordered with dinner that the guests have not finished. The bottle must be corked or capped and placed in a sealed bag so that it does not constitute an "open container" and patrons should be able to produce the receipt from their meal if asked.

CHECKING IDS

Always check IDs, and check them carefully, even for patrons who appear to be well older than the legal drinking age of twenty-one. If you suspect that a customer is trying to pass a false ID, ask the patron to show a second form of ID or verify the information on the ID, such as middle name, date of birth, and address. Politely but firmly refuse to serve customers who do not have any ID, appear to possess a false ID, or do not resemble the picture on the ID.

Water

WATER IS OFTEN THE FIRST ITEM requested after guests sit for a meal and it can be an opportunity for a sale. In your establishment, decide whether water will be served automatically (as many restaurants do) or on request. If yours is a request system, when one guest requests water, ask all of the guests whether they, too, would like water. In addition, asking, "Would you care for ice water or bottled water?" gives guests both a free option and an upscale alternative. Although refills on glasses of ice water are always free, be sure to ask guests before bringing additional bottles of water to the table.

Bottled water comes in two varieties:

Still (nonsparkling) bottled water: Noncarbonated water, usually bottled spring water.

Sparkling bottled water: Carbonated water, which is water containing either naturally occurring or added carbon dioxide.

If the table is not preset with water glasses, tap water—as well as all cold beverages—are served in one of two ways:

Glasses are brought to the table on a beverage tray and placed above each guest's knife. The server then fills each glass with ice water from a pitcher, leaving the glass on the table when pouring. Never let the mouth of the pitcher touch water glasses; keep the pitcher's mouth two to three inches from the water glasses. Fill glasses two thirds to three quarters full.

Filled water glasses are brought to the table on a beverage tray and placed above each guest's knife. Refill glasses according to the instructions above.

Refill water glasses frequently—that is, before each guest has emptied their glass. Alternatively, some restaurants simply leave a pitcher of water on the table so that guests can refill their own glasses.

Bottled water should be opened at the table and served in a glass that looks different enough from the tap water glass so as not to confuse the server, who does not want to pour tap water into a bottled water glass. Do not serve bottled water with ice, unless the ice has also been made from bottled water or unless the guest specifically requests it. Large bottles of water can be left on the table, preferably in an ice bucket.

Ideally, serve water at 38°F. Also consider adding a slice of lemon or lime as a garnish. And periodically taste-test your ice water. If there is an identifiably "off" taste or smell, a water-filtration system may be necessary.

Coffee and Tea

COFFEE AND TEA have long been a part of the U.S. restaurant industry. In fact, an entire restaurant category—coffeehouses—caters to the almost religious experience of coffee drinkers consuming an excellent cup of coffee. Tea shops exist, as well, although without the fervor and intensity found among coffee enthusiasts. Iced tea, however, is the drink of choice in the American South, and is a popular beverage throughout the United States.

Coffee originated in Africa, where it was supposedly discovered by a ninth-century Abyssinian goat herder, who observed lively behavior in goats that had eaten the berries off the coffee shrub. Cultivation of the coffee shrub began in the fifteenth century and the beverage was brought to Europe in the seventeenth century. Today, coffee is widely popular in the United States and is the one drink you can count on being served nearly anywhere, whether at a truck stop or an elegant restaurant.

To create the beverage, the coffee bean is first roasted, a process that affects the color, flavor, and intensity of the brewed coffee (long roasting makes for a darker, stronger, less bitter, more robust coffee than does a shorter roasting time). Arabica beans are the best and most expensive. Dark- and light-roasted beans can be combined into special blends, in order to achieve an almost infinite variety of flavors. After roasting, the beans are ground, either finely or coarsely, depending on how the coffee will be brewed.

AMERICAN COFFEE

The best coffeemakers brew the grounds at 205° to 207°F and hold it at 185°F—but do not leave brewed coffee on the burner for more than twenty-five minutes. Many establishments use a series of small coffeepots (ten to twelve cups) instead of one or two large industrial-size pots, so that the waitstaff can serve directly from the brewing pot at the table, instead of pouring the coffee in the kitchen and carrying full cups on a tray to the guests.

Oils in the beans flavor the coffee, but those oils oxidize easily, which is why ground coffee is vacuum sealed; after the seal is broken, ground coffee should be kept refrigerated. Whole beans can be stored at room temperature for only about two weeks, but last far longer than ground coffee. For this reason, fine restaurants grind whole beans each day as needed to achieve the freshest, most flavorful coffee.

Decaffeinated coffee (which contains only about 3 percent of the caffeine of regular coffee) is now so popular that, in some restaurants, guests request it twice as often as caffeinated coffee. Decaf coffee beans are either soaked in water or exposed to a chemical gas to extract the caffeine from the beans; water extraction (often called "the European method" or "the Swiss water process") is the less toxic—and, in the opinion of many people, has the best flavor—and is requested most often among discerning coffee drinkers. Be sure that decaf coffeepots are easily distinguished by a different-colored handle (usually green or orange).

Coffee may be served black; with cream, half-and-half, or milk; with sugar or artificial sweeteners; and before or after dinner. Serve cream in a small creamer, or serve disposable creamers in a small dish of ice. Coffee used to be served in five- to eight-ounce mugs, but today's mugs are increasingly large—up to twenty ouncesespecially in cafés and coffeehouses. When serving coffee, wipe the spout or mouth of the container, and then place it one or two inches above the rim of the cup and pour slowly. Pour from the right, with the handle in the three o'clock position, and allow room at the top to add cream. Place a teaspoon, milk, cream, and sugar to the right of the cup, either before or after pouring the coffee. The coffee spoon may also be served on the saucer.

Some guests begin the meal with coffee, while others end with it, with or after dessert. If coffee is ordered before or with the meal, offer refills throughout the meal at no charge. Coffee can also be a separate course, usually served after dessert, sometimes with chocolates.

ESPRESSO AND CAPPUCCINO

Espresso is deep, rich, dark-roasted, finely ground coffee that is steamed until it produces a foam on top, called "crema." Espresso is usually served black, in a demitasse (a tiny cup), but it may also be served with sugar and, on request, a lemon twist. Cappuccino, on the other hand, is one-third coffee, one-third steamed whole milk, and one-third foamed whole milk; low-fat and nonfat milk are popular substitutes, as is soy milk for

MAKING ESSPRESSO WITH LOOSE COFFEE

1. Fill the filter with the correct amount of coffee and tamp it down until compact.

2. Insert the arm into the espresso machine and lock it in place.

3. Set warmed cups under the spigots and turn on the steam.

4. (right) Remove the spent grounds from the filter and clean it between uses.

customers who either cannot or prefer not to consume dairy products. A garnish of cinnamon, cocoa, or chocolate shavings may be added to the top of the foamed milk.

An espresso machine brews one or two cups of specialty coffee at a time, and although it does much of the work for you, the coffee has to be ground to the right consistency and properly tamped into the machine. Most coffee suppliers have developed prepackaged, preground espresso servings that are said to produce a more consistent product with a cleaner process. Available in the form of pods, cartridges, or capsules (according to the brand of espresso you use), this style of coffee requires an adapter arm that is provided by the supplier. Some of these preground, preportioned espresso servings are less likely to make a long-lasting crema, but advances are being made continually to the quality of the product.

MAKING CAPPUCCINO

1. Make the espresso as described at left. Fill a pitcher about half full with milk.

2. Position the pitcher so that the steaming nozzle is completely submerged in the milk and turn the steam on.

3. Continue steaming until the milk has doubled in volume and filled the pitcher.

4. (far left) Use a spoon to hold the foam back and pour steamed milk into the espresso. Spoon the foam on top of the espresso. Garnish with cinnamon, cocoa, or shaved chocolate.

5. (left) Wipe down the steamer spout between uses.

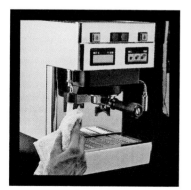

Other Specialty Coffees

In addition to espresso and cappuccino, restaurants serve several other specialty coffees:

LATTE: espresso with more steamed milk than a cappuccino

MACCHIATO: an espresso with a dollop of steamed milk on top

LATTE MACCHIATO: steamed milk with a dollop of espresso on top

DOPPIO: a double espresso

RISTRETTO: espresso made with a little less water, thereby producing a much stronger flavor

LUONGO: Espresso made with a little more water

FREDDO: iced coffee served in a tall glass; espresso freddo (or caffé freddo) is iced espresso; cappuccino freddo is iced cappuccino

CORRETTO: Espresso that has been "corrected" by adding a little alcohol, usually Sambuca.

For cappuccino, the machine should heat the foamed milk to no more than 158°F to avoid a scalded taste. While brewing espresso, cappuccino, or macchiato, the top of the espresso machine should be used only to warm cups and mugs.

Remove the grounds from the arm and rinse it between servings. Wipe off the steamer arm immediately. The espresso machine should not be turned off overnight, to preserve the heating element. The machine should be cleaned and back–washed daily.

HOT TEA

All tea comes from the same plant, the *Camelia sinensis*. The way the tea is picked and processed determines whether the final product is known as green, black, oolong, or white.

Tea, especially green tea, is quickly gaining in popularity because of its healthy antioxidant properties. Green tea comes directly from unfermented tea leaves. Black tea, on the other hand, is fully fermented before it is dried, and is the most popular form of hot tea consumed by Americans. Oolong tea is lightly fermented before it is dried. Herbal tea is not really tea at all but dried herbs and flowers.

Green teas achieve their best flavor when steeped between 160° and 180°F for no more than three minutes, while black teas are best steeped at 190° to 210°F for no more than five minutes. Herbal teas (tisanes) may be steeped as long as the guest deisres. All tea must be stored in a clean, dry container, away from moisture, light, and strong-smelling foods.

If tea bags are served alongside a pot of hot water, allow the guest to add the tea bag to the pot so that they can control the brewing time. If you add it in the waiter's station, they will have no way of knowing how long the tea has been in the water. Some establishments may instead serve a pot of brewed hot tea, perhaps along with a small pot of hot water, instead of bringing bags or loose tea to the guest. Either way, the guest pours their own tea into the mug.

Some tea drinkers add milk (rather than half-and-half) or lemon; be sure to ask when taking the tea order. Sweeteners for tea include sugar (cubes are traditional) and honey. Although some establishments serve just one or two tea varieties, tea aficionados will appreciate a wide variety.

ICED TEA

Iced tea is a popular drink that is usually made from the orange pekoe variety of black tea, although some restaurants now offer iced herbal and green teas. There is the danger of iced tea clouding when chilled or refrigerated, so iced tea batches should be made fresh each day and not refrigerated. (Pouring a small amount of hot water into cloudy tea will help clear it.)

Serve iced tea in a tall glass with ice, a lemon wedge or slice, and an iced tea spoon. Many patrons also add sugar or artificial sweeteners (if these are not on the table, bring them before serving the tea). To make the service of your iced tea more remarkable, offer a simple syrup to sweeten tea. To make simple syrup, a mixture of one part sugar and one part water is brought to a simmer, then cooled, and then transferred to clean bottles or cruets to serve at the table.

Conclusion

THE DRINKS YOU SERVE YOUR GUESTS are just as important to their enjoyment as the foods. Remarkable servers know that the prompt service of beverages as soon as their guests are seated is the best way to welcome them to the restaurant and establish a pleasant tone for the entire dining experience. Knowing which drink goes in which glass, what the correct garnish is for a drink, and the difference between a drink that is served neat and one served on the rocks is part of your education as a server. There are a host of drink options throughout the meal, ranging from apéritifs before the meal to digestifs and cordials served at the end. Coffee, tea, and water all have a place in a fine meal. Showing the proper concern and respect for the service of these beverages is one of the ways you can deliver remarkable service to every guest.

8

Wine Service

WINE IS THE CLASSIC COMPLEMENT
to a fine meal, but many diners lack
confidence in their ability to choose wines
that enhance the flavor of their meals. A
knowledgeable server can alleviate a diner's
apprehension about wine choices—and
will be rewarded for doing so, given that
wine can total as much as 35 percent of the
check for some diners, resulting in a much
larger gratuity. For this reason, be sure to
ask, "Would you care to see our wine list?"
or "Will you be having wine this evening?"
as soon as guests are comfortably seated.

    This chapter shares the ins and
outs of selecting and serving wine to your
guests. For information on serving other
beverages, see chapter 7.

Glassware for Wine Service

GLASSES SHOULD BE BROUGHT TO THE TABLE before the wine, either by carrying them upside down between your fingers or by bringing them on a tray. You can carry two to six glasses between your fingers (see page 144 for instructions and an illustration of carrying stemmed glassware), taking care to handle the glassware only by the stems, never putting your fingers inside the bowls of the glasses. Skin oils can be removed only with detergents, which are far from ideal for glasses. Soiled glasses should be handled by the stem or with two fingers around the base of the bowl.

Always check glasses for spots before bringing them to the table. If you find spots, remove them with a clean, lint-free cloth. To further clean washed glasses, you can steam them over boiling water and wipe them clean with a lint-free cloth.

GLASSWARE DESIGN

Varieties of wineglasses are practically endless—see below for examples of the most common—although using one all-purpose wineglass, along with a flute for sparkling wines. is adequate for most wine service needs. More elaborate wine and beverage programs require a more extensive range of glassware.

The best design for a wineglass is a stable-based, stemmed, bowl-shaped glass with the rim turned in slightly. The white wineglass is tall and the bowl has a

Glassware for wine service. From left to right: Champagne flute, white wineglass, reserve white wineglass, red wineglass, Bordeaux/Tuscany glass, Burgundy/Piedmont glass.

smaller opening to capture and hold the aroma and bouquet; the red wineglass has a wider opening to promote aeration. The stem of the glass must be long enough to allow guests to hold glasses by them (holding by the bowl raises the temperature of the wine). A fluted or tulip-shaped glass for sparking wine lets the wine stay cooler longer, allows for appreciation of the color, and preserves the effervescence.

Most wineglasses hold about eight ounces, but the normal portion of wine is four to five ounces. The extra room in the glass's bowl provides space for the aroma of the wine to accumulate and permits the taster to enjoy the wine's bouquet. Lately the trend has been toward very large glasses, some of which hold as much as twenty fluid ounces. Wine connoisseurs appreciate these glasses because they allow for a more thorough evaluation (and appreciation) of the wine's aromas. However, they can give the impression that your establishment is pouring meager portions of wine. Some restaurants prefer to serve wines in standard-size glasses, but may still have the extra-large glasses on hand for guests that request them.

CLEANING GLASSWARE

Glassware for wine must be impeccably clean, because the aroma and taste of wine can be affected by foreign substances and soap residue. In most establishments, glassware is washed, double-rinsed, steamed, polished, and dried with a cloth. Strong detergents and improper rinsing in industrial machines may leave a residue that can mask the quality of the wine and discourage the effervescence in a sparkling wine. The procedure for steaming and storing glasses appears in chapter 5 on pages 111 to 112.

Grapes

WINE IS THE FERMENTED JUICE OF FRUIT, usually grapes. In the process of wine fermentation, yeast, a living organism found on the skin of ripe grapes, transforms the sugar naturally present in grape juice into alcohol and carbon dioxide. These days, most winemakers choose a specific strain of yeast that was grown in a lab—it's safer than relying on the wild yeast used in spontaneous fermentation.

Wines obtain their distinctive characteristics as result of the climate and soil in which the grapes were grown, the variety of grape, the condition of the grapes when picked, the age of the vines, the control of the fermentation process, as well as the aging and the storage techniques used after fermentation.

The grapes used for the wine and the way that they are handled determine whether the wine will be white, red, or rosé (also called "blush"). The wine's color almost always comes from the skins, which have most of the pigment and tannins. This means that a white wine can technically be made from a red grape—you just have to keep the pale juice away from the skin. Red and pink wines are made from red grapes, and the amount of time the skins spend in the juice helps to determine the depth of color. The longer the juice is allowed to stay in contact with the grape skin, the deeper the color. Some rosés are made by adding red juice or wine to white juice or wine. This is usually a technique that is applied to less expensive wines; however, rosé Champagne, a notable fine wine, is an exception to this general rule.

A final factor in the color of wine is its age. White wines turn more golden or brown as they get older—red wines lose their ruby color and tend towards garnet and then maroon.

FLAVORS

Wine flavors are described in the following terms:

- **Fruit:** When most people say a wine is "fruity," they usually mean it's sweet. Fruit flavors in wine can actually mimic sweetness, so a technically dry wine (one with no residual sugar) can seem sweet. Grapes themselves have a broad range of esters (flavor molecules) that can mimic the flavors of other fruits. Add to this the fact that fermentation also creates other flavors, and you can wind up with aromas of green pepper or strawberry. Remember, most of what we think is taste happens in the nose—so smells turn into flavors. While you might think that you taste sweetness, you are experiencing the aroma of something else (like a peach) that is sweet.

- **Tartness:** The acidity of grapes both preserves the wine and flavors it. The prevalent acid in grapes is malic acid, which is also found in apples. A tart wine helps balance rich foods that are high in fat content. Wines that are high in acid will can make your mouth water.

What's Malo?

Malolactic fermentation occurs when bacteria get into the wine and convert the grapes' malic acid (also found in apples) into lactic acid (also found in milk). Lactic acid is weaker than malic acid, so a wine that has undergone malolactic fermentation feels softer and tastes less sour. Virtually all red wines go through this process, and some whites. Most notably, big oaky California Chardonnays that go through "malo" have a richer aspect because of it.

- **Tannins:** Tannins are found in the skins, pits, and stems of grapes, and although they act as an excellent preservative (they were once used to tan leather), they also can add a bitter, astringent flavor to wines, as well as a drying sensation on the sides of the mouth. Red wines have more tannins than white, and because tannins soften with age, older red wines tend to have a softer mouthfeel, and somewhat less bitterness.

- **Body:** Body refers to the weight, or feeling, of a wine in your mouth. For dry wines, this sensation is usually related to the percentage of alcohol since glycol, an alcohol-related sugar, makes the wine feel thicker. The more alcohol there is, the more glycol there is, and the thicker the wine feels. Body can be important when matching wine with food—big wine (such as a Napa Valley Cabernet) overpowers light food (such as boneless chicken breast) and light wine (like Muscadet) tastes watery with big food (like grilled salmon).

- **Balance:** Balance refers to the combination of fruit, tartness, tannins, and body; that is, how all of the preceding flavors work together. A wine that is neither too fruity nor too tart, with a nice complexity of flavor, gives you a well-rounded drinking experience.

WHITE WINE GRAPES

White wines can can range in color from pale yellow to gold, and some white wines have an almost green hue. White wines can range from light bodied to quite full (as in the case of dessert wines). They may bone-dry or syrupy sweet, depending on the type of grape used and how ripe it is. White wine grape varieties include the following:

- **Chardonnay:** This grape is capable of producing a broad range of wines with flavors that range from simple, clean, and crisp all the way up to full-bodied, rich, and oaky. It is the most popular grape in the U.S. and is increasing in worldwide sales, partly because it can produce many styles and is relatively easy to grow. It is grown in almost every wine-growing country now.

- **Chenin Blanc:** The Chenin Blanc grape is a real chameleon, capable of yielding everything from light, dry, fresh wines, to medium-bodied off-dry wines, and even botrytis-affected rich dessert wines. It is grown around the world, but is most popular in the Loire Valley of France, in the U.S., and in South Africa, where its historic name is "Steen."

- **Gewürztraminer:** This grape produces a spicy, flavorful wine with unusual notes that sometimes include lychee nuts and floral aromas. It is grown mostly in Alsace, France, and in the U.S.

- **Müller-Thurgau:** This is a widely planted grape in Germany and used to be the most-planted grape on the planet. It produces a serviceable everyday wine.

- **Muscat:** Muscat is a family of grapes known almost as well for being delicious table grapes as for wine making. While there are some dry wines made from muscat grapes, the dessert wines may be more familiar, from the light, delicate Moscato d'Asti from Piedmont in Italy to the rich, lightly fortified vin doux naturel Muscat de Beaumes de Venise from the Rhône in France.

- **Pinot Blanc:** The Pinot Blanc grape is grown mostly in Alsace as a basic component for solid, basic wines. It also is used to make the base wine for sparkling crémant wines from the same region. Pinot Blanc is also grown in northern Italy and occasionally in the U.S.

- **Riesling:** Considered one of the most "noble" white grapes, Riesling grapes can produce some of the finest food-friendly dry wines in the world. They can also produce everything from very light, off-dry wines to unctuous, botrytis-affected dessert wines.

- **Sauvignon Blanc:** Popular around the world, this grape is known for its "green" aromas. These smells can be grassy, herbal, or vegetal. It has become a real success story in New Zealand, is very popular in California, and has its original roots in the Loire Valley and Bordeaux regions of France.

- **Sémillon:** The Sémillon grape is most famous as a blending partner for Sauvignon Blanc in Bordeaux. It can have peachy aromas, and its thin skin makes it susceptible to Botrytis cinerea, the "Noble Rot" that can lead to the most famous dessert wine in the world, Sauternes. It is also used in dry wines in France, the U.S., and Australia.

- **Trebbiano:** This grape is the most planted white grape in Italy, and is actually slightly different in each growing region. It tends to produce a light, simple wine that is meant to be consumed young and fresh. It is also grown in France under the name Ugni Blanc, and is used for the base wine that is distilled into both Cognac and Armagnac.

RED WINE GRAPES

Red wines are made from red grapes (as well as purple- or black-skinned grapes) and are fermented with their skins, which give them both color and a good bit of tannin, along with additional flavor compounds. The additional tannin and pigment does, by definition, give red wine a fuller body than white, but there still are some relatively light-bodied red wines. Colors of red wines can range from a pale ruby to almost black depending on the thickness of the grape's skin and how long the skin is in contact with the juice. In addition, rosé or blush wines (which have a pink color) are either the result of mixing red and white wines or are produced by using red wine grapes but fermenting or macerating the wine with the skins for a shorter period of time than red wines. Rosé wines are meant to be drunk young and fresh. Dry rosés are very popular in Europe as they are very flexible with food. Americans tend to prefer fruity wines and so "blush" wines from the U.S. usually have some residual sugar. Red wine grape varieties include the following:

- **Barbera:** The Barbera grape produces a fairly light but intensely flavored wine in the Piedmont region of Italy. Some wineries in California (the "Cal-Ital" producers) have done very well with it, producing a spicy, intense wine with structure.

- **Cabernet Sauvignon:** Considered the most noble of all red grapes, Cabernet Sauvignon produces wines with lots of tannin, dark color, and intense acidity. In Europe (especially Bordeaux), these characteristics are softened by introducing blending grapes, usually Merlot. In California, especially the Napa Valley, it is warm enough for the grape to produce a more balanced wine on its own, although some blending is still done to achieve a more interesting flavor profile. Though perhaps best known as a wine from these premium growing areas, Cabernet Sauvignon is being grown around the world now; it is even used to produce some value wines because of its tremendous marketability.

- **Gamay:** This French grape from the Beaujolais region creates a delicate red wine. Its best-known version is Beaujolais nouveau, a light quaffing wine. More seriously regarded versions come from specific towns and are collectively called Cru Beaujolais, with the most famous wines being Morgon and Moulin a-Vent.

- **Grenache:** This is one of the two most important grapes in the Rhône Valley of France, and is also popular in California and Australia. It gives a spicy, red-fruit profile, and often has a light aroma of ground white pepper. Its finest application may be in the production of Châteauneuf-du-Pape, where it is one of the thirteen varieties allowed in the blend.

- **Merlot:** Merlot grapes produce a wine tends to be low in acid or "soft." This is a plus for people who want to drink red wine by itself, but does not help it to match well with food. That profile is exactly what allows it to be popular by the glass in the U.S. and also to be a good balancing partner for Cabernet Sauvignon in the Old World. It is thus one of the most planted grapes in the world, and produces the most popular red wine in this country.

- **Nebbiolo:** This Italian grape creates an intensely flavored, full-bodied red wine. It is the grape used in the "king of Italian wines," Barolo, as well as the "queen," Barbaresco. These are some of the finest, most expensive wines made in Italy, and because of their relatively robust acidity, can age for many years—sometimes decades.

- **Pinot Noir:** This is the favorite grape of many wine professionals for two reasons. First, its medium body, earthiness, and good acidity make it a great partner for food. Second, it is a grape that is very good at allowing the place of its origin to show through in the glass—in other words, its terroir. It is grown world-wide, but is most popular in Burgundy, France, and in California. Fine examples are starting to come from New Zealand, as well. This grape tends to do well in cooler climates.

- **Sangiovese:** This Italian grape is the main grape in Italy's most famous wine, Chianti. It also makes appearances in Brunello di Montalcino, Vino Nobile di Montepulciano, and Morellino di Scansano. In each case, the wine is medium- to full-bodied, with a round earthiness and good acidity, making Sangiovese wines great food companions. Brunello di Montalcino is arguably the greatest of these wines and can be enjoyed both when it is young and after ten to twenty years of aging. It is often said to have a "velvety" texture.

- **Syrah/Shiraz:** In France, especially in the northern Rhône Valley, Syrah produces wines with deep color and high acid, thus producing wines that age magnificently, such as Hermitage. They tend to have spice aromas as well, such as ground black pepper. As grown in California and Australia, where its name is "Shiraz," more fruit is evident in the resulting wine, with the color and acid still noticeable. The popularity of this delicious wine has made "Shiraz" a very important grape for the U.S. market.

- **Zinfandel:** This grape is grown only in the U.S. For many years, its place of origin was a mystery and some producers even thought that it was brought by aliens. As it turns out, Zinfandel's ancestor is the Primitivo grape of Italy. For many years, "Zin" was the most-planted grape in California—its spicy, earthy flavor and dark fruit reminded many Italian wine makers of the wines that they had left behind. When Americans started looking for lighter wines, Zinfandel vineyards languished, until Sutter Home Winery produced its first "White Zinfandel," an off-dry rosé that led to the coining of the term "blush wine." Ironically, this innocuous beverage led to a renaissance of interest in the wine now termed "red Zinfandel," which can be a lush, full-bodied, spicy, and delicious wine.

How to Think about Wine: The Quadrant System

WITH SO MANY WINES AVAILABLE, you may be looking for a shortcut—that is, a way to recommend wine choices to your customers without having to memorize every available wine and its characteristics. Thankfully, if you know where a wine comes from (and most labels give you this information), you can predict the basic flavors of the wine.

NORTH/SOUTH

In cold northern regions, grapes don't ripen as well as in warmer places, so the resulting wines are lighter-bodied and highly acidic. Wines made from grapes that grow in warmer, southern regions tend to be full-bodied with less acidity. For this reason, recommend a northern wine (from Oregon or the Alto Adige of Italy, for instance) if guests are looking for a light-bodied wine and recommend a southern wine (from the Rhône or Provence, for instance) for more body.

OLD WORLD/NEW WORLD

Wines grown in the Old World (that is, Europe) tend to be earthier, drier, and less fruity, and thus go well with most food choices. Many European wines, because of their lack of fruity sweetness, are meant to be somewhat incomplete since they are designed to accompany food and be complemented by it—not to be consumed on their own. Wines from the New World (the United States, South America, Africa, and Australia), on the other hand, provide a complete flavor and are best consumed on their own, without food. Using this knowledge along with the tenets of northern or southern growing regions, you should be able to find a light-bodied fruity wine by looking for a cold region in the New World, such as Washington State. Instead of memorizing thousands of facts and names, just look at the map of the world broken into four quadrants. This will make it easier to sell wine and please guests at the same time.

Pairing Food and Wine

THE ADAGE THAT RED WINES should be paired with red meats and white wine with "white" foods such as poultry, pasta, and fish is no longer considered gospel. Instead, discerning wine drinkers are encouraged to choose the wine flavors that they enjoy most.

If guests ask which wine they should order, ask about their tastes and preferences, as well as their price range. Keep in mind that a table of four people is likely to order different things, so a finely tuned wine pairing goes out the window anyway, unless you only go with wines by the glass. Usually the best answer is to recommend wines that are flexible with a range of foods—such as Riesling and Pinot Noir. The following table gives you specific pairings for common entrées that you can use to recommend wine to your guests.

Some establishments offer guests wine charts that match wine varieties to the foods with which they are best paired. At other establishments, those charts are only for the staff and include the wine number (for easy identification in the storage rack), name, pronunciation, year, bottle size, price, type (red, white, rosé, sparkling, fortified), origin, serving temperature, characteristics (body, flavor, bouquet), and recommended accompanying dishes. Other restaurants don't have charts at all, so it is wise to know as much as possible about the wines offered at your establishment.

PAIRING FOOD AND WINE

APPETIZERS	Dry, light-bodied wines; sparkling wines such as CHAMPAGNE or PROSECCO
PASTA	
Fettuccine Alfredo (cream sauce)	Frascati, Sauvignon Blanc
Lasagna (tomato sauce)	Chianti, Cabernet Sauvignon
Spaghetti primavera (light sauce)	Soave, Sauvignon Blanc
FISH AND SEAFOOD	
Grilled or broiled fish	Chardonnay, Sauvignon Blanc
Fresh shellfish	Sauvignon Blanc, Johannisberg Riesling
Fried fish	Chardonnay, Johannisberg Riesling
POULTRY	
Chicken with light cream sauce	Chardonnay, Johannisberg Riesling
Barbecued chicken	Gamay Beaujolais
Sweet-and-sour chicken	White Zinfandel, Johannisberg Riesling
BEEF	
New York strip steak	Cabernet Sauvignon, Merlot
Filet mignon with béarnaise sauce	Cabernet Sauvignon, Merlot
Beef Stroganoff	Merlot, Pinot Noir
PORK/VEAL/LAMB/HAM	
Roast pork	Chardonnay, Gamay Beaujolais
Glazed ham	White Zinfandel
Grilled pork chops	Gamay Beaujolais, Zinfandel
Veal parmigiana	Zinfandel, Chardonnay
LIGHT ENTRÉES	
Fruit salad	Johannisberg Riesling
Quiche Lorraine	Sauvignon Blanc, Chenin Blanc
Chicken Caesar salad	Sauvignon Blanc, Chardonnay

If the wine selection in your establishment is well chosen but simple, you will be able to help guests make wine selections without a copious amount of additional wine education. In establishments where the wine selection is vast, a sommelier (wine steward) assists guests in selecting wines. If your establishment does not employ a sommelier and has a large wine list, you may be educated about the wines your restaurant carries through tastings and seminars. In addition, the manager may suggest wines to go with each day's special menu offerings in preservice meetings.

Vintages

A VINTAGE WINE is an exceptional wine from an exceptional year. But most wines, even the unexceptional ones, include a vintage (date) on the wine label from when the grapes were picked, because wines made from the same grapes, in the same region, and at the same winery can taste noticeably different from year to year. A vintage chart lists the quality of grape harvests, but because all wines made in a particular year may not be great wines, a vintage chart does little but give you a general idea of which wines may be better than others.

Older, expensive wines are highly dependent on a particular vintage, and your wine list should reflect whichever vintages are currently available in your selection. However, if guests request a specific vintage that your establishment no longer carries (as can be the case when a vintage runs out and is replaced by a new year), bring a close substitute (preferably the same wine in a different vintage), explain that the vintage requested is not available, and ask whether the substitute is acceptable. Or, if your establishment employs a sommelier, ask him or her to consult with your diners to select a different wine or vintage.

Types of Wine

IN ADDITION TO TRADITIONAL WINE (also known as "still" or "table" wine), there are two other types that may appear on your wine list: sparkling and fortified wines.

STILL WINES

If the carbon dioxide gas that occurs naturally during fermentation is allowed to escape from the wine during fermentation, the product is called "still" or "table" wine. This is the wine most people think of when they ask for wine (e.g., Merlot or Cabernet Sauvignon). In the United States, table wines may contain 7 to 14 percent alcohol. The European Union, on the other hand, defines table wine as any wine that does not meet the appellation standards and is the least distinctive legal category for wines. This has led some people to assume that the term *table wine* means that the wine is somehow inferior to other wines. Table wines may have an alcohol content of 7 to 14 percent and may be sold by the bottle, by the glass, or in a carafe.

SPARKLING WINE

Sparkling wine is often misnamed "Champagne," a term that applies only to grapes grown in the Champagne region of France. Regardless of the origin of the grapes, sparkling wine is made when the carbon dioxide produced during the fermentation process is captured in the wine, producing a fizziness that is absent in still wines. Although most sparkling wines are white, they can also be red or rosé, and the alcohol content is 8 to 14 percent, as with still wine.

Sparkling wines range from very dry to very sweet on the following scale: extra-brut, brut, extra-dry, sec, demi-sec, and doux and are produced in one of three ways:

- **Méthode champenoise:** As with most wines, the fermentation process begins in a large vat, but the wine is then bottled and fermented again, remaining in that bottle until it is opened by the consumer (look for a label that says, "fermented in this bottle"). During the second fermentation process, sugar and yeast are added to the bottle to produce more carbon dioxide and develop additional flavors. This process produces a sediment that must be expelled before shipping the wine, and when the cork is removed to expel the sediment, more sugar may be added.

- **Transfer method:** Due to the trouble inherent in removing sediment from the bottles, some sparkling wine is transferred to a pressurized machine that removes sediment quickly after the second fermentation process is complete. From there, the wine receives a sweetening dosage and is rebottled. The label will say, "fermented in the bottle." The difference between that statement and "fermented in this bottle" reflects the differences in method, and often, in quality and price between méthode champenoise and the transfer method.

- **Charmat or bulk method:** With this method, the wine is kept under pressure in large tanks and it is also given sugar and yeast in order to produce more carbon dioxide, before the sediment is filtered out and the wine is bottled. This method is used for the least expensive sparkling wines, because it is an inexpensive and efficient way to produce sparkling wine.

See the Sparkling Wine Service later in this chapter for information on how to open and serve a bottle of sparkling wine.

FORTIFIED WINE

Fortified wines are wines "fortified" with brandy or other additional alcohols, either to stop the fermentation process (and thereby change the flavor) or just to increase the alcohol content, which is usually between 17 and 22 percent. Apéritif wines are usually a type of fortified wine and are flavored with herbs, spices, flowers, bark, and so on; they are usually served before a meal and may be either sweet or dry. These wines are also called "aromatized wines" because they have an aroma from the added herbs. Vermouth is one such example of an apéritif or aromatized wine.

Another type of fortified wine includes some dessert wines, which are sweet and full-bodied and are usually served after a meal. Port, Sherry, and Madeira are a few examples of dessert wines.

Wine Labels

THE MAIN WINE LABEL gives you four important pieces of information about a particular wine: the type or name of the wine; the vintage; the region; and the producer. The vintage may also be listed on the neck label, if there is one, which makes the vintage easier to identify. Wines sold in the United States must also list the alcoholic content (as a percentage), state whether it's a still or sparkling wine, and warn about the dangers of alcohol consumption.

Tasting Wine

THE MORE WINES YOU HAVE TASTED, the more knowledgeable you will be when guests have questions about the wine list. If your establishment does not offer wine-tasting sessions for servers, ask the dining room manager whether such events can be scheduled. When tasting wines, keep a notebook in which you record the wine's name, vintage, cost, description, and personal impressions.

To taste wine, you first hold the wine up to the light (or a white background) to note its color; then swirl the wine in the glass (do not swirl sparkling wines). Next you smell the wine with your nose down in the glass. Finally, taste the wine, and note the impression left in the mouth after swallowing or spitting the wine out. When going through this process, note the following:

- **Color/clarity:** Holding your glass up to the light or a white background and tipping it to one edge, note the color (from nearly purple to pale yellow) and clarity (that is, whether the wine is clear or shows signs of cloudiness). A few words used to describe a wine's color are: clear, bright, dull, hazy/cloudy, thick/oily, thin/watery, pale, dark, weak, and intense. Red wines lose their bold color as they age, so they start out as a purple-red, and then fade by degrees to ruby, red, red-brown, mahogany, tawny, and amber-brown. White wines, on the other hand, tend to become more colorful with age, changing from a pale green-yellow to straw yellow, gold, deeper gold, yellow-brown, amber-brown, and brown. Rosés become less pink with age, moving from pink to orange to amber. Sparkling wines should have fine, abundant bubbles.

- **Body:** You can make an educated guess about the wine's body based on its alcohol content. The higher the percentage, the more body. To evaluate the body of a wine, swirl the wine in the glass, noting how long it takes for the drippings (also called "legs") to run back down the side of the glass. Dry, light wines will flow quickly (thin legs); thick, full-bodied wines will move more slowly (thicker legs). The best way to judge the body of a wine is to feel its weight on your palette.

- **Aroma/bouquet:** Aroma makes a tremendous difference in how wine is judged. After the wine has sat in the glass for five or ten minutes, swirl the wine in the glass to increase the wine's surface contact with air and intensify its scent. If the scent is fruity or flowery, this is a young wine, and the scent is called an "aroma." For an older wine, the scent is known as its "bouquet," which will be more noticeable with each passing vintage year. Note noticeable scents, including those of flowers, fruits, and spices. Common words used to describe the scent include: perfumed, woody, young, baked, complex, closed, acrid, corky, moldy, skunky, minty, vegetal, or grassy.

- **Taste:** Note the taste by sipping a bit of the wine and exposing it to as many of your taste buds as possible; some people create a whistling sound when they taste wines to achieve this, while others "chew" the wine. Just be sure to expose as much of the tongue as possible, including the front of the tongue, as well as the sides and the back. When tasting, you're judging the acidity (too much is unpleasant; too little is dull), sweetness, and any astringency (judged by whether you pucker up as you taste the wine) that comes from the tannins. Also note the flavors of any fruits, nuts, and spices. Words used to describe the taste of a wine include: syrupy, cloying, hot, biting, raw, harsh, mild, fat, nervous, round, firm, clumsy, flabby, velvety, soft, and generous. After swallowing or spitting, note the finish—that is, whether the wine taste lingers in your mouth (as it will for a complex wine) or whether it "finishes clean" (as it will for a light, crisp wine).

Wine Storage

STORING WINE PROPERLY is essential for maintaining its flavor. Wines are corked to protect them from contact with air, but the bottles must also be kept at a constant temperature (and not extremely hot or cold), away from sunlight, free from vibration, and away from herbs and other foods with strong odors. Therefore, keep all wines in a well-ventilated, dark, odor-free, vibration-free area that is temperature controlled (between 55° and 60°F, with no fluctuations). Controlling vibration and movement is especially important with red wines, which develop sediment with time. Store all wines horizontally (on their sides) to prevent the cork from drying and shrinking, but avoid having bottles roll around the storage area—instead, hold them still in racks or bins. For easy identification and to avoid disturbing the sediment, keep labels up, facing the ceiling. Some establishments also use a numbering system that corresponds to a wine list—wine bottles are tagged with numbers that match those on the list.

Convenient access to the wine storage area from the dining area is essential; otherwise, keeping a par stock (a supply equal to the amount normally needed) in the dining room is advisable.

Taking the Wine Order

WHETHER DONE BY THE SOMMELIER, maître d', or server, the wine order should be taken with elegance and grace. The server should address everyone at the table: "Would you care to see our wine list?" or "Will you be having wine this evening?" If your restaurant offers a selection of wine by the glass, all of the guests at your table may want to see and select from a wine list. Even if yours is a by-the-bottle-only establishment, all guests may want to see the wine list and discuss which bottle to select. Still, if you can identify a host for the party, present the wine list to him or her first, standing on the guest's right side, before handing additional lists to other members of the party who appear interested in it. Then excuse yourself for a few minutes to allow the party time to select a wine.

Do not offer suggestions unless asked, but do answer all questions completely. If guests are struggling with which wine to order, you may want to ask, "What type of wine do you normally enjoy?" You can then suggest similar wines from your list.

Ask the host (or individual guests) whether they want the wine served before or with the meal; if it is served with the meal, determine which course. If the host has given no instructions in this regard, these guidelines should be followed: white and rosé wines should be opened and served with the first course; red wines should be opened and held at room temperature, on the table, immediately following the presentation to the host.

When guests are unsure how much wine to order, especially for a large party, keep in mind that you will be able to pour up to six glasses from one full bottle of wine if you are pouring about four ounces per glass.

When Guests Bring Their Own Wine

Some establishments allow guests to bring their own wine, either as a general policy or for some special occasions. Keep in mind, however, that the lost revenue may be substantial, so the only restaurants that do this routinely are those that do not have a liquor license. Corkage fees are common in bring-your-own establishments—these fees cover the cost of handling, uncorking, and serving the wine, as well as washing the glasses. Fees may be charged per person or per bottle, but generally range from $2 to $5 per person or $10 to $20 per bottle.

Presenting, Opening, and Serving Wine

AFTER GUESTS HAVE ORDERED WINE, you must present the bottle(s) to your guests, open it, and serve it. This requires at least some of the wine-serving equipment shown in the below figure. For service to proceed smoothly, corkscrews, wine buckets, decanters, napkins, baskets, and candles must be ready for use at all times. As always, mise en place is extremely important.

PRESENTING THE BOTTLE AND REMOVING THE CORK

The technique for opening a bottle of still wine is shown on the facing page.

After the bottle has been chilled (if necessary), wipe the bottle dry with a napkin to avoid spilling cold water on your guests, and present the bottle to the person who ordered, by approaching from their right side. Be sure the entire label is visible to the guest as you review the vintage, name, and producer. When your guest indicates approval, place the bottle back in the bucket or on the table, if a bucket is not used, to remove the cork. Never, ever place the bottle between your legs or against your thigh to open it! If your guests do not approve the wine, make the necessary corrections and return with a different bottle.

Cut the covering over the cork (called the "capsule") Draw the blade around the bottle. Remove the capsule and put it in your pocket.

Now you must remove the cork. A captain's corkscrew (also called a "waiter's tool") is a levered, T-type corkscrew; it is the most popular because you can keep it in your pocket. Be sure yours has a spiral worm with at least five curves, with the outsides of the curves grooved to provide a strong grip on the cork. Insert the corkscrew slightly off center at a slight angle, straighten it up after one or two turns, and continue to turn the corkscrew until only one turn of the spiral remains above the cork. Pull the corkscrew straight up, raising your elbow and being careful not to bend the cork or to touch the mouth of the bottle with your hands. Rock the cork back and forth while pulling gently toward the ceiling.

Equipment for wine service.

Using an ah-so cork remover.

OPENING A BOTTLE OF STILL WINE

1. Present the bottle to the person who ordered it, cradling it in a serviette so the entire label is visible and can be read.

2. Place the bottle on a flat surface and remove the foil covering the cork. Cut around the front of the neck of the bottle just below the second lip.

3. Cut the foil around the back of the neck just below the second lip.

4. Peel away the top of the foil, lifting it away using the blade from the corkscrew and holding the neck of the bottle with the left hand.

5. Insert the corkscrew slightly off center at a slight angle and straighten it up with one or two turns.

6. Tilt the corkscrew so that the notch in the lever will rest on the lip of the bottle. Hold it in place with the index finger while bracing the neck of the bottle.

7. Pull the corkscrew straight up while continuing to hold the lever in place and brace the neck of the bottle. Be careful not to touch the lip of the bottle.

8. Twist the cork, holding in a napkin to release it from the bottle opening.

An ah-so cork-removal tool is easy to use—some say it is easier than a corkscrew ("ah, so easy!"). Simply insert the longer prong between the cork and bottle neck and rock back and forth, while applying pressure, until the shorter prong is also inserted. Now rock the handle, continuing downward pressure, until the tool is fully inserted. Then you pull the handle upward, twisting as you pull up to release the cork.

A cork retrieval tool may be necessary for those rare times that the cork or a portion of it falls into the bottle and must be removed before serving the wine. If a piece breaks off but does not fall into the bottle, simply remove and discard the broken piece of cork from the waiter's tool. Carefully insert the worm into the remaining portion of cork, trying to let it catch part of the cork without applying too much downward pressure. Turn the worm as far as possible, connect the lever, and lift.

Both natural cork and synthetic or plastic wine stoppers are removed with either a corkscrew style opener (waiter's tool) or ah-so. These corks are the traditional size and shape. Natural cork is easier to remove than synthetic or plastic stoppers, is biodegradable, and can be used to reseal an open bottle. However, cork may allow some air into the bottle and may introduce trichloroanisole (TCA), the compound chiefly responsible for musty flavors and aromas. Synthetic or plastic stoppers are inexpensive but they are non-biodegradable and are more difficult to reinsert in a bottle.

Metal screw caps make a virtually air-tight seal and can be used to reseal an opened bottle. To remove screw caps, hold the bottle in your non-dominant hand. Wrap your other hand around the cap. Twist sharply to break the seal. You may simply twist the cap off at this point, or for a little showmanship, you can roll the screw cap down one of your forearms toward the palm of your hand to finish unscrewing the cap and then catch the cap as it moves across your palm.

Effervescent wines may be sealed with crown caps like those used to seal sodas or beer. These caps may be replaced with a natural cork and a wire cage before the wine is shipped, but some producers do not replace them. These caps are an effective seal, but do not provide the "show" guests often expect during sparkling wine service, since you simply pop them off the bottle with a lever-style bottle opener.

Glass stoppers are covered by a capsule and a screw cap. Once the capsule and cap are removed, the stopper is pulled from the bottle; no tools are required to remove or reinsert the stopper. These stoppers offer excellent protection from oxidation.

The Zork looks like a traditional bottle stopper covered with a capsule. The stopper itself consists of three parts; a clamp that holds the cap securely onto the bottle, a sheet of metal foil that seals the bottle, and a plunger. To remove the Zork from a bottle, pull on the plastic "ribbon" holding the cap in place. Pull the cap away from the bottle to open the seal and lift out the plunger. The plunger recreates the sound of a cork's "pop" during the opening ceremony and seals the bottle up when the Zork is reinserted.

The cork is presented to the host to make sure the cork is neither too moist nor too dry and to confirm the vineyard. Crown caps and screw caps will not provide this information and they are not typically presented. To avoid staining the tablecloth, the cork should be presented on a small plate as shown in the photograph at right.

Presenting the cork

Place the cork just to the right of the glass of the person who ordered the wine or on a small dish. Now wipe the lip and mouth of the bottle and pour about one ounce into the glass, keeping the label facing the guest; this is known as the tasting pour. A standard tasting pour is shown below. At this time—as well as each time you finish pouring any wine—lift and twist the mouth of the bottle to avoid dripping wine down the side of the bottle. If the wine is accepted, pour wine for all guests (women first, then men) pouring last to the person who ordered. At this point, remove the cork from the table.

If a guest complains of not liking a wine or of a wine tasting bad, take back the bottle and serve another. Chances are, it's a bad bottle, and your wine distributor will give your establishment a credit for the bottle. In fact, about one in ten bottles goes bad and must be discarded. One potential fault is cork mold (called "corkiness") or some other form of mildew or mustiness in the wine. A storage area that is too hot can lead to a wine being cooked (a situation referred to as "volatile acidity" or "maderization"). If nothing's wrong with the wine, you can sell the rest of it by the glass to cover the cost or it can be used for a staff tasting at the end of the night.

POURING

No wineglass should be filled more than half full. This leaves space for the wine to be swirled and to release the bouquet.

The tasting pour

Two general rules of thumb apply for filling wineglasses: White wineglasses should be filled about half full, with four to five ounces of wine; this size pour means that the guest can drink the wine while it is still chilled, leaving the remainder of the wine to stay chilled in the bottle. Red wineglasses are filled about one-third full, with five ounces of wine. For large glasses (with a capacity greater than eight ounces), you should fill the glass with a four- or five-ounce portion of water and notice how full the glass is, then pour up to the same level when serving wine.

If separate wines are to be served for different courses, the next wine should be poured before the previous glass is removed. Depending on the style of service, the house rules may allow the server to ask the guest if they may remove the old glass.

WINE BUCKETS AND OTHER WINE HOLDERS

A wine bucket sits on the table or next to it on a stand, filled three-quarters full with a mixture of two parts ice to one part water, in order to chill the wine to the desired temperature. A cloth napkin should be draped on the wine bucket for service. Chilling takes approximately fifteen minutes. For sparkling and fortified wines, leave the bottle in the bucket throughout the meal to retain a temperature of 41° to 47°F. White wines and rosés, on the other hand, do not need to sit in ice after they're opened because they should remain at a temperature of 44° to 54°F. If guests prefer, these wines can remain in a bucket after serving, but for better flavor, remove the bucket and place the wine bottle on a coaster or in a holder. Red wines are never placed in a wine bucket, as they are served at 50° to 55°F for light red wines and 55° to 65°F for medium and full-bodied red wines.

A few other ways of presenting wine at the table are as follows:

- **Coaster or holder:** A coaster or holder is a place for the wine bottle to rest during the meal.

- **Basket:** Used only with red wines, a wine bottle sits in the basket until it is decanted or served. The primary function is to facilitate gentle transferring of a mature red wine from cellar to table for decanting.

- **Decanter:** Older, delicate red wines may be poured into a decanter (known as "decanting") before they are served, because this allows the wine to breathe.

DECANTING WINE

Decanting does more than move the wine from the bottle into a decanter. It also aerates the wine and separates it from the sediment in the bottom of the bottle, which is why you must take great care to never empty the entire wine bottle into the decanter. Some establishments decant all red wines to avoid serving the sediment to guests. (White wines are not usually decanted, even if they have sediment, unless requested by the guest.) The sediment in red wine comes from tannins and color pigments. This sediment has an unpleasant and bitter taste and should never be allowed into a guest's glass.

Decanting wine.

To decant a bottle of wine, hold the shoulder of the bottle in front of a candle so that you can see through the bottle clearly. Pour a few drops of wine into the decanter, swirl them, and then empty this into a wineglass. This ensures that nothing in the decanter contaminates the taste of the wine. Pour more of the bottle's contents into the decanter until sediment appears in the shoulder; at this moment, stop pouring immediately! Proceed as usual, pouring a glass for the host, and then serving the other guests. Leave both the decanter and the empty wine bottle on the table.

OPENING SPARKLING WINES

1. Present the bottle to the person who ordered it, cradling it in a serviette so the entire label is visible and can be read.

2. Holding the bottle in the serviette, remove the foil covering the wire cage.

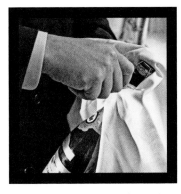

3. Holding the thumb on top of the cork and applying slight pressure, loosen the wire cage with the other hand.

4. Holding the base of the bottle in one hand, place the serviette over the cork. Hold the cork still while twisting the bottle. As the cork pushes out, hold it tightly. The cork should come out slowly and make a slight "shhh" sound.

5. Gently remove the cork from the bottle.

Sparkling Wine Service

TO SERVE SPARKLING WINE, first chill the bottle in a wine bucket, keeping in mind that sparkling wine bottles are thicker than white wine bottles, so they require more chilling time. The technique for opening a bottle of sparkling wine is shown on page 219. With the bottle in the wine bucket, place the bottle at a 45-degree angle, place a napkin over the top of the bottle, and loosen the foil capsule. Hold your thumb over the cork as you untwist the wire cage that holds the cork in place.

Directing the cork away from guests (while maintaining the 45-degree angle), release the cork slowly, allowing pressure to escape. Remove the cork completely and present it to the host. Wipe the mouth of the bottle with a napkin, and then wipe excess water from the bottle. As you pour, be sure the label is facing the host.

As with table wines, pour about an ounce into a glass for the host's approval. Once approved, pour one or two ounces for the next guest, let the foam dissipate, and then pour another two to three ounces, as shown below. (This double pouring is called "pouring in two motions" or "priming the glass"). Leave the sparkling wine in the bucket.

1. Use a serviette to wipe the water from the bottle.

2. Pour about one ounce, slowly, into the glass. Let the foam subside in the glass.

3. Continue pouring the sparkling wine into the glass, adding another 2 to 3 ounces to each glass.

Conclusion

REMARKABLE WINE SERVICE depends upon the server's ability to understand the house wine list and the characteristics of the wines. With that knowledge in hand, making helpful suggestions to the guest concerned about which wine to choose for the table, or even an individual guest's selection of a glass of wine to enjoy with an entrée, is much easier.

Once the wine is selected, the service of the wine should be a pleasure for the guests. Learning to use a waiter's tool and other bottle-opening devices, as well as the other accoutrements of wine service—buckets, baskets, and decanters—means that you can make the show of presenting and opening the wine smooth and elegant. Preparing and setting the correct glassware is yet another key to success. When it is finally time to pour the wine, you should be able to gauge just how much to put in each glass so that every glass has the perfect amount.

9

Banquet Service for Special Functions

HOSTING AND CATERING SPECIAL FUNCTIONS—whether a wedding reception, professional meeting, retirement or birthday party, or other event—offers your establishment the chance to provide the highest level of professional hospitality for your most important guests. A banquet is an elaborate, often ceremonial meal prepared and served to a great number of guests. (Information about reservations for groups is introduced in chapter 4, page xxx.) They are frequently held in honor of a person, an organization, or an occasion. Regardless of the nature of the event, a banquet is a special meal, one that requires a great deal of planning. All of the factors involved—lighting, linen, wine selection, menu composition, and pace—must be planned in advance. Without proper planning, the affair cannot be executed to perfection.

Venues for affairs such as banquets and receptions fall into four categories:

- An establishment that does on-premises and off-premises catering
- An establishment or company that does off-premises catering exclusively
- A restaurant with full catering facilities
- A restaurant with limited catering facilities

Planning and execution are usually the functions of the catering department in larger operations such as a hotel, but in smaller establishments they often become the responsibility of the dining room staff. It may be appropriate to work with an event or wedding planner or directly with the host, depending upon your client's preference.

Throughout this chapter we will refer to catering and banquets mainly as they pertain to restaurants, even though many professional servers have made a career of catering service.

Advantages of Catering

IN CATERING, all sales are booked in advance. Consequently, the number of guests and the amount of food to be served are all known beforehand. This can offer some distinct advantages. For the restaurant, there are other benefits:

- Cash deposits, which ensure an adequate supply of working capital
- Efficient portion and cost control
- Controlled labor costs, with a set number of hours and employees required for a function
- Reduced inventory costs (specialty items can be rented, and costs passed on to the client)
- Accurately forecasted sales and profits
- Use of facilities and equipment during normally unproductive hours or days when the restaurant is closed
- Revenue that can be used for upgrading facilities and equipment or for additional advertising—without having to raise menu prices
- Introduction of the restaurant to new, potentially regular, customers

For the server, a catered affair means the prospect of a guaranteed gratuity and the possibility of additional tips for special service.

Banquet Service

BANQUETS USE SEVERAL TABLE SERVICE STYLES: American, platter, butler, or buffet service. Some events may use a combination of service styles, such as butler service for hors d'oeuvre and buffet service during dinner. To be successful, catering personnel require a mastery of a variety of service styles and a total understanding of all the details of a function and its timing in order to provide the high level of professional hospitality that makes these special occasions memorable.

It is important to keep in mind that no matter how routine banquet service is for the server, for the guests it is a special, perhaps once-in-a-lifetime event, and every effort should be made to make it perfect for them. The flow of the entire banquet is of paramount concern. The sequence of service should be consistent and timely for all tables and should follow the standards established ahead of time. Teamwork is vital during banquets. Every table should feel that they received remarkable service, that their needs were anticipated as if by a mind reader, and that there was nothing more that could have been done to make it better.

Careful planning is required, no matter which service style is employed. If established service procedures for table setup or service (for instance, presetting all of the silver for the entire meal, serving from trays, using rental items such as glassware or chairs) are to be altered, these changes or variations must be organized and all service personnel briefed on the changes well before the event.

The importance of constant communication between the dining room and the kitchen during a banquet cannot be emphasized enough. The timing of courses may need to be coordinated with the band (or DJ), Champagne toast, blessing, welcome speech, cake-cutting ceremony, and so on.

A meeting for the service staff is usually held prior to the catered affair to ensure that all servers have been briefed about their duties and have the information they may need to perform well before, during, and after the event.

The banquet manager's and the client's planned schedule of events should be fully understood by the banquet headwaiter, the chef, the band, the photographer, and the videographer. Last-minute changes to the schedule on the day of the event must also be communicated to all concerned.

Particular points to be covered prior to the function are:

- Menu and floor plan
- Number of tables and covers per waiter and per captain, if applicable
- Sequence of events, food and beverage service, and entertainment

- Mise en place, with attention to special equipment

- Specific points to remember, such as specialty presentations, styles of service, or special requests

Staffing for a Banquet

THE NUMBER OF SERVICE PERSONNEL needed for a banquet depends on the total number of guests and the style of service. If American service is used at the banquet, one server should be allowed for every twenty guests; for Russian service, two servers for every thirty guests; for a buffet, one server for every thirty guests. For cocktail receptions or for butler service of hors d'oeuvre, one server should be scheduled for every thirty to forty guests.

Setting Up for a Banquet

WHEN SETTING UP THE DINING ROOM, the head table should be positioned for optimal visibility by all of the guests. A dais, or raised platform, can be used if necessary, to allow viewing of the head table. The rest of the table plan depends on the type of function, the size and shape of the room, the number of guests to be seated, and the preferences of the organizer. Round tables are ideal for banquets, since they allow for easy conversation among guests.

Square footage allotments for banquets vary, depending on the specific service details, such as size of dance floor, placement of cake or gift table, and so on. For sit-down affairs, from twelve to fifteen square feet per person should be allowed. Buffet service requires a little less space, ten to twelve square feet per person.

All tables, with the exception of the head table, should be numbered. Table numbers can be mounted on stands and should be visible to guests as they enter the room. Guests can obtain their table numbers from either a master seating chart or a special table set up to supply table numbers.

The seating chart should be drawn up prior to the affair. The host may wish to create the seating chart, or prefer to review and approve it once generated by either the maître d' or the event organizer. The seating chart becomes an important organizational tool to check that all necessary arrangements have been made, such as ordering the correct number of floral arrangements and so forth. It also allows the management to station servers effectively as well as to plan solutions for any difficulties that might arise.

Any good seating plan has an allowance for extra guests. A good rule of thumb is to anticipate that there may be a minimum of five to ten percent more guests than the number the of RSVPs the host received, but this number is always discussed with the host or organizer ahead of time.

Preparing the Banquet Room

WHEN GUESTS WALK INTO THE BANQUET ROOM, their first impression should be overwhelmingly positive. Tablecloths should be laid in an organized and systematic manner. Any overlap of cloths on a table should face away from the main entrance so that it will be less visible to guests viewing the room on arrival.

The tableware should reflect the occasion as well as the menu. All tableware should be laid according to the style and sequence of service. Its placement should be extremely precise. There may be a lot on the tabletop, so it is important that servers do their best to make each cover as neat and compact as possible to give guests enough room to enjoy their meal as well as to permit servers to do their work efficiently and safely.

DECORATION

Consulting with the florist is part of the planning process. It is imperative to know the layout of the décor ahead of time, so that any potential disruption to the placement of serving pieces can be resolved. Servers need to know how to set the tables in conjunction with the decorations on the table. Generally, the florist is scheduled to arrive just after the tablecloths are laid but before covers are in place, so the centerpieces can be set up. The florist may require assistance or may drop the centerpieces off earlier in the day for the servers to place them.

Servers should be careful to avoid spilling the water in the vases or disturbing the floral arrangements. If there are any spills while setting up the room, you may need to replace the cloth an completely reset the table. Centerpieces should be either short enough to fall below eye level or positioned on stands that are well above eye level so that the guests can see each other across the table.

Garland runners may be used for rectangular banquet tables or the head table. If there are place settings planned for the end position of the table, the runner should not extend the full length of the table, but should leave enough room for the cover to be set without forcing you to place dishes on top of the flowers. Garlands may be used along with centerpieces but they need to be placed prior to other items, such as the salt and pepper shakers and candles.

Note: It is a tradition that the centerpiece is taken home by one of the guests at the table. If not, the host may have other specific requests for the centerpieces. Before you remove the centerpieces, find out if there are such plans.

CANDLES

The florist may also supply candleholders. Candles should be lit before the guests arrive at the banquet. Whenever candles are used, servers need to be especially watchful: guests often toss their napkins or programs too near the candles when they rise from the table to dance or speak with friends. Placing candles in hurrican lamps or small glass vases keeps them visible but takes away the danger of an open flame at the table.

Presetting the Table

ALTHOUGH IT IS PROPER to set all food and beverages after the guests are seated, at banquet, some courses may be properly preset on the table. This may be the preferred option when a cocktail/hors d'oeuvre hour is held in a separate room from the dinner or when there is a limited amount of time for the event.

Preset items can save service time and allow more time for dancing or other planned events. Ice water glasses, bread and butter, and a cold appetizer may be in place when the guests arrive in the dining room. If a toast is planned upon seating, Champagne can be poured as well, though it is better to pour as guests are seated to avoid pouring for places occupied by anyone who might not care for Champagne or for seats that will not be occupied. This certainly avoids waste, and also gives the server a chance to begin interacting with the table.

NOTE: Since many people do not drink Champagne, the client may choose to have Champagne and sparkling cider or other nonalcoholic sparkling beverages offered, butler style, as the guests enter the dining room.

SETUP FOR BUFFET SERVICE

Buffets can be as elegant or informal as the client wishes. Foods are arranged on tables, which may include floral or edible arrangements, ice carvings, and other special decorative touches, such as fountains. A variety of techniques for arranging and setting up the buffet is shown below. Particular concerns of buffet service setup include the following:

- If space for the length of the buffet line is limited, create wider tables by setting additional eight-foot tables on four-inch-square blocks behind and overlapping the other eight-foot tables. The blocks should have small notched holes for the feet. The holes prevent the legs of the table from sliding off the blocks, which could cause the entire table to collapse. Using deeper holes in the front can provide a slight sloping of the table toward the guests.

- If skirting is not available for the table, use tablecloths. A seventy-two-inch cloth will cover the tabletop and drape to the floor on one side of an eight-foot table. Another cloth of the same size will cover the other side of the table to the floor and the tabletop. This economical way of skirting can be disguised by using colored forty-five-inch squares placed at an angle, creating a bent diamond over the edge of the table.

Create two levels by raising one table on blocks.

Use colored square clothes as an overlay on top of skirting made from tablecloths.

Create height on the table by draping and covering crates.

- To add height and create more visual interest, place items on the table on a variety of improvised platforms, including inverted empty glass racks or inverted empty milk crates covered with a cloth.

The artichoke fold protects the linens from drips.

- Use underliners beneath sauces and dips to catch any drips. A soiled underliner can be replaced more quickly and easily than the entire cloth. Keep sauces and dips close to the table edge so that guests won't have to reach very far for them; this will result in less spillage.

- Hand-wipe plates for the buffet line before service. Dishwashing machines do not always get all of the food off the plates. It is very unappetizing for a guest to pick up a plate and find dried food adhering to it.

- Either place flatware at the buffet line (preferably at the end rather than the beginning so that the guests do not have to carry it through the line with them) or preset it at the tables. Extra china and flatware should always be available.

Bar Service for Banquets

THERE ARE DIFFERENT KINDS OF BAR SERVICE: open bar, consumption bar, and cash bar. An open bar means that guests may have as much to drink as they like during a specified time period. Guests are not charged for drinks because the host pays a prearranged rate per hour. A "consumption bar" operates like an open bar, as far as guests are concerned. Rather than paying an hourly rate based upon an estimate, the host pays for what is actually consumed, based upon the difference between the opening and closing inventory. At a cash bar, guests pay for their drinks when they are ordered. Generally one bartender is assigned for every fifty people at either an open or cash bar.

At banquets, you are responsible for adhering to liquor laws. You should ask for identification if a guest might be underage. Very often bar service is discontinued during dinner, when wine is normally served. The bar may reopen when dessert is served, so guests may order cordials or other after-dinner drinks during the dancing phase of the event.

When a facility has no physical bar, two clothed and skirted eight-foot tables can serve as front and back bars. The bartender must be especially careful to handle all bar items in a sanitary manner under such conditions. An ice scoop, for example, is mandatory.

Flying service is a substitute for bar service in which servers provide beverages on trays (called "flying platters") to guests as they stand and mingle. Flying service may also include trays of hors d'oeuvre served butler style.

Platter Service

THE MAIN GOAL OF PLATTER SERVICE is to serve fully cooked food while it is still hot and to serve it in an elegant manner. It is particularly useful at banquets or wherever large groups of people must be quickly served. Platter service can be an addition to preplated American-style service—for example, when offering extra main-course helpings.

All food is fully cooked, and placed on silver or porcelain platters or in soup tureens. Servers bring the platters to the dining room, present them to the head of the table, and show them to the guests before serving. The server stands with feet together, to the left of the guest. The platter rests on the palm of the left hand, which is protected by a folded side towel. The server bends at the waist, advancing the left foot slightly, and brings the platter close to the rim of the guest's dinner plate. Food is plated with the aid of a serving spoon and fork with the server's right hand.

Considerable skill, strength, and dexterity are required to perform proper platter service. Trays can be heavy and hot and must be held firmly in the left hand while the food is being served with the right hand from the guest's left. Practice is required to prevent dropping or damaging the food or spilling the sauce.

Rules for Platter Service

A few basic rules for platter service should be observed. The suggestions that follow will make it run smoother:

- Serve food from the guest's left; move counterclockwise around the table.

- Set in clean plates from the guest's right; move clockwise around the table.

- Remove soiled plates from the guest's right; move clockwise around the table.

- Serve beverages from the guest's right; move clockwise around the table.

To both set and remove the plates, stand at each guest's right side, moving clockwise around the table. To serve beverages, stand at each guest's right side, again moving clockwise around the table.

Precise timing and organization are essential if the food is to reach the guests at its peak. The personnel in the kitchen must calculate the exact moment to platter the food so that it is presented to the guest promptly. Carving must be done in a minimal amount of time. Coordination for plating and serving throughout the meal can be achieved only if there are open and free-flowing lines of communication between the kitchen and the dining room.

While speed of service is essential, the food should still be arranged attractively and correctly. This is especially true when the dishes are accompanied by different garnishes that must blend perfectly with the principal ingredient. Traditionally, the protein is placed on the portion of the plate closest to the guest, using the appropriate utensils, and the accompaniments placed neatly above the protein. They should be arranged on the guest's plate in the same form and shape as they appear on the platter. The food should be handled as little as possible to avoid breaking and changing its appearance.

Teams of servers are sometimes used in platter service, since plattered foods or soups usually require a separate garnish, accompaniment, or sauce. The back waiter follows the front waiter in the same direction around the table, serving the accompaniment. The following are additional suggestions for successful platter service:

- Know the number of portions expected from each platter.

- Use a clean serving spoon and fork for each dish.

- To prevent dripping ladles, touch the bottom of the ladle to the surface of the soup in the tureen after filling the ladle. Any soup that is clinging to the bottom of the ladle will fall back into the tureen.

- Lift and place the food gracefully. Never slide it onto the guest's plate.

- Become adept at the proper use of service fork and spoon before attempting to serve the guests.

The primary disadvantage of platter service is that by the last guest, the food on the platter may look ragged and unappetizing. Another disadvantage is that guests may ask for additional portions, leaving too little for the last guest. One final disadvantage is that the entire effect will be ruined if the server spills or drips on a guest, and care should be taken not to spill or drip on the table, as well.

Buffet Service

BUFFET SERVICE STYLES can incorporate many different types of service. Guests may serve themselves at a buffet, or they may be helped by a carver at the carving station, or they may be able to watch a cook preparing pasta at the pasta station. Servers may be stationed at the buffet line to assist with the service of some foods, both to make the guests' experience more pleasant and to keep waste to a minimum by offering standard portions (though it is always appropriate to let guests point out the portion they wish or to have a bit more or less than the standard portion). Even if servers are not stationed on the line to assist with service, they must keep it at the top of their concern. The buffet should always be well stocked and clean; as soon as an item is running low, the kitchen should be alerted so that a fresh item can be prepared for the line.

Servers are responsible for pouring wine as well as cold and hot beverage service at the table, clearing, and setting coffee cups, sugars, creamers, and so on.

- During a buffet, be sure to keep the table well stocked and presentable for the guests.

- Keep the buffet table and surrounding area clean, as guests frequently drop or spill food on the table or floor.

- Sometimes a buffet cannot be replenished from behind the buffet line, which means you will have to replenish from the same side as the guests are using to serve themselves. When bringing in fresh food, remember that the guests have the right of way.

- Check to be sure that the correct serving tools are on the buffet so that guests are not left stranded in front a of dish with no way to serve themselves.

Vendor Meals

If the band (or the event planner, florist, or photographer) is to receive a meal (often contracted at half price), it is advisable to work out a schedule for their meals that does not compromise the timing of the event. For instance, when the band stops to eat, the guests can be encouraged to come to their seats for their meal. By the time the guests are at the tables and have enjoyed their main course, the band has returned and begun to play so that the dancing can begin again.

Coffee Service

SOME HOSTS OPT FOR A COFFEE STATION, while others may prefer that coffee and tea be poured at the table. The advantage of a coffee station is that it encourages the guests to get up from the table. The advantage of pouring at the table is that the guests are served both dessert and coffee at once.

Coffee cups and saucers may be preset at breakfast and luncheon events, or if the dinner is meant to precede a meeting or fund-raising event. When the banquet calls for a coffee station, extra care should be taken to keep the station free of debris. Sugar packets, disposable creamers, stir sticks, and the like tend to accumulate quickly. While it's wise to have a small basket on the table for discards, guests sometimes ignore it. Servers should monitor the cleanliness of the station at all times. Milk and cream should be served from insulated, and clearly labeled, containers. Individual milk or cream packets should be kept on ice.

Even with buffet-style meals, though, the host may prefer that coffee be poured at the table. After the dinner plates have been cleared, the creamers and sugar caddies should be placed on the table; two of each would be sufficient for large rounds of ten. A table of twelve will need three sugar caddies and three creamers. If the cups are not preset, part of the preparation for the event should be to stack ten saucers in the center of a beverage tray and set ten cups around the edge of the tray. At coffee time, the server can simply place a cup on the top saucer, then place the saucer on the table to the right of the guest with the handle of the cup in the four o'clock position. The server should proceed around the table clockwise, while another server follows with pots of regular and decaffeinated coffee.

Note: If the client requests it, an espresso cart may be rented to offer espresso and cappuccino. Orders can be taken by the server on a table-by-table basis or the guests can go to the espresso cart themselves. Although the word *espresso* means "fast," it can take a long time to serve a large quantity of these hot beverages. As china espresso cups are not usually available as rentals, the client should be informed in advance if paper cups have to be used.

Conclusion

THE SERVICE OF BANQUETS is much like professional service at other times. All of the same skills are required, but in addition to the server's normal duties, a greater awareness is required. Even more than usual, the server must be part of a smoothly coordinated team.

With events of this scale, very careful attention to money is crucial to the success of the restaurant or caterer. It makes sense that these large affairs be handled with contracts and deposits.

10 Tableside Service

THE PRACTICE OF TABLESIDE PREPARATION of food has been around for a long time, partly because it's a very special experience. There are few things we can do in the restaurant industry that are more impressive, or ultimately as satisfying, as cooking in the dining room.

There is a business side to this as well. First of all, cooking (or finishing or carving) food in the dining room can take some of the load off a busy station in the kitchen. Second, you can charge more money for tableside service. The cost of ingredients for a Caesar salad is the same whether it's made in the kitchen or at the table, but the restaurant can charge more for that salad when it's prepared in front of the guests, because of the added show.

The excitement and satisfaction of the guest, of course, can lead to the financial success of a restaurant in less obvious ways. Return business and word of mouth are hard to measure, but both are sure to increase as you boost the value perceived by the guests. Performing some food preparation in the dining room can be a valuable tool in that regard.

The Show

IT CAN BE INTIMIDATING to have guests watching intently as you work with a sharp knife to disjoint a Cornish hen or ignite alcohol so that flames shoot up from a copper pan. The only way to assuage the fear is experience: As the waiters repeat the preparation over and over, they will become more comfortable with it—and maybe even be able to enjoy the showmanship involved.

Tableside preparation can be appropriate to several types of establishment—it's not just the province of the most formal French restaurants. In fact, a casual eatery might be a great place to introduce flaming after-dinner coffees, which gives the server a chance to up-sell.

THE EQUIPMENT

The type and cost of tableside cooking equipment depends on which dishes are going to be prepared. At a bare minimum, say for a cold salad, the waiter needs a flat, stable surface at a convenient height, as well as the equipment to prepare the dish. With the move to more complex preparations and hot food, the need for specialized equipment increases. Here are some items that you should be familiar with when entering into the world of tableside preparation:

- **Guéridon:** Originally, the word guéridon referred to a small table that held a lamp or vase, supported by a tall column or sculpture of a human or mythological figure. However, in modern dining rooms the guéridon (at right) is a rolling trolley with a few shelves—the bottom ones used for storage of equipment and flatware, the top as the work surface. Guéridons should be easy to maneuver through the dining room. Typically, a restaurant will have one or two for the entire dining room.

- **Salad bowl:** A good-size unfinished wooden salad bowl is used for Caesar salads as well as other tableside salads. Unfinished wood is the material of choice because its mildly rough surface allows the waiter to crush the garlic and anchovy fillets into a paste that will dissolve into the dressing. A smooth-surfaced bowl would leave chunks of garlic and anchovy in the dressing, which could be jarring to the palate.

- **Réchaud:** The term *rechauffer* means "to reheat" in French, and the réchaud is a heating unit or burner that is used to heat up or cook food in the dining room (shown on page 240). Fuel sources vary, the most old-fashioned being

Guéridon with réchaud,
ready for service.

Réchaud with crêpe suzette pan.

alcohol. Canned heat (or Sterno) came into favor for a while, but the current popular choice is the portable butane or propane burner. There are equipment companies that make attractive metal holders that hide the workmanlike burners from the guests' view. Also available are guéridons that have built-in refillable butane burners. These trolleys are not inexpensive, but their sleek appearance adds a soigné touch to the dining room.

◻ **Copper pans:** Any cooking that will take place in the dining room should be done in attractive cookware. Copper is the most traditional and attractive metal surface (as well as the most expensive and difficult to maintain) of any sauté pans to be used in the dining room. Copper is also an excellent conductor of heat and will shorten the amount of time required to preheat the pan for cooking.

 Bimetal pans have a stainless-steel or tin interior surface that is bonded to the copper exterior. A stainless-steel lining is more durable and more common these days; a tin lining will eventually wear away, and the pan will have to be retinned.

 For many applications, most notably fish (both flat and round), an oval pan is usually best. However, the traditional crêpes suzette pan (shown on the réchaud at left) is a wide, round, shallow pan that allows the whole crêpe to be coated in sauce before it is folded into its serving shape.

◻ **Zabaglione pan:** One of the easiest tableside desserts is zabaglione (warm, whipped egg yolks with sugar and Marsala wine) served over fresh fruit. It is usually prepared in a hemispherical solid copper pan with a handle. The cooking is done over a réchaud or Sterno.

◻ **Café diablo set:** The dramatic coffee preparation café diablo requires a pan similar to a zabaglione pan, with a stand that holds the pan over a heat source so that the waiter can use both hands during the preparation.

◻ **Miscellaneous small equipment:** Cutting boards, carving and boning knives, pepper mills, soup tureens, and ladles are needed for various tableside dishes and must be in good working condition (i.e., knives sharpened) as well as attractive. Also, the serving spoon and fork should be the same length, to make one-handed service of food easier.

THE FOOD

When preparing food in the dining room we can't taste the food to check the seasoning, but there are two ways to deal with this limitation. One is to use ingredients that are inherently salty or well seasoned to begin with, such as anchovies, Parmigiano-Reggiano cheese, Worcestershire sauce, and prepared mustard. The other way to ensure you prepare well-seasoned food is to preseason some of the mise en place before it comes to the dining room. The server must depend upon the kitchen staff to achieve the goal of a well-seasoned dish.

Doneness of meat or fish is perhaps an even thornier problem. The most important factor is the amount of experience that the waiter has had preparing the dish. Uniformity of portion size is also important here. The fillet for steak Diane should be pounded to the same thickness every time, and the size of fish should stay within a narrow range. This will help to make cooking times similar. Whoever is involved in making this dish—the kitchen staff preparing the mise en place, the servers who will perform the tableside cooking—should have a chance to practice the dish at least once before making it for a guest.

It's not just seasoning that is difficult to do in the dining room. You may need to thicken a cream sauce directly in the sauté pan when there really isn't enough time to reduce it. The trick is that the kitchen staff has either reduced the cream ahead of time or added just enough arrowroot powder or other thickening agent to the cream to make it thicken as soon as the pan gets hot while you are preparing the sauce.

Flaming Alcohol

Adding a flammable substance (such as a liqueur) to a sauté pan that is right above an open flame can be very dangerous. If the stream of alcohol coming from the bottle is too close to the burner's flame, the fire can travel up that stream and into the bottle, causing the contents to explode and sending flaming alcohol and broken glass all over the guests and your staff. Such a tragedy can be avoided by removing the pan from the réchaud before adding the liqueur. Another method is to pull the pan halfway off the réchaud, add the liqueur to the back of the pan, then tilt it forward so the alcohol rushes to the front of the pan, where it ignites; this method is best suited for more experienced servers.

TABLESIDE COOKING TIPS

◻ Never, ever touch any of the food with your fingers (touching a banana's peel is fine, however).

◻ During most tableside cooking, hold the fork in your left hand, spoon in your right. Spoon and fork are held in the same hand only for serving.

◻ Put the mise en place on the guéridon in the order in which it will be used. It helps you to stay organized when nerves take over.

◻ If you need to clean off the spoon while cooking, don't bang it on the side of the sauté pan—just wipe off the bottom of the spoon with the fork.

◻ When sautéing, preheat the pan before adding the food. To avoid splattering the guest with hot fat, large pieces of meat or fish should be laid in the pan toward you—the opposite of what you would do in the kitchen.

◻ When moving the finished product to the plate, be careful not to let any of the food fall from the serviceware.

◻ If you drop something on the floor, don't acknowledge it, make a face, or even look at it—most of the guests will never notice. When you have finished plating, place a serviette over the dropped item and pick it up.

◻ Don't be overly meticulous. You don't have to turn over every banana slice or every shrimp in the pan. Guests get bored.

◻ Keep dishes relatively simple. Don't go overboard with the number of ingredients or complexity of the method.

Caesar Salad

This is one of the most famous salads in the world. It was created by Caesar Cardini when some regular customers came by his restaurant in Tijuana, Mexico, for a late-night snack. The kitchen was closed, and he didn't have a whole lot to work with, but he ended up creating a classic. Although we regard the pounded anchovy in the salad as necessary for an authentic flavor and balance in the salad, the truth is that Cardini used Worcestershire sauce, according to the "original" recipe he gave to Julia Child.

EQUIPMENT

Guéridon or work surface

Large wooden salad bowl, unfinished

Service spoon and fork

Peppermill filled with black peppercorns

Two chilled salad plates

INGREDIENTS

1 clove of garlic, peeled

1 anchovy fillet

1 tablespoon Dijon mustard

1 pasteurized egg yolk

½ lemon, seeds removed

4 ounces extra-virgin olive oil, in gooseneck bottle

1 head romaine lettuce, washed and dried, torn into bite-size pieces, rolled in clean cloth napkin

4 tablespoons grated Parmigiano-Reggiano

¾ cup croutons

METHOD

1. Place the garlic clove in the bowl. Break up the clove into small pieces with the fork. When the pieces are small enough, crush them with the back of the spoon to create a paste. Rub the garlic paste into the wooden bowl, leaving no visible pieces of garlic.

Hint: While crushing and rubbing the garlic, hold the bowl with the free fingers of your left (fork) hand.

2. Repeat first step with the anchovy fillet. Again, when finished there should be no visible sign of the garlic or anchovy.

3. Add mustard to the bowl and distribute evenly over the bottom of the bowl.

4. Add egg yolk, whisking lightly to combine with the mustard and to incorporate the flavor from the garlic and anchovy.

5. Take the lemon half and stick the fork into the cut side, just below the center, with the spoon held just below the fork. The fork will catch any pits that the prep cooks missed, while the juice drips into the spoon. Add the lemon juice to the bowl. Whisk it into the egg-mustard mixture with the fork.

6. Drizzle the olive oil in a circle around the side of the bowl, about halfway down from the edge. This allows the oil to pick up the anchovy and garlic flavors that were rubbed in. Whisk in the oil, creating the finished dressing. It should be slightly thick, with a pleasant yellow color, and should be heady with the aromas of garlic, anchovy, mustard, and lemon.

7. Add the lettuce to the bowl, along with half of the grated cheese. Toss the salad lightly to coat with the dressing and cheese.

8. Ask the guests if they would like some ground black pepper, and comply with their wishes. Add the croutons and toss again to combine.

9. Divide the salad between two chilled salad plates and garnish with the remaining grated cheese.

YIELD 2 SERVINGS

Steak Diane

A s with many other classic dishes, the origins of this dish are shrouded in the past. One story is that it was created for a member of the Vanderbilt family on her private train; another is that it's named after Diana, the Roman goddess of the hunt and the moon.

EQUIPMENT

Guéridon with réchaud

Copper sauté pan

Ramekins for mise en place

Peppermill filled with black peppercorns

Service spoon and fork

2 heated dinner plates

INGREDIENTS

Salt

2 three-ounce beef tenderloin medallions, pounded to ⅜-inch thick

2 ounces olive oil, in gooseneck bottle

1 ounce unsalted butter, in pieces

2 tablespoons finely minced shallots

1 tablespoon lemon juice

1 teaspoon Worcestershire sauce

1 ounce Armagnac or cognac

4 ounces demi-glace

1 tablespoon Dijon mustard

2 ounces heavy cream

1 tablespoon chopped parsley

METHOD

1. Light the réchaud, set on medium-high heat, and start preheating the pan.

2. Sprinkle salt and grind black pepper onto both sides of each medallion.

3. Put some olive oil in the pan and add a little butter. Remember, don't put too much fat in the pan—it's hard to remove it later before making the sauce.

4. When the pan is almost smoking, lay the meat into the pan toward yourself to avoid splattering the guests with hot fat.

5. If there are hot spots in the pan, move the steaks around the pan to achieve even browning. Once the first side is well browned, turn the steaks over.

6. While the steaks brown on the other side, add the shallots to the coolest area of the pan and stir them around until fragrant and translucent.

7. When the steaks are brown but still a bit undercooked, remove them from the pan and place on one of the warmed dinner plates. Invert the other plate over the steaks to keep them warm as you prepare the sauce.

8. Lower the heat to medium, then add the lemon juice and Worcestershire sauce to the pan. Add the Armagnac or cognac and scrape up the browned bits from the pan and let them dissolve into the sauce.

9. Add the demi-glace to the pan and whisk in the mustard with the fork.

10. Pour in enough cream to thicken the sauce without lessening its intensity. Allow it to reduce until just before nappé, then return the steaks and their juices to the sauté pan.

11. When the steaks have been coated in and warmed by the sauce, move them to the plate that covered them, and spoon sauce over the top. Garnish with parsley. Potatoes and vegetables should be brought warm from the kitchen as a side dish.

NOTE: *The dish can be prepared for two if the steaks are cut thicker, the searing temperature is lowered, and the sauce ingredients are doubled.*

YIELD 1 SERVING

Bananas Foster

T his dish was invented at Brennan's Restaurant in New Orleans in the 1950s, the result of Owen Brennan's request that the chef come up with a banana recipe for the breakfast menu. At the time, New Orleans was the major port of entry in the United States for South American bananas, and Brennan wanted to showcase the fruit. It's been said that Brennan's goes through 35,000 pounds of bananas annually just for this dish. It is simple to prepare and absolutely delicious. The bananas can come out of the kitchen already cut into slices, or you can use the method below.

EQUIPMENT

Guéridon with réchaud

Copper sauté pan

Ramekins for mise en place

Service spoon and fork

Utility knife or sharp dinner knife

Bottles with pour spouts for crème de banane and dark rum

Cinnamon shaker

INGREDIENTS

2 ounces unsalted butter, chilled, cut into pieces

2 ounces brown sugar

2 bananas, unpeeled

1 ounce crème de banane

1 ounce dark rum, such as Myers's

Powdered cinnamon, to taste

2 bowls vanilla ice cream

METHOD

1. Light the réchaud and set on a low flame. Put all the butter and sugar in the pan and set it over the flame to melt while you prepare the bananas.

2. Cut the banana peel at the base of the stem. Make two longitudinal cuts in the peel from the cut at the stem down to the base, approximately 1 inch apart. Switch from knife to fork and slip a tine of the fork under one segment of the peel, close to the stem cut. Roll one segment of banana peel off toward yourself (like opening a sardine can), leaving the rest of the peel in place.

3. Pick up the knife again and cut the banana into slices, from stem to bottom, while still inside the banana skin. The last cut should be right above that little nub at the

bottom. The very end of the banana has a tannic taste to it and should be left behind during step number 7.

4. Repeat the above steps with the second banana.

5. While preparing the bananas for cooking, you should have been keeping an eye on the sauce to make sure that it didn't burn. Now raise the heat of the réchaud, and stir the melted butter and sugar using the spoon and fork.

6. Remove the pan from the heat, add the crème de banane, return the pan to the réchaud, and stir until the sauce is smooth.

7. When the sauce has come together, add the bananas to the pan. Hold each banana close to the pan and parallel to it—you want to avoid splashing yourself or a guest with the hot sauce. Use the spoon to lift the upper edge of the banana peel away from the slices and gently pull at the slices with the service spoon. The slices should fall easily out of the banana peel and into the pan.

8. Stir the banana slices with some vigor so that they will be covered in sauce and heated on both sides. It is too time-consuming to flip each banana piece individually, so just turn over the ones that seem a bit raw on top. When the edges of the banana slices begin to look a little rounded, they are probably heated through. Very ripe bananas are more yielding, so be careful not to turn them into mush.

9. With the spoon, move the banana slices and most of the sauce to the half of the pan closest to you to make a clear space for the flambé. Place that area of the pan above the flame. For the rum to ignite, it has to be vaporized by contact with a hot pan—the alcohol vapor is what burns.

10. When the cleared part of the pan begins to smoke a bit or shows some signs of browning, pull the pan off the flame, add the rum to it, and roll the alcohol toward the front of the pan. As it flames up, put down the rum bottle and pick up the cinnamon shaker. Before the flames die down, add two shakes of cinnamon to the pan. The cinnamon adds a nice flavor, and also sparkles as it passes through the flame, sending a lovely aroma through the dining room.

11. Stir to combine, then serve over vanilla ice cream.

YIELD 2 SERVINGS

Caffè Stanzione

This flaming coffee is a crowd-pleaser, both because of the entertainment value and because it's delicious. The three liqueurs used can be mixed and matched, depending on the cuisine of the restaurant. There are, though, some rules. The first and last liqueurs are flambéed, so they should be around 80 proof (which is 40 percent alcohol). The proof level of the middle liqueur doesn't matter. In fact, the middle ingredient doesn't have to have to be alcohol at all; it could be a flavored syrup such as the ones used in coffee shops. Mix and match—experiment with different ingredients to create a signature coffee drink for your restaurant.

EQUIPMENT

Two heat sources (Sterno works fine)

Two heatproof stemmed glasses

Guéridon

Bottles with pour spouts for liqueur

Silver coffee server

Container for whipped cream

Metal ladle with pouring lip

Two cloth napkins, ready to be tied around the glasses

Two small plates lined with doilies

INGREDIENTS

1½ ounces brandy

10 to 12 ounces strong black coffee (decaffeinated if requested)

2 ounces dark crème de cacao

¾ cup whipped cream, unsweetened

2 ounces orange liqueur, such as Gran Gala or Grand Marnier

METHOD

1. Light heat sources.

2. Hold the glasses by the stem, with pinkies under the base for stability. Tilt the glasses over the two flames and rotate them slowly above the flames. The idea here is to heat

the glasses enough that the brandy will flame. Rotating the glasses keeps them from being shattered from the direct heat of the flame.

3. When the glasses are heated, place them on the guéridon and add half the brandy to each glass. Pick up the glasses and tilt them toward the flames. The flames will jump into the glasses.

4. Pour the flaming brandy from glass to glass five or six times. This is for show, but if the guests ask why you do this, tell them that it's to warm the glasses to keep the coffee from getting cold.

5. Put down the glasses again and add half the coffee to each glass. This will put out any flames that are still burning. Leave about 1½ inches of space at the top of the glass.

6. Add half the dark crème de cacao to each glass.

7. Add the whipped cream to the top of each drink—you want it to float on top.

8. Heat the metal ladle over one of the flames. Add all the orange liqueur to the ladle and hold it over the heat source until it flames.

9. Ladle half the flaming liqueur into each of the coffee glasses. Start with the ladle close to the glass, then raise the ladle as you pour, creating a stream of blue fire going into the glass. The more confident you get, the higher you can go.

10. Wrap or tie the napkins around the glasses, place them on the doily-covered plates, and serve.

NOTE: *To use this method, it has to be prepared two at a time because of the initial flambéing style, which was originally developed by legendary mixologist "Professor" Jerry Thomas at the El Dorado Bar in San Francisco for his Blue Blazer cocktail.*

YIELD 2 SERVINGS

11

A Clean and Safe Dining Room

A LASTING IMPRESSION is instantly conveyed by things like a stained tablecloth, soiled or water-spotted silverware, dirty glasses, or dirty fingernails. No matter how well designed the operation or how inventive the menu, poor hygiene reflects badly on the cleanliness and safety of the entire restaurant.

Cleanliness

SURVEYS CONDUCTED BY THE NATIONAL RESTAURANT ASSOCIATION have consistently ranked cleanliness as one of the most important customer considerations when choosing a restaurant. Here are a few of the several areas that need a systematic approach to maintaining a positive public image:

Salt and pepper shakers and sugar bowls: Every week, these should be emptied and run through the dishwasher as an evening closing duty, preferably on separate nights. Drying them overnight will enable an opening server to fill them at the beginning of the following shift. Salt and pepper shakers should be filled and wiped off daily, making sure the caps are tight.

Coffee cups: Since these become stained from tea and coffee, they may need to be soaked in special stain-removing chemicals available from detergent suppliers. Bleach should not be used to remove the stains. It can erode the enamel coating of the china, making the stains permanent.

Coffeepots: The pots used for serving coffee should be polished and clean at all times. Coffee oil residues on the inside may be removed with special coffee-stain remover. The brewing pots can be washed with soap and water, ice cubes and salt, or soaked with the stain remover. Proper rinsing is crucial.

Table bases: Table bases should be checked daily. Any that are dirty, or in need of paint, can negatively affect the dining experience.

Table tents: Table tents and other promotional materials should be checked for cleanliness and wear daily. They should be wiped clean, or replaced, as needed.

Windows and doors: All glass should be cleaned thoroughly before service. Doorknobs should be wiped clean (germs collect on doorknobs and can transfer to staff and guests).

Restrooms: A male and female employee should be assigned to check the restrooms on an hourly basis for cleanliness and the need for supplies.

Hygiene and Sanitation

GOOD HYGIENE IS IMPORTANT for everyone's well-being. It is just the start of the attention to the safety of the guest that is the concern of any professional server. Whenever you serve foods, you must practice sound sanitary practices. Since it is easy to pass a food-borne illness or toxin from one surface to another, keeping everything as clean as possible as safely as possible is in everyone's interest. Every establishment should have at least one employee who is knowledgeable about specific local and state health codes. Regardless of local laws, strict observance of the following rules is essential:

- Have physicals and dental examinations at least once a year.

- Take baths or showers daily.

- Use deodorants, but refrain from perfumes and colognes that can conflict with the food aromas or irritate your guests or coworkers.

- Keep hair clean, neat, and under control (no one wants to find hair in their food).

- Wear clean, suitable clothing at all times.

- Wash hands frequently with germicidal dispenser soap and hot water before starting work, after using the toilet, after smoking, and before preparing food.

- Remove jewelry or hair ornaments that may drop into food.

- Keep fingernails clean and unpolished.

- Cover any burns or cuts with clean rubberized finger bandages (finger cots).

- Keep hands away from hair, faces, arms, and eyes.

- Do not smoke, spit, whistle, or chew gum in the restaurant (or on the premises, if these activities are banned by the management).

- Cover your mouth and nose when sneezing or coughing and wash your hands immediately.

- Use an ice scoop or tongs for handling ice cubes—but don't leave scoops or tongs in the ice. Instead, keep them in a clean container or hung up on a hook.

- Never chill a bottle in the ice that is intended for service in a beverage.

- Use a first-aid kit immediately to treat minor accidental cuts or burns.

- Stay at home when ill to avoid spreading contagious diseases such as colds and flu. (Even if you are suffering from something noncontagious, guests may not know that and worry about their own health.)

- Use a clean spoon or fork each time you taste a food. For sauces, soups, and foods with a similar texture, use the two-spoon technique: Use a clean spoon to dip up a small amount and transfer it onto a second clean spoon. Clean and sanitize all equipment and utensils properly.

- Use only clean and sanitary side towels; replace them whenever they become soiled.

- Handle only the edges of plates, carry glasses by the stems or near the base, and touch silverware only by the handles when serving or clearing. (This topic is covered in greater detail in chapter 5.)

- Discard all perishable items from a bussed table (cream, butter, or bread). They could have been contaminated.

- Wear gloves or use utensils whenever handling uncooked foods, bread, butter, or garnishes (herbs, olives, fruit garnishes, and similar items).

Foot Care

Service personnel are required to stand for long periods of time, so special care must be taken to keep the feet and legs comfortable. Well-fitting, sturdy shoes will prove to be a worthwhile investment. Shoes should be selected that have ample room for toe movement and provide adequate arch support. For extra comfort, try wearing support hose and purchasing cushion insoles. During long work periods, changing shoes and socks will refresh tired feet and the application of foot powder or spray will help to reduce perspiration. Having several pairs of work shoes prevents having to wear the same shoes two days in a row.

After work, muscle tension can be relieved by that old standby, a warm bath. When soaking the feet, very hot water should be avoided —tired feet may not accurately gauge the temperature of the water and can be scalded.

Dishwashing

REGULAR, EFFECTIVE CLEANING of china, glassware, and flatware will prevent the spread of disease and infection. County, city, and state health regulations vary from place to place. It is best to contact the local health department to assure compliance with local requirements, water properties, and temperature levels.

An automatic dishwashing machine can maintain clean and sterile dishes only if it is operated properly. Certain basic steps must be followed in order to achieve clean dishes:

- Scrape all dishes thoroughly.

- Prerinse.

- Stack the dishes ready for racking.

- Do not overload the racks.

- Invert cups, glasses, and bowls.

- Wash flatware in a single layer.

- Make sure enough detergent is used.

- Maintain the proper water temperature—a minimum of 120°F for washing, and 190°F for sterilization. Where equipment or facilities cannot reliably produce or maintain these temperatures, chemical sanitizers can be injected during the rinse cycle.

- Drain, dry, and stack prior to storing in a clean cabinet.

- Do not handle serviceware more than necessary.

Glass washing is, no doubt, the most difficult part of the dishwashing operation. If possible, run glassware through the machine before other dishes for best results, or have a separate washing operation. Prior to washing, look for (and remove) lipstick or any other foreign material that may be difficult to remove in the wash cycle. After a banquet, wash the glasses after the china and flatware, but be sure that the machine has been refilled with clean water.

Place flatware in warm water and detergent for presoaking in order to loosen any food particles. After this procedure, run it through the machine on a wire rack, in single layers, for effective cleaning. Flatware should not be sorted and placed into divider cups—they can become "nested," preventing washing liquids from reaching all parts of the flatware. Air dry flatware and store it with the handles protruding to prevent any contamination.

Replace all chipped or cracked china and glassware. Not only are they difficult to clean and sanitize properly, but they may injure patrons as well. Some establishments do not allow employees to take chipped items home as this may lead to an increase in "accidentally" chipped items.

After the completion of all dishwashing, the area around the dish table and the machine must be thoroughly cleaned. Screens, spray arms, and rinse pipes should be removed and cleaned thoroughly. All water should be drained dry and the tank and machine properly cleaned inside and outside.

Food Safety

ONE OF THE GOLDEN RULES OF FOOD SAFETY is hot food hot and cold food cold. Keeping foods at safe temperatures matters to everyone. Soups should always be properly heated in the kitchen before they are placed in a steam table or in the service area, and the temperature should be monitored to make sure that it stays above 140°F. Perishable foods like milk, soft cheeses, butter, and salad dressings must be kept below 40°F.

Use the FIFO rule (first in, first out) to keep stocks rotated and fresh, and check expiration dates periodically.

Snacking and Drinking while Working

Snacking during set-up and service is not allowed as it involves the placing of fingers in or near the mouth. Those fingers then touch guest plates, bar fruit, glasses, and numerous other items that could spread germs. In fact, those fingers already touched menus, doorknobs, and coffeepot handles (potentially laden with other people's germs) before they went to the server's mouth—possibly exposing the server to disease. These are good reasons for frequent hand washing with soap and hot water.

Whatever you are eating or drinking, do it in an appropriate area, away from the dining room. The containers should be clearly marked with their owners' names. An uncovered container can spill and contaminate food, surfaces, or serving utensils, which could make others sick.

Many items needed for service are kept in the walk-in refrigerator along with kitchen items. Raw meat products (such as chicken, beef, pork, and fish) should be stored below other items so they will not drip on, and possibly contaminate, the contents of the refrigerator. Milk, butter, lemons, and other server needs should be stored on higher shelves, above the meat and fish.

With more and more concern about health and sanitation, many restaurants have developed HACCP (Hazard Analysis Critical Control Point) plans for perishable items, designed to reduce the possibilities of food-borne illnesses. While HACCP plans were originally created for use in the kitchen, systems may be set up for dairy products. For example, an inventory list may be developed for the replenishment of pantry items for each day's service. This list could include a place to record the temperature of the refrigerator and next to each item a column could be available for the expiration date listed on the carton or package. This becomes a constant reinforcement for the servers to check on critical information. Spoiled milk may not make someone ill, but it reflects poorly on the restaurant when it curdles in a guest's coffee.

Sanitation is also an issue when serving takeout or "doggie bags." Since the restaurant has no idea how the guests will handle the food when it leaves, written instructions can be helpful. Even a verbal reminder to guests not to leave the leftover chicken leg in the hot car while shopping can prevent a bout of food poisoning—and will be appreciated.

Safety

A CONSCIENTIOUS EFFORT must be made to assure the personal safety of everyone in the facility—guests and fellow workers alike.

Accidents do not just happen. More appropriately called "incidents," they are usually caused by neglect, carelessness, thoughtlessness, and ignorance. Therefore, most incidents can be avoided. This rest of this chapter's focus is on safety practices in the dining room.

FALLS

People can easily fall over furniture, cords, and equipment. For this reason, nothing should be left in paths of traffic. Never leave anything in stairwells or near doors. To minimize the chance of tripping, electrical cords should be kept off the floor. Furniture, if temporarily moved, must be put back where it belongs as soon as possible—and equipment should be put away immediately after its use. Falls on stairs may be caused by a loose carpet thread or a faulty step or railing. Such disrepair should be reported to the manager at once. Be sure to keep chairs out of dining room traffic aisles. All servers should be aware of women's purses under the tables since the handles may trip someone in the aisles. If a bag or its strap is discovered protruding into or obstructing a walkway, servers should not move them, but ask its owner to move it to a safer place.

Falls account for the largest percentage of accidents in food-service operations. Some additional causes are

- Wet or oily floors, or spills that have not yet been wiped up. Spills are often caused by someone whose hands are already too full—therefore when a spill occurs, it should be wiped up by the first available employee (rather than waiting for the person who caused the spill to clean it). Someone should stand guard by the spill to alert others while another employee gets the tools and materials necessary for cleaning up the spill.

- Unsuitable shoes can cause accidents. Shoes that are perfect in the dining room are not necessarily safe in the kitchen. Safe nonskid rubber soles can be applied to any shoe bottom.

- Unsafe ladders, chairs, and windowsills (a safe ladder is one that is tall enough to permit working comfortably while standing at least one step from the top).

LOADING, LIFTING, AND CARRYING OF FOOD TRAYS

Many restaurant incidents can be prevented through the correct handling of trays in the dining room. Proper balance, with equal distribution of items, is essential for transporting food and related items. Certain guidelines should be followed in loading a tray to ensure safe and sanitary handling:

- Use a tray with a cork or nonskid surface or one that is covered with a damp serviette to prevent items from slipping.

- Stack and lift heavy trays properly (see chapter 6, page 142, for more details).

Carrying a stack of plates.

- Open plates containing food should be held well away from the server's hair.

Practice is essential in developing tray and dish-handling skills. Never carry more than you can manage. The way you carry dishes without a tray is just as important as on a tray or in a bus tub. Resting a stack of plates in the bend of the arm should be avoided, as the stack may collapse. Instead, to carry a stack of clean plates, cover the stack with a clean napkin and carry directly in front of, and slightly away from, the body as shown on facing page.

LIFTING AND CARRYING TRAYS

The carrying of heavy trays or awkward loads should not be attempted until the server has practiced enough (see photo to right) to do so confidently.

Carrying a tray.

When lifting a tray, six inches of the tray should project over the edge of the tray stand, side table, shelf, or counter on which the tray is resting. Place the flattened palm under the edge of the tray, toward the middle of its broad side, and grip the edge of the tray with the free hand. If the tray is heavy, the hand should be kept there. Bend carefully at the knees and lift with the legs and back, not the arms. The server slides the tray out and onto the flattened palm or fingertips. To carry a tray at shoulder level (known as a "high carry"), hold the upper arm close to the body and keep the elbow securely against the body. Resting the tray on the shoulder does give some additional support, but should be avoided as the tray can easily become unbalanced, allowing items to slide off and fall. The high carry is particularly effective when a tray must be carried through a crowd.

When carrying a tray at waist level (such as a cocktail tray), the shoulders should be kept back. Slouching forward will make the tray unstable. While the tray may touch the forearm, the load should not rest there. Rest the weight of the tray on the hand. If the weight rests on the forearm, the tray can easily tip.

To maneuver through a crowd, guard the tray with the unoccupied hand. Guests must never be allowed to remove drinks from a cocktail tray unless the server is supporting the tray with both hands. When a tray is supported by only one hand, the sudden shift in the balance of weight will cause it to tip.

Some servers prefer to rest the tray on their spread fingertips instead of their flattened palm. They feel it gives more balance and maneuverability. Only experience can tell what will work best for a particular person. Try both methods but practice with an empty tray first, then when that feels comfortable, practice with a loaded tray.

If a door is hinged on the right, the tray is carried on the left hand; if hinged on the left, the tray is carried on the right hand. This leaves you with a free hand to open the door and protect or balance the tray as you walk through. However, if either the right or left hand is not strong enough to support a loaded tray, the stronger hand should be used.

BUS TUBS

Bus tubs or boxes are often used in operations with a high turnover rate, where speed is important. When loading a bus tub, rest it either on a rolling cart or a tray stand. Bus tubs, like trays, should never be set directly on tables or chairs.

- Place refuse into one corner of the bus tub.

- Load the largest dishes first.

- Place heavy items in the center. Items like cups and bowls may be nested.

- Glasses should be placed upright to one side; do not put anything into glasses that might cause them to chip, crack, or tip over.

- Flatware should go on the opposite side from the refuse so it is not accidentally tossed in the trash.

- Load butter dishes, creamers, or other food receptacles last.

- If no rolling cart is used, carry the bus tub over the shoulder or in front of the body, ideally with a clean cloth covering the soiled wares.

TEN RULES OF RESTAURANT SAFETY

1. Safety is serious. Don't take chances with your own or others' welfare. If you see a spill or broken glass on the floor, alert those around you and either stay there yourself to warn others or get someone else to do so until it is cleaned up.

2. If a guest has a handbag or some other personal object on the floor by the table ask the owner to move it or offer to move it or place it in the coat check. Members of the floor staff might trip over it and hurt themselves or the guests.

3. Report all injuries to management, no matter how slight, and get immediate first aid.

4. Never run in the restaurant. It is easy to get hurt, or hurt someone else. Also, if guests see someone running, it can make them nervous, thinking that something might be wrong.

5. Use the correct doors into and out of the kitchen. When using the in door, go all of the way in without stopping. There is a good chance that someone is right behind you walking just as fast as you are. By stopping in the doorway, you can both get hurt. Same goes with the out door.

6. Avoid horseplay and practical jokes. Harmless fun can result in injury.

7. Report all defective equipment. Obey safety rules when you are working with any equipment.

8. Avoid backing up or making sudden, jerky movements.

9. Always wear shoes with nonskid soles.

10. Always store cleaning chemicals far away from any food products or serviceware.

FIRE SAFETY

Fires are dangerous for two main reasons: First, there are the injuries and destruction caused by the actual fire, and second, there is the panic that overcomes people in a fire that stops them from thinking and acting rationally. Practicing fire safety encompasses both preventing fires and doing the right thing if a fire breaks out.

The best way to fight fire is to prevent its occurrence. As with "incident" prevention, fire prevention depends on the application of common sense by everyone in the operation. Service personnel must be sure to follow these measures:

- See that ashtrays and receptacles are provided and used in all appropriate areas of the dining room.

- If candles or oil lamps are in use, watch to be sure that napkins or menus do not catch fire.

- Take care in cleaning ashtrays. They should never be emptied directly into wastebaskets or other rubbish containers.

- Never use defective electrical outlets. They should be reported to the manager.

- Never use an improper extension cord (too long or rated too low for intended use), or adapters (plugs have three prongs because the ground is important—do not attempt to defeat their purpose through the use of two-pronged adapters).

- Never overload a circuit.

- Report all frayed cords and loose connections to the manager.

- Take special care when lighting gas jets or alcohol burners on guéridons.

- Extinguish all flames before moving a guéridon in the dining room.

- Exercise extreme caution when flambéing food in the dining room. Always remove the pan from the flame before pouring the alcohol. Keep guéridons at a safe distance from the guests, draperies, sprinklers, and heat sensors.

Every establishment must have a prefire plan in effect. This is an orderly sequence of steps that is coordinated with the local fire department, in compliance with local building codes.

If a fire does break out, the emergency action taken in the first five minutes is extremely important. To be prepared in the event of a fire, the staff should be trained to know the floor plan of the area and the entire building, be familiar with exit routes and alternatives, and know the exact location of fire extinguishers and how to use them. Every member of the staff should be trained in assisting guests to leave the building safely in the event of an emergency.

If a fire breaks out:

- Do not panic.

- Pull the nearest fire alarm box.

- Notify the main switchboard and fire company as to the exact location and nature of the fire.

- Take the reservation list and logbook from the front desk (it contains information about the number—and locations—of people inside the building).

- Assist guests to safety.

- Send someone to explain any special concerns to the firefighters when they arrive.

BURNS

Some dining room equipment and utensils can cause severe burns.

Always move or position hot plates and platters with the aid of a serviette. Verbally inform guests and other service staff whenever any serviceware is hot. Leave a side towel draped over the cover or at the edge of any hot service items. Hot beverages are another potential hazard (tea is brewed with boiling water, and coffee is best brewed between 205° and 208°F). Remember, service should never be rushed: take care in transporting hot liquids, especially when moving through a crowded dining room.

All serious burn injuries should receive medical treatment immediately.

CHOKING

Choking on food is one of the leading causes of accidental death. Unless treated, a choking victim will die in four minutes. Choking victims may exhibit some of these symptoms:

- Panic

- Inability to breathe

- Inability to speak

- Clutching their throats

- Blue skin

- Collapse

Very often, other guests do not notice that someone is choking—because they tend to pay the most attention to someone who is speaking.

The Heimlich maneuver is generally considered the best first aid for choking. Caution is recommended, however. Any administrator of first aid must, according to law, exercise "reasonable care and skill" or else be liable for negligence. It is recommended that dining room personnel be certified in the use of the Heimlich maneuver and in CPR.

EMERGENCY PROCEDURES

In order to be prepared for any kind of accident or emergency, each food-service establishment must have its own specific course of action. As there is seldom time to consult a book when faced with an emergency, be aware beforehand of what to do and how to do it. In a dining room, there can be a variety of emergencies, some of which can be dealt with easily by defusing a situation with a calm, reasoned approach. Others are more serious and require additional action, and perhaps the involvement of others to keep everyone safe.

As soon as the emergency has been handled, write a report covering the details, location, and severity of the accident.

Emergency exits must be kept clear and the doors should open easily. Fire extinguishers should be in working order and easy to locate. Contact phone numbers should be kept current. These procedures and other general emergency strategies should be reviewed periodically.

Here are some general guidelines to follow whenever an emergency occurs:

- Do not panic.

- Call or send for help immediately and give explicit details as to the location and nature of the emergency. If calling emergency services, do not hang up until they do. More information may be required, or they may be able to offer some advice over the phone about temporary assistance to be administered until professional help arrives.

- Do what needs to be done in a logical order.

- When giving first aid, do not attempt more than you are qualified to do.

- Things can be replaced, people cannot. Do not endanger yourself or anyone else.

Conclusion

A CLEAN, SAFE DINING ROOM is the foundation of good service. Safety matters to everyone, from the owner to the staff to the guest. Maintaining food safety, preventing fires, avoiding accidents like slips and falls, and having a plan in case of fires and other emergencies are all part of your professional training.

Appendix

This Appendix contains a number of resources that can help readers of this book to become more remarkable servers. The Glossary of Technical Terms defines some of the terminology that is unique to the profession. Because some of these terms sound very like one another, a second glossary, called Frequently Confused French Culinary Terms, has been included. A third listing of terms and expressions, a Glossary of Restaurant Slang Terms, is included to clarify some of the more mysterious—and sometimes amusing—aspects of our professional jargon. The Bibliography suggests a number of excellent books that can aid in the acquisition of professional knowledge, as do the listings of Periodicals, Trade and Professional Groups, Internet Sources, and Recommended Videos/DVDs.

GLOSSARY OF TECHNICAL TERMS

À LA CARTE (Fr.) A means of meal selection in which the guests compose their own meals by selecting from the menu, where each item is separately priced.

A menu of this type.

Opposite of prix fixe.

À LA RUSSE (Fr.) Russian service, traditionally performed by setting an empty plate in front of each guest from their right side, then serving the food from platters from the guests' left side. Service is provided by moving counter clockwise around the table.

À LA MINUTE (Fr.) cooked at the moment.

À LA SERVIETTE (Fr.) Served on a fancy folded napkin on china.

AL DENTE (It.) Literally, "to the tooth," usually refers to pasta or vegetables that have not been over-cooked—that is, they still maintain a bit of crispness.

AMUSE-GUEULE or AMUSE-BOUCHE (Fr.) Either term is commonly used to refer to a small complimentary canapé or hors d'oeuvre served after the order has been taken.

APÉRITIF Literally, "to open," this is the first drink offered. It should be dry since it is meant to enhance the appetite rather than sweet, which would satiate the appetite. Dry fortified or aromatized wines, bitters, vermouths, or wine cocktails such as kir and kir royale are most common.

ASSIETTE (Fr.) Plate, dish

AU PLATEAU (Fr.) Served on a platter.

BANQUET SERVICE Refers to type(s) of service used to serve parties, i.e. Russian, American, butler, buffet, French, or any combination of the above.

BIMETAL Heavy-gauge oval or round pan with white metal inside and copper outside. Used for tableside cooking and service.

BRUT Very dry sparkling wine.

BUSSING Clearing off tables and dining areas.

CANAPÉ Cold hors d' oeuvre on a piece of toast, bread or cracker.

CAPITAINE (Fr.) Captain in French service. Working captain in charge of a maximum of three rings. Seats customers, oversees service and actively helps on the floor with the preparations when needed.

CARTE DES METS (Fr.) À la carte menu in French.

CARTE DES VINS (Fr.) Wine list in French.

CARVING This term applies to an array of preparations on the dining room floor, replacing the following French classical terms:

> Slicing charcuterie or pâtés, "couper à travers."
>
> Slicing meat, "couper en tranches."
>
> Portioning small game or poultry, "decoupage."
>
> Deboning and filleting fish, "desossage"
>
> Peeling and cutting fruits, "épluchage"

CHEESE BOARD Can be any shape or material (depending on needs) but it should offer between four and eight cheeses. The cheeses offered should consist of a total of five ounces per person.

CORNICHON (Fr.) A very small sour pickle often served with pâté.

COUVERT (COVER) (Fr.) Individual set-up for one guest.

CRUDITÉS (Fr.) Small cuts of fresh vegetables offered with a dip, generally served as a stationary hors d'oeuvre.

DÉBARRASSAGE (Fr.) To clear off the table.

DECANTER A wine carafe used to separate the sediment from older wines and fortified wines. To decant: remove the entire foil in order to see through the neck of the bottle. Place a candle on the table so the flame shines through the neck. Slowly empty the liquid contents of the bottle of wine into the decanter, leaving the sediment in the bottle. Decanting is performed at the beginning of the meal to allow the wine to get to room temperature and to "breathe."

DE-CRUMBING Cleaning the guest's table of the bread crumbs and other debris. In all types of service this should be done at least once during the meal, usually before dessert. Use the crumber or a rolled napkin and sweep debris onto a service plate.

DÉCOUPAGE (Fr.) To disjoint and portion; refers to poultry and flying game served via French service.

DÉGUSTATION (Fr.) A tasting menu of wines and sometimes food, in which many dishes are offered in small portions.

DEMITASSE Literally, "half cup," a small cup used for espresso.

DEMI-SEC Literally, "half sweet," the term refers to a sweet sparkling wine.

DEUCE (slang) A table for two.

EN PAPILLOTE (Fr.) Cooked in a parchment package.

ENTRÉE (Fr.) In the U.S., it means the main course of the meal, or the protein component of a plate. In Europe, entrée refers to a separate course served before the main course. An entrée can be any of the following:

> Vegetable dish
>
> Eggs
>
> Starch
>
> Offal
>
> Composed salad
>
> Fish, shellfish, mollusk
>
> White meat or poultry
>
> Red meat or game

ENTRECÔTE (Fr.) "Between the ribs," a cut of meat. Sized from petite to double. Carved like Chateaubriand when large.

ENTREMET (Fr.) "Between courses." Simple sweet course made from fruits, puddings, mousses, pies, bavarians, tarts, simple cakes, sherbet, sorbet, ice cream, or any combination of the above.

FILET/FILLET The choice undercut of meat (such as filet mignon) or fish served off the bone.

FLAMBÉ (Fr.) Dramatic tableside preparation in which brandy or liqueur is poured over a food item, then set aflame to complete the cooking.

FLATWARE Service eating utensils, "silverware" implies it is silver rather than stainless.

FRIANDS (Fr.) A little something extra—similar to mignardises.

GRANITÉ A sweet ice with no fat or egg.

GRATINÉE (Fr.) French onion soup, topped with a crouton and cheese, and browned under a salamander or broiler.

GRATIN (Fr.) A baked dish that is often topped with cheese and/or bread crumbs, then browned under a salamander or broiler.

GUÉRIDON (Fr.) A rolling service cart.

HOLLOWWARE Soup tureens, water pitchers, coffeepots, large bowls, platters, silver trays, etc.

HORS D'OEUVRE (Fr.) Traditionally a warm appetizer, but often includes any tidbit served before the meal, either passed butler style, at a station where the food is carved or prepared, or in a stationary display.

INTERMEZZO (It.) A light course that acts as an "intermission" between the heavier courses of a long meal. Traditionally served after the fish course. Usually a small glass of ice, sorbet, or trou normande. Used to cleanse the palate or ease digestion.

LAGNIAPPE (Fr.) A small complimentary treat, "a little something extra."

LINEN Or napery, any cloth used by the servers or on the tables or side stands; napkins, table cloths, serviettes.

LOG BOOK Calendar book kept in restaurants to store information used in predicting, number of covers, and the effect upon future business of weather or outside events.

MANDOLINE A kitchen tool for making thin slices of vegetables.

MIGNARDISES (Fr.) The "sweetest of the sweets," served with coffee including; truffles, chocolates, caramels, dipped fruits and nuts, macaroons, mints, or small cookies.

MISE EN PLACE (Fr.) "To put everything in its place," a set-up of required items or ingredients.

MOLLETON (Fr.) Undercloth on a table used to absorb noise and spills. Otherwise known as a silence cloth.

NAPPE (Fr.) Tablecloth, or the description of a food item covered with sauce.

NAPPER (Fr.) To coat with a sauce.

NAPPERON (Fr.) Top cloth.

N.V. No vintage; in reference to wines.

PLACE SETTING Individual set-up for the guest. See couvert.

PLAT (Fr.) Dish, plate

PLATEAU (Fr.) Platter

POINT SYSTEM A system of distributing gratuities according to seniority or rank in the service brigade. More common in Europe.

PROTOCOL Set of rules concerning priorities in arriving, seating, and sequence of service during official or casual events like state dinners or dining in a restaurant.

> **Social:** Children first, then elderly ladies, ladies, elderly gentleman, gentleman by age

> **Diplomatic:** By rank

> **Corporate:** By importance

> **Clergy:** By hierarchy

Usually the guest of honor is the first and the host is the last to be seated and served. The host will taste the wine first and be served last.

RÉCHAUD (Fr.) Hot plate, food warmer, cooking utensil used mostly for guéridon service.

REDRESSER (Fr.) To plate and garnish dishes with food taken from pans, platters, or bowls.

RESERVATION BOOK Calendar book used in restaurants to record the name, time, amount of people, special requests, and telephone number.

RINCE-DOIGTS (Fr.) Finger bowl

RÔTI (Fr.) Literally, "roasted," the main course.

SAUCES (see "Frequently Confused French Culinary Terms")

SAUCE BOAT China or silver hollowware container for sauce served on the side.

SAVORIES Salty hors d'oeuvre or seeded bread rolls served in lounges, pubs, and bars used to increase liquor sales; also a course near the end of a classic seventeen-course French dinner.

SERVICE PLATE A plate with a napkin folded in four on top. It is used to bring serviceware to the table. Sometimes referred to as STP (silverware transport plate).

SERVICE SET Set of serving fork and spoon.

SERVICE TOWEL A napkin folded in three parts along its length, draped over the left arm during service. It is used to handle clean or hot items and should be replaced if soiled.

SERVIETTE (Fr.) Napkin.

SHERBET Frozen fruit juice and sugar with milk, cream, or egg.

SILVER Silver or silver-plated flatware.

SMORGASBORD Scandinavian-style buffet, also hors d'oeuvre buffet

SOIGNÉ (Fr.) French term for service. Literally "caring" or "excellent."

SORBET (Fr.) Frozen fruit juice or tea with sugar, an ice made without fat or egg yolk. Egg white may be used in some sorbets. Used as an intermezzo after the fish course to cleanse the palate for the next course. Replaced the trou normande.

STATLER A square table with flip-up sides to make a larger, usually round table.

STEMWARE Stemmed glassware.

TABLE D'HÔTE (Fr.) Pre-set multicourse menu offered at a set price.

TROU NORMANDE (Fr.) A precurser to sorbet as the intermezzo, a traditional trou normande was a bottle of Calvados (from Normandy) encased in a small block of ice. This was meant to "burn a hole" (trou) in one's stomach to make room for the next course. A room temperature brandy was often substituted.

UNDERLINER Additional larger plate on which plated food is served.

FREQUENTLY CONFUSED FRENCH CULINARY TERMS

SAUCES

AÏOLI Garlic mayonnaise.

AMORICAINE (sometimes seen as "Americaine") Lobster butter added to tomato sauce.

BÉARNAISE Hollandaise with vinegar and tarragon.

BÉCHAMEL White sauce made with milk, flavored with onions and cloves, and thickened with white roux.

BEURRE BLANC White wine and butter.

BORDELAISE Demi-glace, red wine, shallots, butter, and peppercorns; garnished with marrow.

BOURGUIGNONNE Demi-glace with Burgundy, shallots, butter and peppercorns.

HOLLANDAISE Egg yolks, lemon juice, and butter.

JUS Juice from roasting.

JUS LIÉ Thickened jus to make a gravy.

MORNAY Béchamel with egg yolks, Parmesan, and Gruyère.

PÉRIGOURDINE Demi-glace with foie gras purée; garnished with truffles.

POIVRADE Demi-glace with pepper, mirepoix, herbes, red wine, and butter.

PROVENÇALE Shallots, garlic, white wine, tomato concassé, fines herbes, and butter.

RÉMOULADE Mayonnaise, capers, Dijon mustard, anchovies, and gherkins

INGREDIENTS

POISSON Fish.

POUSSIN Young hen.

COOKWARE

TERRINE A container for making pâté. The pâté itself is often referred to as a terrine.

TUREEN A large container with ladle holding several portions of soup. This can be used for family service as well as Russian, French, or English service.

COOKWARE

Terrine

Tureen

POTATOES

Darphin

Dauphine

Dauphinoise

POTATOES

DARPHIN Shredded potatoes that have been formed into a flat round pancake and sauteéd in oil, then baked.

DAUPHINE Puréed potatoes that have been mixed with choux batter, rolled into croqûettes and deep fried.

DAUPHINOISE Thinly sliced potatoes typically layered with cream, butter, and cheese then baked. Similar to the American scalloped potatoes.

DUCHESSE Pureéd potatoes that have been enriched with egg yolks and piped from pastry bag.

FRITES Deep-fried battonets of potato (French fries).

GAUFRETTE (Fr.) Potatoes, thinly sliced with a waffle cut on a mandoline and deep-fried.

OTHER

NAPPE Tablecloth.

NAPPER To coat with a sauce.

NAPPERON Top cloth.

PÂTE A batter used for baking.

PÂTÉ A mixture of ground meats formed in a terrine.

GLOSSARY OF RESTAURANT SLANG TERMS

86:

1. No longer available, as in "86 veal chop"—important in communicating to the service staff.

2. No longer of any use so it should be thrown away, as in "86 it."

Supposed Origin(s):

1. Possibly from the depression era; soup pots held 85 cups of soup so when the pot was empty, it was called out, "86 soup."

2. Believed to be from a nautical term: the ship must be at 86 fathoms before garbage can be thrown overboard.

3. Suggested to have originated as the last stop on a Chicago train line, "86—all out."

4. The term (enthusiastically adopted by bartenders and restaurant employees) actually originated in soda-fountains during the 1920s. All of the soda jerks' codes were numeric, such as "55" for root beer, "99" for the boss, "98" for the second in command (also "pest"), and "87 1/2" for "there's a good-looking girl out front." (Mary Morris and William Morris, *Morris Dictionary of Word and Phrase Origins,* 2nd ed. New York: HarperCollins, 1988).

68: The item is once again available. For example, if the veal was delivered late and was just fabricated prior to opening, the service staff would be notified, as in "68 veal chop." Usage not as common as 86.

ACE: A single diner at a table.

ALL DAY: A total count of a certain menu item by adding up all the dupes. May be in a variety of stages of preparedness.

COVER:

1. the mise en place for a single place setting.

2. a guest, as in the number of covers served.

DEUCE: A two-top, or a table for two.

DROP: To serve or present the item, as in "Drop the check on table 21."

DUPE: Abbreviation for duplicates, can be hand-written or computer-generated (sometimes referred to as a "chit")

F & B: The food and beverage department.

FIRE: Start preparing the next course. Can be fired by the service staff or chef/expediter, depending on house procedures; as in "Fire main course on table 16." Appetizers and desserts are generally automatically fired when ordered unless otherwise indicated by the server.

FOUR-TOP: A table for four. Similar uses include those for other size tables, such as "six-top," or "eight-top."

IN THE WEEDS: More multiple tasks required than can be handled; needing to be in several places at once. Also referred to as "weeded." Result of being "slammed."

LAGNIAPPE: Louisiana Creole term for "a little something extra."

ON THE FLY: Needed right away, usually as a result of an error or miscommunication, as in "One trout on the fly."

PICK-UP: Announcing to the kitchen line that the table is ready and flatware in place for the next course, as in "Pick-up pasta course on table 34."

REACH-IN: A free-standing refrigerator unit. If below a counter top, it may be referred to as a "low-boy."

SLAMMED: Having your entire station seated at once. This often results in slamming the kitchen as well, but can be avoided by getting the order to the kitchen as each order is taken rather than taking all the orders at once, and delivering them together.

SOS: Sauce on the side.

STIFF: To leave a restaurant without leaving a tip (see walk-outs).

STP: Silverware transport plate. The plate with folded napkin used to take clean flatware to a table.

WALK-IN:

1. the large refrigerator that you can walk into. Usually stores butter and milk products for front of house.

2. guests without a reservation. Avoid referring to them as "walk-ins" (see chapter 4).

WALK-OUTS: Guests who leave the restaurant without paying for their meals.

Bibliography

The bibliography includes a number of excellent books that can aid in the acquisition of professional knowledge. In addition, there are listings of periodicals; government, trade, and professional groups; Internet sources; and recommended videotapes.

BOOKS

Amendola, Joseph. *Ice Carving Made Easy*. New York: National Restaurant Association, 1969.

Andrioli, Sergio. *Tableside Cookery*. New York: Van Nostrand Reinhold, 1990.

Aresty, Esther B. *The Delectable Past: The Joys of the Table—from Rome to the Renaissance, from Queen Elizabeth I to Mrs. Beeton. The Menus, the Manners—and the Most Delectable Recipes of the Past, Masterfully Re-created for Cooking and Enjoying Today*. New York: Simon and Schuster, 1964.

Axler, Bruce H. *Profitable Catering*. Indianapolis: ITT, 1974.

Axler, Bruce H., and Carol A. Litrides. *Food and Beverage Service*. New York: Wiley, 1990.

Brett, Gerard. *Dinner Is Served: A Study in Manners*. Hamden, CT: Archon Books, 1969.

Collins, Philip. *The Art of the Cocktail: 100 Classic Cocktail Recipes*. San Francisco: Chronicle Books, 1992.

Cullen, Max O'Rell. *How to Carve Meat, Game, and Poultry*. New York: Dover Publications, 1976.

Dahmer, Sondra J. *The Waiter and Waitress Training Manual*. Boston: Cahners Books, 1974.

Dalby, Andrew, and Sally Grainger. *The Classical Cookbook*. Malibu, CA: J. Paul Getty Museum, 1996.

FitzGibbon, Theodora. *The Pleasures of the Table*. Oxford: Oxford University Press, 1981.

Flower, Barbara, and Elisabeth Rosenbaum. *The Roman Cookery Book: A Critical Translation of The Art of Cooking by Apicius for Use in the Study or Kitchen*. London and New York: Peter Nevill Ltd., 1958.

Fuller, John. *Modern Restaurant Service: A Manual for Students and Practitioners*. London: Hutchinson, 1983.

Gauntner, John. *The Sake Handbook*. Singapore: Yenbooks (Charles E. Tuttle Co.), 1997.

Giblin, James. *From Hand to Mouth, or How We Invented Knives, Forks, Spoons, and Chopsticks, and the Table Manners to Go with Them*. New York: Crowell, 1987.

Ginders, James R. *A Guide to Napkin Folding*. Boston: CBI Publishers, 1980.

Gluck, Sandra. *The Best of Coffee*. San Francisco: Collins, 1994.

Griffin, Jill. *Customer Loyalty: How to Earn It, How to Keep It*. San Francisco: Jossey-Bass, 1997.

Gutek, Barbara A. *The Dynamics of Service: Reflections on the Changing Nature of Customer/Provider Interactions*. San Francisco: Jossey-Bass, 1995.

Harris, R. Lee. *The Customer Is King!* Milwaukee: ASQC Quality Press, 1991.

Hazlitt, W. Carew. *Old Cookery Books*. London: Eliot Stock, 1886 (reissued Detroit: Gale Research Co., 1968).

Herbst, Sharon Tyler and Ron Herbst. *The New Food Lover's Companion*. 4th ed. Hauppauge, NY: Barron's, 2007.

Hetzer, Linda. *The Simple Art of Napkin Folding: 94 Fancy Folds for Every Tabletop Occasion*. New York: Hearst, 1991.

Illy, Francesco, and Riccardo Illy. *The Book of Coffee*. New York, London, and Paris: Abbeville, 1992.

Jenkins, Steven. *Cheese Primer*. New York: Workman, 1996.

Kahan, Nancy. *Entertaining for Business*. New York: Crown, 1990.

Kalish, Susan S. *The Art of Napkin Folding*. Philadelphia: Running Press, 1988.

Katona, Christie. *Cappuccino/Espresso: The Book of Beverages*. San Leandro, CA: Bristol, 1993.

Kemp, Jim. *Stylish Settings: The Art of Tabletop Design*. New York: Gallery Books, 1990.

Ketterer, Manfred. *How to Run a Successful Catering Business*. Rochelle Park, NJ: Hayden, 1982.

King, Carol A. *Professional Dining Room Management*. 2nd ed. New York: Van Nostrand Reinhold, 1988.

Knox, Kevin. *Coffee Basics: A Quick and Easy Guide*. New York: Wiley, 1997.

Koch, Maryjo. *Coffee: Delectables for All Seasons*. San Francisco: Collins, 1995.

Kolpan, Steven, Brian Smith, and Michael Weiss. *Exploring Wine*. New York: Wiley, 1996.

Kramer, Matt. *Making Sense of Wine*. New York: Morrow, 1989.

Labensky, Steven, Gaye G. Ingram, and Sarah R. Labensky (compilers). *Webster's New World Dictionary of Culinary Arts*. 2nd ed. Upper Saddle River, NJ: Pearson Prentice Hall, 2006.

Lash, Linda M. *The Complete Guide to Customer Service*. New York: Wiley, 1989.

Latham, Jean. *The Pleasure of Your Company: A History of Manners and Meals*. London: A. and C. Black, 1972.

Lillicrap, Dennis R., and John A. Cousins. *Food and Beverage Service*. 7th ed. London: Hodder Arnold, 2006.

Lipinski, Robert A. *Professional Beverage Management*. New York: Van Nostrand Reinhold, 1996.

Litrides, Carol A., and Bruce H. Axler. *Restaurant Service: Beyond the Basics*. New York: Wiley, 1994.

Maresca, Tom. *The Right Wine*. New York: Grove Weidenfeld, 1990.

Marshall, A. C. *The Waiter*. 3rd ed. London: Barrie and Rockliff, 1967.

Mennell, Stephen. *All Manners of Food: Eating and Taste in England and France from the Middle Ages to the Present*. Oxford and New York: Basil Blackwell Ltd., 1985.

Michaelson, Gerald A. *Building Bridges to Customers*. Portland, OR: Productivity Press, 1995.

Müller, Marianne, and Ola Mikolasek, with Hans Tapper. *Great Napkin Folding and Table Setting*. Trans. Elisabeth R. Reinersmann. New York: Sterling, 1990.

Murphy, Claudia Quigley. *The History of the Art of Tablesetting, Ancient and Modern: From Anglo-Saxon Days to the Present Time, with Illustrations and Bibliography, For the Use of Schools, Colleges, Extension Workers, Women's Clubs, Etc.*. New York: n.p., 1921.

Nantet, Bernard, et al. *Cheeses of the World*. New York: Rizzoli, 1993.

Nutley, Joyce. *Advanced Service Techniques*. London: Hodder and Stoughton, 1992.

Plotkin, Robert. *The Bartender's Companion: A Complete Drink Recipe Guide*. 4th ed. Tucson, AZ: Barmedia, 2003.

Revel, Jean François. *Culture and Cuisine: A Journey Through the History of Food*. Trans. Helen R. Lane. Garden City, NY: Doubleday, 1982.

Root, Waverley Lewis. *Eating in America: A History*. New York: Morrow, 1976.

Rudman, Theo. *Rudman's Complete Guide to Cigars*. 3rd ed. Chicago: Triumph Books, 1996.

Ruffel, Denis. *The Professional Catering Series*. New York: Van Nostrand Reinhold, 1989.

Saint George, Amelia. *Amelia Saint George's Table Decorating Book: With 8 Pages of Pull-out Designs*. North Pomfret, VT: Trafalgar Square, 1995.

Schivelbusch, Wolfgang. *Tastes of Paradise: A Social History of Spices, Stimulants, and Intoxicants*. Trans. David Jacobson. New York: Vintage, 1993.

Simon, Joanna. *Wine with Food*. New York: Simon and Schuster, 1996.

Southey, Paul. *The Expert Carver: How to Carve Meat, Poultry, and Game*. London: Century, 1987.

Splaver, Bernard. *Successful Catering*. New York: Van Nostrand Reinhold, 1991.

Stiel, Holly. *Thank You Very Much: A Book for Anyone Who Has Ever Said "May I Help You?"* Berkeley, CA: Ten Speed Press, 1995.

Sullivan, Jim and Phil "Zoom" Roberts. *Service that Sells! The Art of Profitable Hospitality*. Denver: Pencom International, 1991.

Takahashi, Kuwako. *East Meets West Table Setting: Table Design and Food*. Tokyo: Shufunotomo, 1991.

Tannahill, Reay. *Food in History*. 2nd ed. New York: Crown, 1988.

Tapper, Hans, and Helena York. *Napkin Folding and Place Cards for Festive Tables*. Trans. Elisabeth Reinersmann. New York: Sterling, 1989.

Tuor, Conrad. *Wine and Food Handbook: Aide-Mémoire du Sommelier* 2nd Ed. London: Hodder and Stoughton, 2002.

Ukers, William H. *The Romance of Coffee: An Outline History of Coffee and Coffee Drinking Through a Thousand Years*. New York: Tea and Coffee Trade Journal Co., 1948.

Visser, Margaret. *Much Depends on Dinner: The Extraordinary History and Mythology, Allure and Obsessions, Perils and Taboos, of an Ordinary Meal*. New York: Grove Press, 1986.

Visser, Margaret. *The Rituals of Dinner: The Origins, Evolution, Eccentricities, and Meaning of Table Manners*. New York: Grove Wiedenfeld, 1991.

Weiss, Edith, and Hal Weiss. *Catering Handbook*. New York: Van Nostrand Reinhold, 1991.

Wirth, Barbara. *The Elegant Table*. Trans. Danielle Lawrence de Froidmont. New York: Harry N. Abrams, 1988.

Wolk, Michael. *Designing for the Table: Decorative and Functional Products*. New York: Library of Applied Design, PBC International, 1992.

Zraly, Kevin. *Windows on the World Complete Wine Course 2009 edition*. New York: Sterling, 2008.

Periodicals

AMERICAN MIXOLOGIST

Robert Plotkin's Barmedia

P.O. Box 14486

Tucson, AZ 85732-4486

Phone: (800) 421-7179

(520) 747-8131

Fax: (520) 903-0540

Web: barmedia.com/amo/amo.htm

ART CULINAIRE

40 Mills Street

P.O. Box 9268

Morristown, NJ 07960

Phone: (973) 993-5500

Fax: (973) 993-8779

Web: www.getartc.com/

CHEF

The Chef's Business Magazine

Talcott Communications Corp.

20 W. Kenzie, Suite 1200

Chicago, IL 60654

Phone: (312) 849-2220

Fax: (312) 849-2174

Web: www.chefmagazine.com

CIGAR AFICIONADO

M. Shanken Communications, Inc.

387 Park Avenue South

New York, NY 10016

Phone: (212) 684-4224

Fax: (212) 684-5424

Web: www.cigaraficianado.com/

DECANTER

IPC Media

Blue Fin Building

110 Southwark Street

London SE1 0SU

United Kingdom

Phone: +44 (0) 3148-5000

Web: www.decanter.com/

FOOD ARTS

Food Arts Publishing, Inc.

387 Park Avenue South

New York, NY 10016

Phone: (212) 684-4224

Fax: (212) 684-5424

Web: www.mshanken.com

HOSPITALITY

Sophie Allcock

Trinity Court

34, West Street

Surrey SM1 15H Sutton

United Kingdom

Phone: +44(0) 20-8661-4915

Web: www.instituteofhospitality.org.uk

NATION'S RESTAURANT NEWS

A Publication of Lebhar-Friedman Inc.

425 Park Avenue, 6th floor

New York, NY 10022

Phone: (800) 453-2427

Web: www.nrn.com/

RESTAURANT BUSINESS

90 Broad Street, Suite 402
New York, NY 10004
Phone: (646) 708-7300
Fax: (646) 708-7399
Web: www.restaurantbiz.com/

RESTAURANT HOSPITALITY

Penton Media, Inc.
1300 E 9th Street
Cleveland, OH 44114-2543
Phone: (216) 931-9373
Fax: (215) 245-4060
Web: restaurant-hospitality.com/

SANTÉ

On-Premise Communications, Inc.
P.O. Box 4678
100 South Street
Bennington, VT 05201-4678
Phone: (802) 442-6771
Fax: (802) 442-6859
Web: www.isantemagazine.com/

TEA AND COFFEE JOURNAL

Lockwood Publications, Inc.
26 Broadway, Floor 9M
New York, NY 10004
Phone: (212) 391-2060
Fax: (212) 827-0945
Web: www.teaandcoffee.net/

THE WINE ADVOCATE

P.O.Box 311
Monkton, MD 21111
Phone: (410) 329-6477
Fax: (410) 357-4504
Web: www.erobertparker.com

WINE AND FOOD COMPANION

P.O. Box 639
Lenox Hill Station
New York, NY 10021
Phone: (800) 888-1961
Fax: (212) 737-7629
Web: www.globalgourmet.com/food/egg/
fdnews.html

WINE AND SPIRITS

2 W 32nd Street, Suite 601
New York, NY 10001
Phone: (212) 695-4660
Web: www.wineandspiritsmagazine.com

WINE BUSINESS MONTHLY

Smartwired Inc.
110 W Napa Street
Sonoma, CA 95476
Phone: (707) 939-0822
Fax: (707) 939-0833
Web: smartwine.com/wbm/swwbm1.htm

WINE SPECTATOR

387 Park Ave. South
New York, NY 10016
Phone: (212) 684-4224
Fax: (212) 684-5424
Web: www.winespectator.com/

Trade and Professional Groups

AMERICAN CULINARY FEDERATION, INC. (ACF)

180 Center Place Way

St. Augustine, FL 32095

Phone: (904) 824-4468

Fax: (904) 825-4758

E-mail: acf@acfchefs.net

Web site: www.acfchefs.org

AMERICAN INSTITUTE OF WINE AND FOOD (AIWF)

213-37 39th Avenue

Bayside, NY 11361

Phone: (800) 274-2493

Fax: (718) 522-0204

Web site: http://www.aiwf.org/

FEDERATION OF DINING ROOM PROFESSIONALS

1417 Sadler Road, Suite 100

Fernanadina Beach, FL 32034

Phone: (909) 491-6690 or (877) 264-FDRP

Fax: (904) 491-6689

Web site: www.fdrp.com

INTERNATIONAL ASSOCIATION OF CULINARY PROFESSIONALS (IACP)

1100 Johnson Ferry Road, Suite 300

Atlanta, GA 30342

Phone: (404) 252-3663

Fax: (404) 252-0774

E-mail: info@iacp.com

Web site: www.iacp.com

INTERNTATIONAL COUNCIL ON HOTEL, RESTAURANT
AND INSTITUTIONAL EDUCATION (ICHRIE)

2800 N Parham Road, Suite 230

Richmond, VA 23294

Phone: (804) 346-4800

Fax: (804) 346-5009

E-mail: membership@chrie.org

Web site: www.chrie.org

INTERNATIONAL FOOD INFORMATION COUNCIL (IFIC)

1100 Connecticut Avenue, NW, Suite 430

Washington, DC 20036

Phone: (202) 296-6540

Fax: (202) 296-6547

E-mail: foodinfo@ific.org

Web site: www.ificinfo.org

SOMMELIER SOCIETY OF AMERICA

P.O. Box 20080

West Village Station

New York, NY 10014

Phone: (212) 679-4190

Fax: (212) 255-8959

Web site: www.sommeliersocietyofamerica.org

WAITERS ASSOCIATION

1100 West Beaver Avenue

State College, PA 16801

Phone: (800) 437-7842

WOMEN CHEFS AND RESTAURATEURS

455 S Fourth Street, Suite 650

Louisville, KY 40202

Phone: (502) 581-0300 or (877) 927-7787

Fax: (502) 589-3602

Web site: www.womenchefs.org

WOMEN'S FOODSERVICE FORUM

1650 W 82nd Street, Suite 650

Bloomington, MN 55431

Phone: (952) 358-2100 or (866) 368-8008

Fax: (952) 358-2119

Web site: www.womenfoodserviceforum.com

Internet Sources

APPELLATION OF AMERICA INC.
http://www.appellationamerica.com

FOOD AND NUTRITION INFORMATION CENTER (FNIC)
http://fnic.nal.usda.gov/

ROBERT MONDAVI WINERY
http://www.robertmondaviwinery.com/

WAITERS/WAITRESSES: CALIFORNIA OCCUPATIONAL GUIDE
http://www.calmis.cahwnet.gov/file/occguide/WAITER

WINES.COM
http://www.wines.com/

Recommended Videos/DVDS

Art of Folding Table Napkins, The. The Food and Beverage Institute, 1997. (Available at 1-800-285-8280, ask for VT 1498)

Bar Code: How Alcohol Affects the Body. National Restaurant Association, n.d. (Available at 1-800-765-2122)

Bar Code: The Law and your Responsibility. National Restaurant Association, n.d. (Available at 1-800-765-2122)

Bar Code: Service in Difficult Situations. National Restaurant Association, n.d. (Available at 1-800-765-2122)

Bar Code: Techniques for Responsible Alcohol Service. National Restaurant Association, n.d. (Available at 1-800-765-2122)

Basic Table Service Skills, Part 1. The Culinary Institute of America, 1993. (Available at 1-800-285-8280, ask for VT 244)

Basic Table Service Skills, Part 2. The Culinary Institute of America, 1993. (Available at 1-800-285-8280, ask for VT 245)

Basic Table Service Skills, Part 3. The Culinary Institute of America, 1993. (Available at 1-800-285-8280, ask for VT 246)

Brewing Coffee. The Culinary Institute of America, 1985. (Available at 1-800-285-8280, ask for VT 191)

CARE: Controlling Alcohol Risk Effectively. Educational Foundation, 1993. (Available at 1-517-372-8800)

Exceeding Expectations: Service Tips and Techniques to Keep your Customer Coming Back. The Culinary Institute of America. (DVD, Available at 1-800-285-8280, ask for ISBN 1-58315-330-6)

Espresso 101. Bellissimo, 1998. (Available at 1-800-655-3955)

Heimlich Maneuver: How to Save a Choking Victim. AIMS Multimedia, 1982. (Available at 1-800-367-2467, ask for catalog no. 20951)

How to Give Exceptional Customer Service, Volumes 1–4. Career Track, 1989. (Available at 1-800-334-1018, ask for catalog no. 40435)

Kevin Zraly Wine Tasting. The Culinary Institute of America, 1993. (Available at 1-800-888-7850 or at www.ciaprochef.com, ask for VT 1115)

The Perfect Match: Wine and Food. The Culinary Institute of America. (DVD, Available at 1-800-285-8280, ask for ISBN 1-58315-332-2)

Service that Sells. Pencom International, 1998. (Available at 1-800-247-8514)

Toolkit: Challenging Guests. The Culinary Institute of America. (Download. Visit www.ciaprochef.com)

Toolkit: Front-of-the-House Sanitation. The Culinary Institute of America. (Download. Visit www.ciaprochef.com)

Toolkit: Wine Service. The Culinary Institute of America. (Download. Visit www.ciaprochef.com)

Toolkit: Improve Your Bottom Line Through Upselling. The Culinary Institute of America. (Download. Visit www.ciaprochef.com)

Wine Service for Waitstaff. The Culinary Institute of America, 1990. (DVD, Available at 800-888-7850 or at www.ciaprochef.com, ask for VT 232)

Index